Ready® Classroom
Mathematics

Grade 8 • Volume 1

NOT FOR RESALE

978-1-7280-1302-2
©2021–Curriculum Associates, LLC
North Billerica, MA 01862
No part of this book may be reproduced
by any means without written permission
from the publisher.
All Rights Reserved. Printed in USA.
2 3 4 5 6 7 8 9 10 11 12 13 14 15   22 21 20

Curriculum Associates

Contents

UNIT 2

Geometric Figures

Transformations, Similarity, and Angle Relationships

iii

Contents (continued)

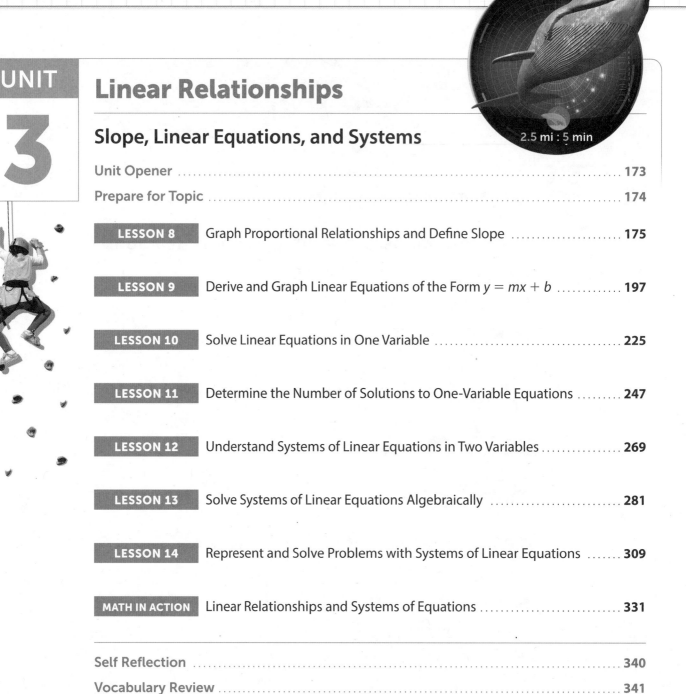

UNIT 3

Linear Relationships

Slope, Linear Equations, and Systems

2.5 mi : 5 min

UNIT 4

Functions

Linear and Nonlinear Relationships

Contents (continued)

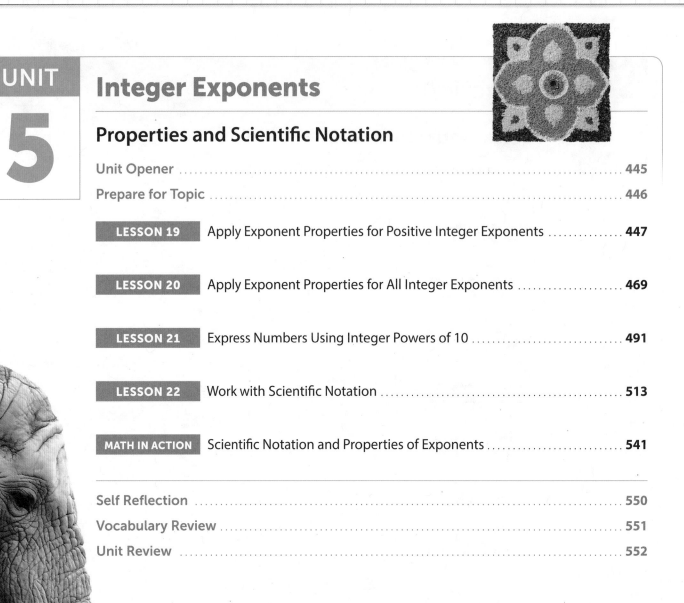

UNIT 5

Integer Exponents

Properties and Scientific Notation

Real Numbers

Rational Numbers, Irrational Numbers, and the Pythagorean Theorem

$A = 9$ in.^{2}

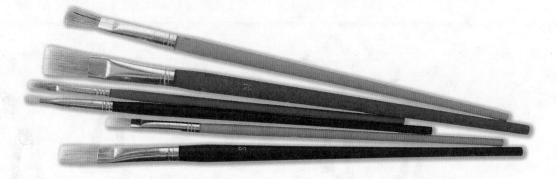

Contents (continued)

Unit 1

Geometric Figures

Rigid Transformations
and Congruence

 **Self Check** | Before starting this unit, check off the skills you know below.
As you complete each lesson, see how many more skills you can check off!

I can . . .	Before	After
Recognize translations, reflections, and rotations as rigid transformations.	☐	☐
Understand that rigid transformations do not change the size and shape of a figure.	☐	☐
Perform translations, reflections, and rotations in the coordinate plane.	☐	☐
Describe a rigid transformation that maps a figure onto an image.	☐	☐
Understand that two figures are congruent if one can be mapped exactly onto the other by a sequence of one or more rigid transformations.	☐	☐
Perform sequences of translations, rotations, and reflections in the coordinate plane.	☐	☐
Describe a sequence of translations, rotations, and reflections that maps a figure onto an image.	☐	☐
Use math vocabulary and precise language to describe the effects of rigid transformations on a figure.	☐	☐

Prepare for Rigid Transformations and Congruence

➤ **Think about what you know about representing relationships and information in the coordinate plane. Find and label one example of each item in the image below. You can use more than one label for the same point, line, or figure.**

a. point and its ordered pair	**e.** angle and its measure
b. vertical line	**f.** line segment and its length
c. horizontal line	**g.** vertex and its coordinates
d. parallel lines	

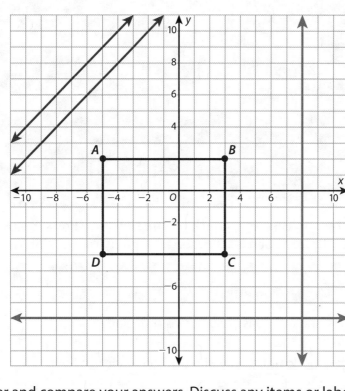

Meet with a partner and compare your answers. Discuss any items or labels that you do not agree about. You may revise or add to your work as needed.

Dear Family,

This week your student is exploring rigid transformations of figures. A **rigid transformation** is a movement that slides, flips, or turns a figure without changing its size or shape. Your student will be learning about three types of transformations:

- A **translation** slides a figure from one place to another.
- A **reflection** flips a figure over a line.
- A **rotation** turns a figure around a given point.

Show how to transform figure *A* in three different ways.

➤ **ONE WAY** to transform figure *A* is to translate it. You can slide figure *A* to the right.

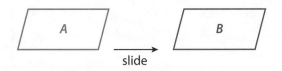

➤ **ANOTHER WAY** to transform figure *A* is to reflect it. You can flip figure *A* across a line of reflection to the right of the figure.

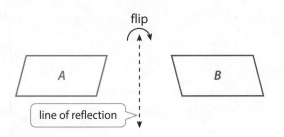

➤ **ANOTHER WAY** to transform figure *A* is to rotate it. You can use the bottom right vertex of *A* as a **center of rotation** and turn figure *A* to the right, or clockwise, around this point.

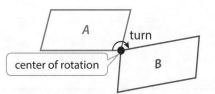

 Use the next page to start a conversation about rigid transformations.

Activity Thinking About Rigid Transformations Around You

➤ **Do this activity together to investigate rigid transformations of figures in the real world.**

Some patterns can be made by transforming a figure repeatedly. This is true for many household features, such as wallpaper designs.

The wallpaper pattern on the right uses a parallelogram. The pattern can be described in many ways. One way is that each column is a flip, or reflection, of the column next to it.

? What other patterns of transformed figures do you see in and around your home?

Explore Rigid Transformations

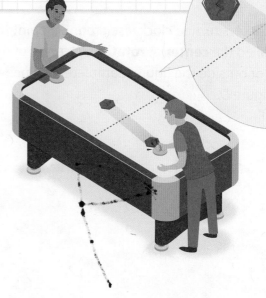

Model It

➤ **Complete the problems about sliding a figure and flipping a figure.**

1 **a.** You can slide figure *A* to the right to get its **image**, figure *B*. Complete the image by drawing the missing sides of figure *B*.

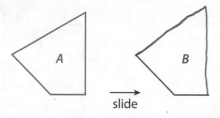

slide

b. A movement that slides a figure is a called a **translation**. What is the same about figure *A* and figure *B*? What is different?

Both figures have the same size and strength. What's different is that they had to translate the shape.

2 **a.** You can flip figure *A* across a **line of reflection** to get its image, figure *C*. Complete the image by drawing the missing sides of figure *C*.

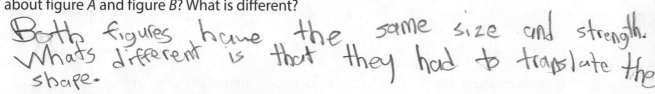

line of reflection

flip

b. A movement that flips a figure is called a **reflection**. What is the same about figure *A* and figure *C*? What is different?

Figure C is a mirror image of figure A.

DISCUSS IT

Ask: How did you know how to complete the image after the translation? After the reflection?

Share: I knew that the missing sides . . .

Learning Targets   SMP 2, SMP 3, SMP 5, SMP 6, SMP 7
Verify experimentally the properties of rotations, reflections, and translations.
• Lines are taken to lines, and line segments to line segments of the same length.
• Angles are taken to angles of the same measure.
• Parallel lines are taken to parallel lines.

Model It

➤ **Complete the problems about turning a figure.**

3 **a.** Figure *A* is turned clockwise around a point to get its image, figure *D*. The point is called the **center of rotation**. A center of rotation can be any point inside, on, or outside the figure. Complete the image by drawing the missing sides of figure *D*.

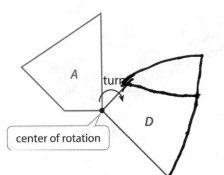

DISCUSS IT

Ask: How would a different center of rotation change the way a figure rotates?

Share: A way I think about a rotation is . . .

b. A movement that turns a figure is called a **rotation**. What is the same about figure *A* and figure *D*? What is different?

c. A **transformation** describes a change in location, orientation, or size of a figure. Translations, reflections, and rotations belong to the subcategory of transformations called **rigid transformations**. Why do you think these are called rigid transformations?

4 **Reflect** How is a rotation like a reflection? How is a rotation different from a reflection?

Prepare for Rigid Transformations

1 Think about what you know about geometric figures and parallel lines. Fill in each box. Use words, numbers, and pictures. Show as many ideas as you can.

In My Own Words	My Illustrations

parallel lines

Examples	Non-Examples

2 Identify all the pairs of parallel sides of each figure.

LESSON 1 Understand Rigid Transformations and Their Properties   **7**

➤ **Complete problems 3–5.**

3 Figure *S* is a translation of figure *R*. Complete the image by drawing the missing sides of figure *S*.

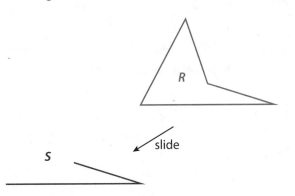

4 Figure *T* is a reflection of figure *R* across the line of reflection. Complete the image by drawing the missing sides of figure *T*.

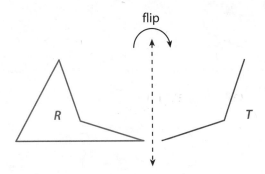

5 Figure *U* is a rotation of figure *R* counterclockwise around the center of rotation. Complete the image by drawing the missing sides of figure *U*.

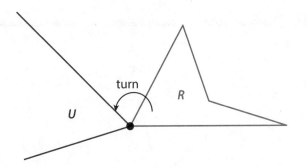

Develop Understanding of Rigid Transformations and Their Properties

Model It: Corresponding Sides

➤ **Try these two problems involving rigid transformations.**

1 Figure *PQRSTU* is a transformation of figure *ABCDEF*.

a. Is figure *PQRSTU* a *translation, reflection,* or *rotation*? Explain your reasoning.

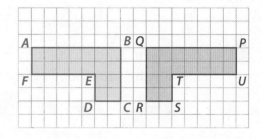

b. Draw an arrow to show how figure *ABCDEF* moved. Add the center of rotation for a rotation or the line of reflection for a reflection.

2 When figures are the same shape, you can identify corresponding parts between the figures. Angles in the same relative position are called **corresponding angles**. Sides in the same relative position are called **corresponding sides**.

a. When you name figures that are the same shape using vertex labels, it is important to use corresponding vertices in the same order.

Figure *PQRSTU* is the image of figure *ABCDEF*. Identify the corresponding sides.

$\overline{AB}$ and _____ $\overline{EF}$ and _____   _____ and $\overline{RS}$

_____ and $\overline{UP}$ $\overline{BC}$ and _____   _____ and $\overline{ST}$

b. How do the lengths of the corresponding sides compare? How do you know?

c. In figure *ABCDEF*, $\overline{AB}$ is parallel to $\overline{FE}$. You can write this using parallel line notation as $\overline{AB} \parallel \overline{FE}$. In figure *PQRSTU*, is $\overline{PQ} \parallel \overline{UT}$? How can you tell?

d. Look at the other pairs of parallel sides in figure *ABCDEF*. What do you notice about the corresponding pairs of sides in figure *PQRSTU*?

> **DISCUSS IT**
>
> *Ask:* Why is it important to correctly identify the corresponding sides of an original figure and its image?
>
> *Share:* Once I identify corresponding sides...

Model It: Corresponding Angles

➤ **Try these two problems about rigid transformations.**

3 Figures *ABCYE, HIJKL,* and *PQRST* are images of figure *VWXYZ*. Identify each image as a *translation, reflection,* or *rotation*.

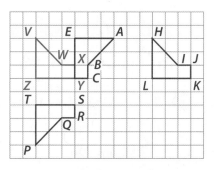

4 **a.** In problem 3, figure *PQRST* is an image of figure *VWXYZ*. Identify the corresponding angles.

∠*V* and _____   _____ and ∠*S*   ∠*Z* and _____

∠*X* and _____   _____ and ∠*Q*

b. How do the measures of the corresponding angles in problem 4a compare? How do you know?

CONNECT IT

➤ **Complete the problems below.**

5 Look at the two **Model Its**. How can corresponding parts help you to determine that an original figure and its image are the same size and shape?

6 Transform figure *JKLMN* to make an image, figure *ABCDE*. Draw and label figure *ABCDE*. Identify the transformation you used. Then use corresponding parts to show that the figure and image are the same size and shape.

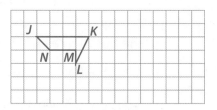

Practice Understanding Rigid Transformations and Their Properties

➤ **Study how the Example shows ways to analyze properties of a figure and its image after a transformation. Then solve problems 1–4.**

Example

Figure *Q* is a transformation of figure *P*. Compare the properties of the figures. Tell what is the same and what is different about figure *P* and figure *Q*. Identify the transformation.

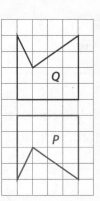

Same: The figures have the same shape and size. Parallel sides in figure *P* correspond to parallel sides in figure *Q*. The lengths of corresponding sides are the same, and the measures of corresponding angles are the same.

Different: Figure *Q* is in a different location than figure *P* and facing a different direction. Figure *Q* is a mirror image of figure *P*.

The transformation is a reflection.

① Figure *A* was transformed to make figures *B, C,* and *D*.

a. Which figure is a translation of figure *A*?

Draw an arrow to show the direction of the translation.

b. Which figure is a reflection of figure *A*?

Draw the line of reflection.

c. Which figure is a rotation of figure *A*?

Is the center of rotation inside, on, or outside the figure?

Vocabulary

reflection
a transformation that flips (reflects) a figure across a line to form a mirror image.

rotation
a transformation that turns (rotates) a figure a given angle and direction around a point.

translation
a transformation that moves (slides) each point of a figure the same distance and in the same direction.

2 Figure *WXUY* is a transformation of figure *STUV*.

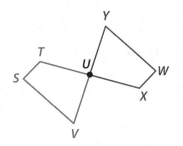

a. Identify the transformation.

b. Figure *WXUY* is the image of figure *STUV*. Identify the corresponding side or angle for each given side or angle.

$\overline{ST}$ and _____   _____ and $\overline{UY}$ $\overline{TU}$ and _____

_____ and $\overline{YW}$ $\angle S$ and _____   _____ and $\angle X$

$\angle TUV$ and _____   _____ and $\angle Y$

c. Describe how you could compare the corresponding sides and angles of figure *WXUY* and its image, figure *STUV*.

d. What does comparing the corresponding parts of an original figure and its image tell you about the transformation that was performed?

3 Mr. Patel drew figure *A* and its image, figure *K*, on the grid. Amelia says figure *K* is a rotation of figure *A*. Kareem says it is a reflection. Can both students be correct? Explain.

4 How could you use parallel sides to compare figures *A* and *K* from problem 3?

Refine Ideas About Rigid Transformations and Their Properties

Apply It

➤ **Complete problems 1–5.**

1 **Justify** Luis says figure *Y* is a rotation of figure *X*. Explain Luis's error.

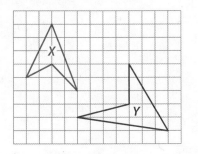

2 **Explain** Does figure *B* appear to be a reflection of figure *A* for each pair of figures? Explain why or why not.

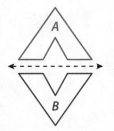   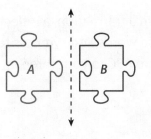

3 **Predict** Zara translates figure *P* to make figure *Q*. If she translates figure *Q* 4 units to the right to make figure *R*, where will figure *R* be located? Explain your reasoning.

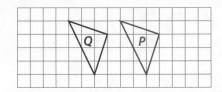

4 Akira draws some figures on grid paper. Some of the figures are transformations of figure C.

PART A Which figures appear to be rigid transformations of figure C?

PART B Explain how you can verify or prove that the figures you answered in Part A are rigid transformations of figure C.

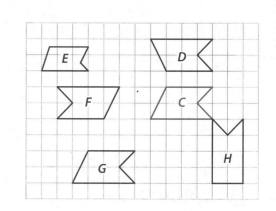

PART C Identify the transformation Akira used to get each image of figure C.

5 **Math Journal** Perform a translation, a reflection, and a rotation on figure ABC. Use words and symbols to compare the size and shape of figure ABC to your three images.

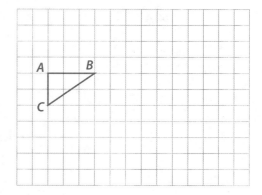

End of Lesson Checklist

☐ **INTERACTIVE GLOSSARY** Find the entry for *transformation*. Draw and label three different examples of a transformation.

Dear Family,

This week your student is learning about working with transformations in the coordinate plane. Previously, they learned about transformations that slide, reflect, or rotate a figure without changing its size or shape. Now, they will identify the coordinates of the vertices of the image of a figure that has been transformed in the coordinate plane.

When a figure is transformed, the resulting image is often named using prime notation. For example, if point A is translated 3 units up, the image is often named A'. This is read "A-prime." Your student will be solving problems involving transformations in the coordinate plane, like the one below.

Lola translates $\triangle ABC$ to make a design pattern. Lola draws $\triangle ABC$ in the coordinate plane as shown and then translates $\triangle ABC$ 7 units to the right to form $\triangle A'B'C'$. What are the coordinates of the vertices of $\triangle A'B'C'$?

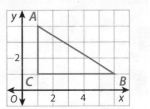

➤ **ONE WAY** to find the coordinates of the vertices of $\triangle A'B'C'$ is to trace $\triangle ABC$ onto tracing paper and then slide it 7 units to the right. Then identify the coordinates.

➤ **ANOTHER WAY** to find the coordinates of the vertices of $\triangle A'B'C'$ is to think about how the translation moves $\triangle ABC$. All of the vertices move **right 7 units**, so **add 7** to each x-coordinate.

$A(1, 4) \longrightarrow (1 + 7, 4) \longrightarrow A'(8, 4)$

$B(6, 1) \longrightarrow (6 + 7, 1) \longrightarrow B'(13, 1)$

$C(1, 1) \longrightarrow (1 + 7, 1) \longrightarrow C'(8, 1)$

 Use the next page to start a conversation about transformations in the coordinate plane.

Activity Thinking About Transformations in the Coordinate Plane

➤ **Do this activity together to investigate transformations in the coordinate plane.**

Many people like to draw pictures that involve shapes and patterns. Often without realizing it, the pattern may show a shape that has been transformed.

Look at the patterns below. Describe the transformations you see.

PATTERN 1

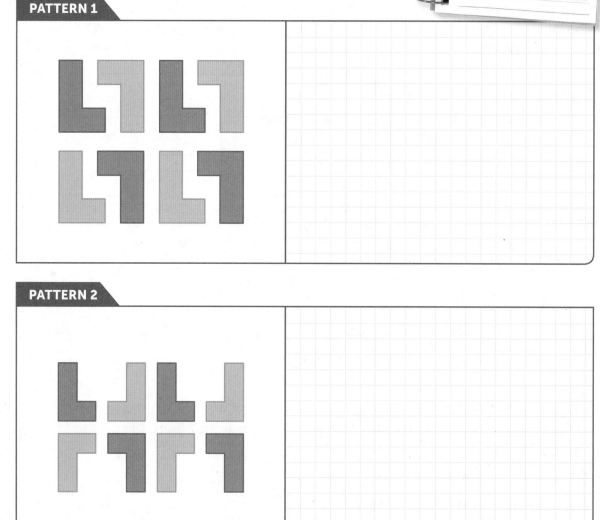

PATTERN 2

> **?** What do the two patterns have in common? Could you add to either of the patterns?

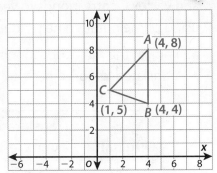

Explore Translations in the Coordinate Plane

Previously, you learned about rigid transformations. In this lesson, you will learn about rigid transformations in the coordinate plane.

➤ **Use what you know to try to solve the problem below.**

Roberto uses a computer design program to make stickers. He draws △ABC in the coordinate plane as shown. Then he translates △ABC 5 units to the left to form △A′B′C′. What are the coordinates of the vertices of △A′B′C′?

TRY IT   **Math Toolkit** graph paper, tracing paper, transparency sheets

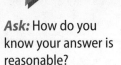

DISCUSS IT

Ask: How do you know your answer is reasonable?

Share: I knew . . . so I . . .

◎ **Learning Target**   SMP 1, SMP 2, SMP 3, SMP 4, SMP 5, SMP 6, SMP 7
Describe the effect of dilations, translations, rotations, and reflections on two-dimensional figures using coordinates.

CONNECT IT

1 **Look Back** What are the coordinates of the vertices of △A′B′C′? How do you know?

2 **Look Ahead** In Roberto's design, △ABC transforms to, or maps onto, △A′B′C′. This means vertex A corresponds to vertex A′, vertex B corresponds to vertex B′, and vertex C corresponds to vertex C′. A′ is read "A-prime." Naming an image using prime notation helps identify corresponding vertices.

a. Look at the table. How do the coordinates of a point change when it is translated left or right?

Original	Translated 2 units left	Translated 4 units left	Translated 2 units right	Translated 4 units right
(4, 8)	(2, 8)	(0, 8)	(6, 8)	(8, 8)

b. Look at the table. How do the coordinates of a point change when it is translated up or down?

Original	Translated 2 units up	Translated 4 units up	Translated 2 units down	Translated 4 units down
(4, 8)	(4, 10)	(4, 12)	(4, 6)	(4, 4)

3 **Reflect** What are the coordinates of the point (x, y) translated 5 units down? Explain.

Prepare for Transformations in the Coordinate Plane

1 Think about what you know about geometric figures and vertices. Fill in each box. Use words, numbers, and pictures. Show as many ideas as you can.

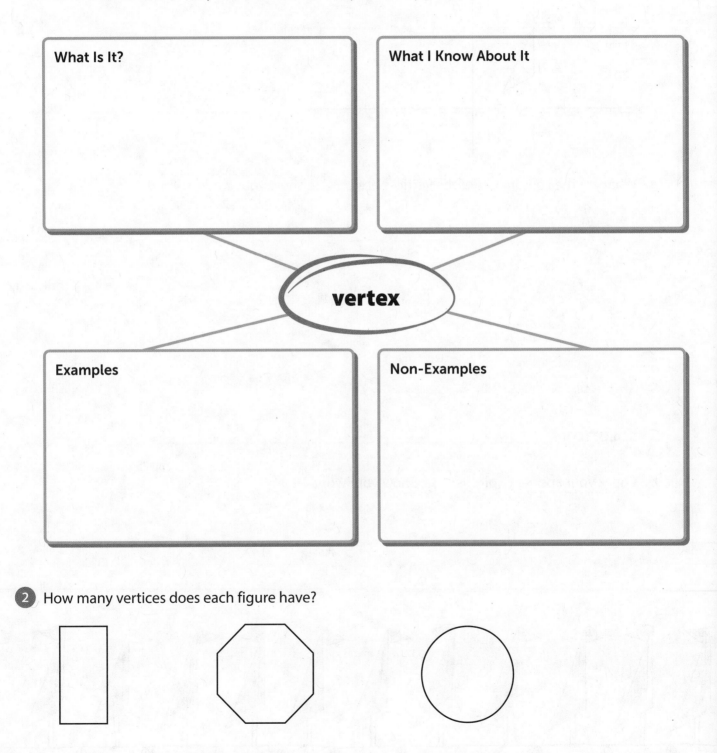

What Is It?

What I Know About It

vertex

Examples

Non-Examples

2 How many vertices does each figure have?

3 Winona is planning a border design using triangles. She begins by drawing △JKL in the coordinate plane. Then she translates △JKL 6 units to the right to form △J'K'L'.

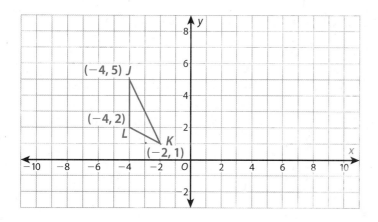

a. What are the coordinates of the vertices of △J'K'L'? Show your work.

SOLUTION _____

b. Check your answer to problem 3a. Show your work.

Develop Performing a Reflection in the Coordinate Plane

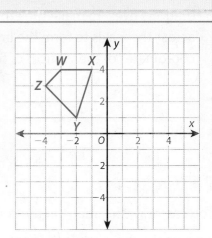

Make a Paper Dragon

➤ **Read and try to solve the problem below.**

Alyssa is making a paper dragon puppet as part of her family's Chinese New Year celebration. She lays her tissue paper over the coordinate plane. Then she draws figure *WXYZ* for one of the dragon's eyes. To make the other eye, she reflects figure *WXYZ* across the *x*-axis to form the image, figure *W′X′Y′Z′*. What are the coordinates of the vertices of figure *W′X′Y′Z′*?

TRY IT

Math Toolkit graph paper, tracing paper, transparency sheets

DISCUSS IT

Ask: What did you do first to find the coordinates of figure *W′X′Y′Z′*?

Share: At first, I thought . . .

➤ **Explore different ways to reflect a figure in the coordinate plane.**

Alyssa is making a paper dragon puppet as part of her family's Chinese New Year celebration. She lays her tissue paper over the coordinate plane. Then she draws figure *WXYZ* for one of the dragon's eyes. To make the other eye, she reflects figure *WXYZ* across the *x*-axis to form the image, figure *W'X'Y'Z'* What are the coordinates of the vertices of figure *W'X'Y'Z'*?

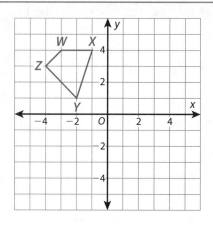

Picture It

You can draw the image in the coordinate plane.

In this case, the *x*-axis is the line of reflection.

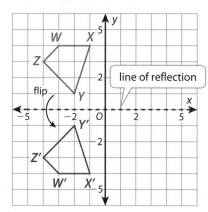

Model It

You can now identify the coordinates of the vertices of the image.

Make a table to compare corresponding vertices.

WXYZ	W(−3, 4)	X(−1, 4)	Y(−2, 1)	Z(−4, 3)
W'X'Y'Z'	W'(−3, −4)	X'(−1, −4)		

➤ **Use the problem from the previous page to help you understand how to perform a reflection in the coordinate plane.**

1 Look at **Picture It**. How does the distance of each vertex of figure *WXYZ* to the line of reflection compare to the distance of its corresponding vertex of figure *W′X′Y′Z′* to the line of reflection?

2 Look at **Model It**. What are the coordinates for vertices *Y′* and *Z′*? Complete the table.

3 The table shows how the coordinates of a point change when it is reflected across either the *x*-axis or the *y*-axis. Describe how the coordinates of a point change when it is reflected across each axis.

Original	(2, 3)	(−1, 4)	(−5, −1)	(3, −6)
Reflected across *x*-axis	(2, −3)	(−1, −4)	(−5, 1)	(3, 6)
Reflected across *y*-axis	(−2, 3)	(1, 4)	(5, −1)	(−3, −6)

4 What are the coordinates of the point (x, y) when it is reflected across the *x*-axis? When it is reflected across the *y*-axis? Explain why only one coordinate changes when you reflect a point across an axis.

5 **Reflect** Think about all the models and strategies you have discussed today. Describe how one of them helped you better understand how to solve the **Try It** problem.

Apply It

➤ **Use what you learned to solve these problems.**

6 Seth reflects △ABC across the x-axis to form △DEF. Draw △DEF. What are the coordinates of the vertices of △DEF?

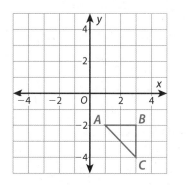

7 Isabel is planning a design that uses different colored wooden triangles. She starts by drawing △JKL in the coordinate plane. She then reflects △JKL across the x-axis to form △J′K′L′. Draw △J′K′L′ in the coordinate plane. What are the coordinates of the vertices of △J′K′L′?

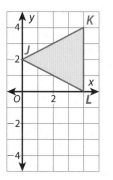

8 Malik draws quadrilateral STUV in the coordinate plane with vertices at $S(-5, -4)$, $T(-4, -1)$, $U(-1, 0)$, and $V(-3, -3)$. Then Malik reflects quadrilateral STUV across the y-axis to form quadrilateral S′T′U′V′. What are the coordinates of the vertices of quadrilateral S′T′U′V′? Show your work.

SOLUTION _____

Practice Performing a Reflection in the Coordinate Plane

➤ **Study the Example showing a reflection across the *y*-axis. Then solve problems 1–5.**

Example

Tessa is using reflections to design a pattern. She draws figure *GHIJ* in the coordinate plane. How might she have reflected figure *GHIJ* across the *y*-axis to form figure *G′H′I′J′*?

Tessa could have counted the number of units from each vertex to the *y*-axis. Then she could have counted the same number of units on the other side of the *y*-axis to plot the corresponding vertices of figure *G′H′I′J′*.

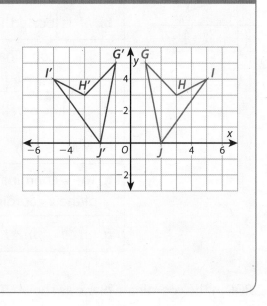

1 Tessa can now use her graph in the Example to find the coordinates of the vertices of figure *G′H′I′J′*. How could she have found these coordinates without drawing the reflection of figure *GHIJ*?

2 Jabari draws figure *GHIJ* in the coordinate plane. He wants to reflect figure *GHIJ* across the *x*-axis to form figure *WXYZ*.

a. Draw a dashed line to show the line of reflection.

b. Show where Jabari should draw figure *WXYZ*.

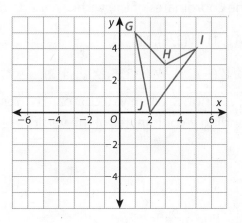

3 Figure *JKLMN* is reflected across the *x*-axis to form figure *J'K'L'M'N'*. Tell whether each statement is *True* or *False*.

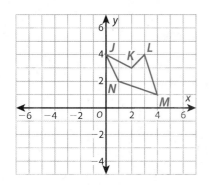

	True	False
a. *L'* is located at $(-3, 4)$.	○	○
b. *M'* is located 1 unit below the *x*-axis.	○	○
c. The *y*-coordinate of *K'* is the opposite of the *y*-coordinate of *K*.	○	○
d. The line of reflection is the *y*-axis.	○	○
e. $N'M' = NM$	○	○
f. The *x*-coordinate of *N'* is the opposite of the *x*-coordinate of *N*.	○	○
g. $m\angle J' = m\angle J$	○	○

4 Noor draws △*PQR* in the coordinate plane as shown. Then she reflects △*PQR* across the *y*-axis to form △*P'Q'R'*. Doug incorrectly says the coordinates of *Q'* are $(-3, 2)$. What is the correct answer? How might Doug have gotten his answer?

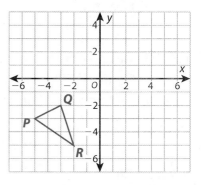

5 Below are the coordinates of the vertices of △*VWX* and its image after a reflection.

△*VWX*: *V*(2, 1), *W*(3, 5), *X*(4, 2)

△*V'W'X'*: *V'*(−2, 1), *W'*(−3, 5), *X'*(−4, 2)

a. What do you notice when you compare corresponding *x*-coordinates and corresponding *y*-coordinates of the vertices of △*VWX* and △*V'W'X'*?

b. What is the line of reflection?

Develop Performing a Rotation in the Coordinate Plane

➤ **Read and try to solve the problem below.**

Jamal draws △*PQR* in the coordinate plane as shown. He rotates △*PQR* 90° counterclockwise around the origin to form the image △*P'Q'R'*. What are the coordinates of the vertices of △*P'Q'R'*?

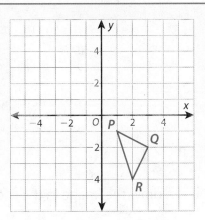

 TRY IT

Math Toolkit graph paper, tracing paper, transparency sheets

DISCUSS IT

Ask: How did you choose that strategy to find the coordinates of the vertices of △*P'Q'R'*?

Share: At first, I thought . . .

➤ **Explore different ways to rotate a figure in the coordinate plane.**

Jamal draws △PQR in the coordinate plane as shown. He rotates △PQR 90° counterclockwise around the origin to form the image △P'Q'R'. What are the coordinates of the vertices of △P'Q'R'?

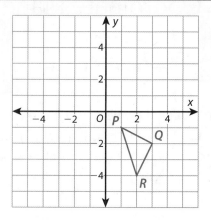

Picture It

You can draw the image in the coordinate plane.

You can think of a rotation as moving in a circle. Since 90° is $\frac{1}{4}$ of 360°, 90° is $\frac{1}{4}$ of a full turn of a circle.

Think of each vertex as being on a circle. Then move the vertex counterclockwise one quarter turn of that circle.

△P'Q'R' is the image of △PQR rotated 90° counterclockwise around the origin.

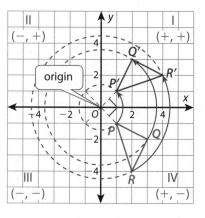

Model It

You can identify the coordinates of the vertices of the image in the coordinate plane.

Make a table to compare corresponding vertices of △PQR and △P'Q'R'.

△PQR	P(1, −1)	Q(3, −2)	R(2, −4)
△P'Q'R'	P'(1, 1)		

➤ **Use the problem from the previous page to help you understand how to rotate a figure in the coordinate plane.**

1 Use the graph in **Picture It** to complete the table in **Model It** with the coordinates for vertices Q' and R'.

2 The table shows how the coordinates change when you rotate a point 90° counterclockwise around the origin. Compare the coordinates of the image point to the original point.

Original	(2, 1)	(−1, 3)	(−4, −2)	(6, −5)
Rotated 90° counterclockwise	(−1, 2)	(−3, −1)	(2, −4)	(5, 6)

3 The table shows how the coordinates change when you rotate a point 90° clockwise around the origin. Compare the coordinates of the image point to the original point.

Original	(2, 1)	(−1, 3)	(−4, −2)	(6, −5)
Rotated 90° clockwise	(1, −2)	(3, 1)	(−2, 4)	(−5, −6)

4 What are the coordinates of the image of a point (x, y) that is rotated 90° counterclockwise around the origin? That is rotated 90° clockwise around the origin?

5 **Reflect** Think about all the models and strategies you have discussed today. Describe how one of them helped you better understand how to solve the **Try It** problem.

Apply It

➤ **Use what you learned to solve these problems.**

6 Carter rotates figure *JKLM* 90° clockwise around the origin to form figure *WXYZ*. Draw figure *WXYZ*. What are the coordinates of the vertices of figure *WXYZ*?

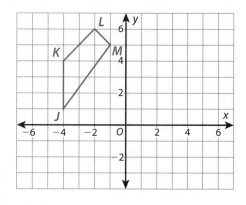

7 Shanika draws figure *ABCD* in the coordinate plane. She rotates figure *ABCD* 180° clockwise around the origin to form figure *A'B'C'D'*.

a. Draw figure *A'B'C'D'*. What do you notice when you compare corresponding *x*-coordinates and corresponding *y*-coordinates of the vertices of figures *ABCD* and *A'B'C'D'*?

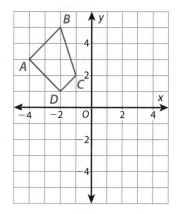

b. How would the coordinates of the vertices of figure *A'B'C'D'* change if Shanika rotated figure *ABCD* 180° counterclockwise instead? Explain.

8 Diego draws △*FGH* in the coordinate plane with vertices *F* (−1, −3), *G* (−3, −5), and *H* (−5, −2). He rotates △*FGH* 90° counterclockwise around the origin to form △*F'G'H'*. What are the coordinates of the vertices of △*F'G'H'*? Show your work.

SOLUTION _____

Practice Performing a Rotation in the Coordinate Plane

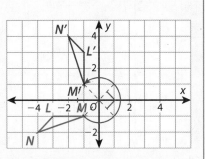

propeller

➤ **Study the Example showing a 270° counterclockwise rotation around the origin. Then solve problems 1–5.**

Example

Samuel is designing a propeller for a model plane. He draws △*LMN* in the coordinate plane. He rotates △*LMN* 270° counterclockwise around the origin to form △*L'M'N'*. How might Samuel have performed the rotation on △*LMN* to form △*L'M'N'*?

Samuel could have drawn a circle, centered at the origin, passing through vertex *M* of △*LMN*. Since 270° is equal to three 90° turns, Samuel could have rotated vertex *M* three 90° counterclockwise turns to vertex *M'*. Then he could have counted 2 units up from *M'* to find *L'*, and then 1 unit up from and 1 unit to the left of *L'* to find *N'*.

1 Compare the coordinates of the corresponding vertices of △*LMN* and △*L'M'N'* in the Example. Describe the effect of the 270° counterclockwise rotation on the vertices. What other rotation of △*LMN* would have the same effect?

2 Emily drew quadrilateral *ABCD* and its image *A'B'C'D'* in the coordinate plane. Draw a 180° rotation and a 90° clockwise rotation of quadrilateral *ABCD* around the origin.

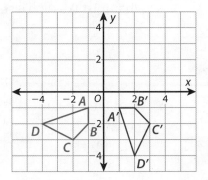

3 Ximena draws an X shape in the coordinate plane as shown. Draw the images of her X shape rotated 90° counterclockwise, 180°, and 270° counterclockwise around the origin. Label each image with the degree of rotation and direction.

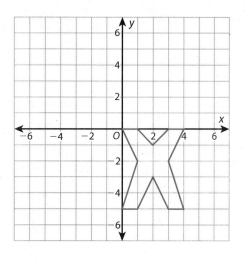

4 Michael rotates △ABC to form the image △A′B′C′. The table shows the corresponding vertices for △ABC and △A′B′C′. What degree of rotation and direction did Michael rotate △ABC to form △A′B′C′?

△**ABC**	A (2, 3)	B (4, 4)	C (3, 0)
△**A′B′C′**	A′(3, −2)	B′(4, −4)	C′(0, −3)

5 Destiny plots △EFG in the coordinate plane. Then Destiny's teacher asks her to rotate △EFG 90° clockwise around the origin to form its image △E′F′G′. Her original figure and image are shown in the coordinate plane.

a. What mistake did Destiny make?

b. What are the correct coordinates of the vertices for the image?

c. Draw the correct image △E′F′G′ in the coordinate plane.

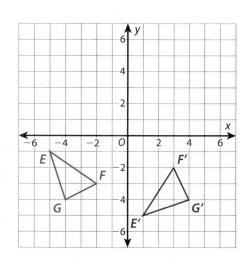

Develop Describing Single Rigid Transformations in the Coordinate Plane

➤ **Read and try to solve the problem below.**

Juan draws △A in the coordinate plane. He uses a single transformation to form the image △A'. What single transformation did Juan use?

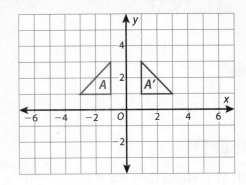

Math Toolkit graph paper, tracing paper, transparency sheets

DISCUSS IT

Ask: How did you figure out which transformation Juan used?

Share: I know that . . . so I . . .

➤ **Explore different ways to describe single rigid transformations in the coordinate plane.**

Juan draws △A in the coordinate plane. He uses a single transformation to form the image △A'. What single transformation did Juan use?

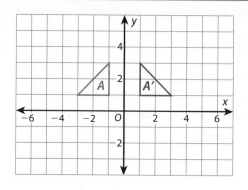

Model It

You can reflect the figure across an axis.

If you reflect △A across the y-axis, you can map the figure onto its image, △A'.

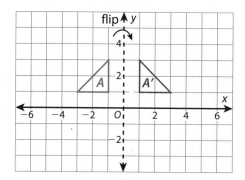

Model It

You can rotate the figure around the origin.

If you rotate △A 90° clockwise around the origin, you can map △A onto its image, △A'. You could also use a 270° counterclockwise rotation around the origin.

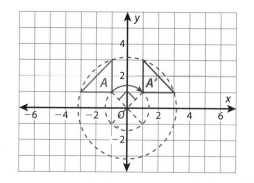

➤ **Use the problem from the previous page to help you understand how to describe single rigid transformations in the coordinate plane.**

1 Look at both **Model Its**. Why is it impossible to tell whether Juan used a reflection or a rotation to transform △*A* just by looking at the image?

2 Triangle *A* is shown with its vertices labeled *XYZ*. Label △*X'Y'Z'* first to show a reflection of △*XYZ*. Then label △*X'Y'Z'* to show a rotation of △*XYZ*.

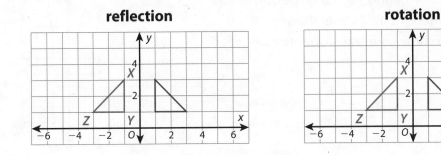

reflection   **rotation**

3 In problem 2, can you tell whether a reflection or a rotation was used to transform △*XYZ* just by looking at the image? Explain.

4 How do labeled vertices help you identify which transformation was used to transform a figure?

5 **Reflect** Think about all the models and strategies you have discussed today. Describe how one of them helped you better understand how to solve the **Try It** problem.

Apply It

➤ **Use what you learned to solve these problems.**

6 Brett and Sofia each perform a single transformation on figure *JKLM* to form image *J'K'L'M'*. Brett translates figure *JKLM* up 4 units. Sofia rotates figure *JKLM* 90° counterclockwise around the origin.

a. Label the vertices of each student's image.

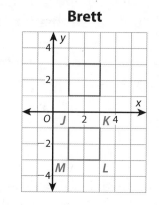

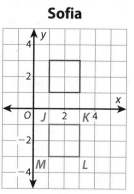

b. What is another single transformation you could perform on figure *JKLM* to form image *J'K'L'M'*? Label the vertices of the image at the right to show your transformation.

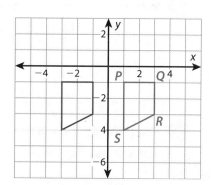

7 Rosa transforms figure *PQRS* to form its image *P'Q'R'S'*. Label the vertices of figure *P'Q'R'S'* and tell what single transformation Rosa used. Is there another single transformation you could perform on figure *PQRS* that would cause you to label the vertices of figure *P'Q'R'S'* differently? Explain.

8 Andre transforms figure *ABCDEF* to form its image *A'B'C'D'E'F'*. What single transformation did he use? How do you know?

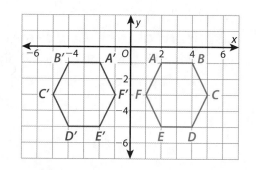

Practice Describing Single Rigid Transformations in the Coordinate Plane

➤ **Study the Example showing how to describe a single rigid transformation in the coordinate plane. Then solve problems 1–4.**

Example

Hai used a single transformation to map figure *A* onto its image *A′*. What is one way Hai could have mapped figure *A* onto figure *A′*?

Hai could have translated figure *A* 8 units up to map figure *A* onto figure *A′*.

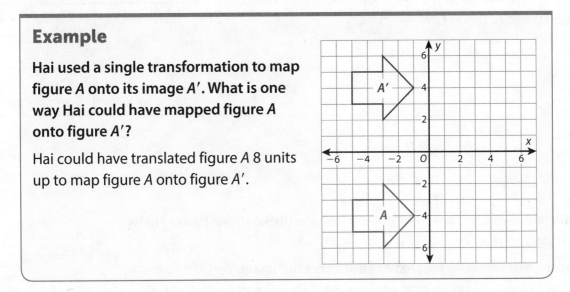

1. **a.** Describe another single transformation that maps figure *A* onto figure *A′* in the Example.

   b. What is a transformation that would not map figure *A* onto figure *A′*? Explain.

2. Sarah uses a digital art program to draw figure *Y* and its image *Y′*. What are two ways Sarah could have made the image using a single transformation?

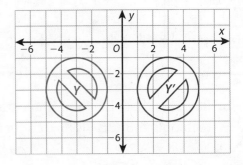

③ Imani is drawing octagon Q and its image Q' in the coordinate plane. She wants to be able to identify at least two single transformations that will map octagon Q to octagon Q'.

Draw and label a possible octagon Q and its image Q' that Imani could use. What single transformations could you use to map octagon Q onto octagon Q'?

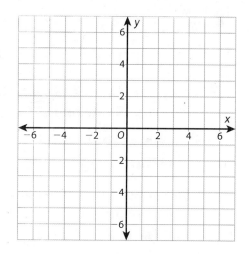

④ Ravi draws rectangle ABCD in the coordinate plane. He uses a single transformation to form the image rectangle A'B'C'D'.

a. What transformation could Ravi have used? Label the image vertices to show two different ways Ravi could map rectangle ABCD onto rectangle A'B'C'D' and identify each transformation.

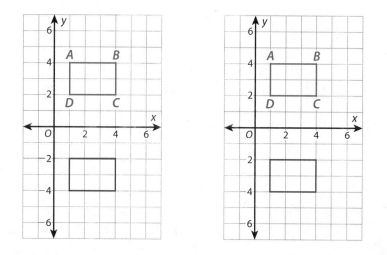

b. Ravi says there is a third single transformation that maps rectangle ABCD onto rectangle A'B'C'D'. Is Ravi correct? Explain.

Refine Working with Single Rigid Transformations in the Coordinate Plane

➤ **Complete the Example below. Then solve problems 1–8.**

Example

Aisha rotates △*XYZ* 90° clockwise around vertex *Z*. What are the coordinates of the image △*X′Y′Z*?

Look at how you can show your work using the coordinate plane.

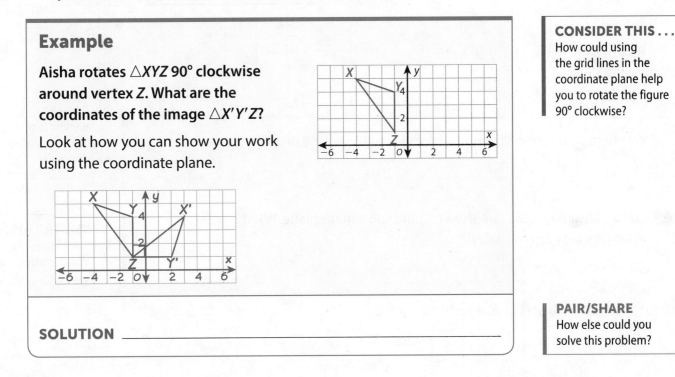

SOLUTION _____

CONSIDER THIS . . .
How could using the grid lines in the coordinate plane help you to rotate the figure 90° clockwise?

PAIR/SHARE
How else could you solve this problem?

Apply It

1 Darius transformed figure *TUVW* to form its image *T′U′V′W′* using two different transformations. Identify the single transformation he used to map figure *TUVW* onto figure *T′U′V′W′* in each graph.

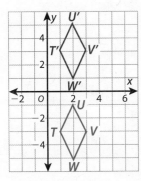 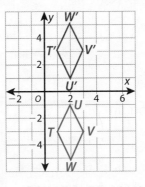

CONSIDER THIS . . .
How can the labels on the corresponding vertices help you identify the transformation?

PAIR/SHARE
How else could you identify each transformation?

2 Point *D* is shown in the coordinate plane. Plot the image point for each single transformation of point *D*. Then write the coordinates.

a. image *A*: reflection across the *x*-axis

b. image *B*: translation 7 units to the right

c. image *C*: rotation 90° counterclockwise around the origin

CONSIDER THIS . . .
Could it help to identify the quadrant each image is in?

PAIR/SHARE
Explain how to check whether your answers are reasonable.

3 △*H* and its image △*H'* are shown in the coordinate plane. What single rotation maps △*H* onto △*H'*?

CONSIDER THIS . . .
One way to think about a rotation is to think of it as a turn.

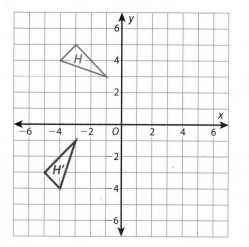

A 90° clockwise rotation around the origin

B 180° clockwise rotation around the origin

C 180° counterclockwise rotation around the origin

D 270° clockwise rotation around the origin

Hiroko chose A as the correct answer. How might she have gotten that answer?

PAIR/SHARE
What is another way to rotate △*H* to map it onto the same image?

4 Figures *A–G* are all images of figure *W*. Which figures can you not map figure *W* onto using a single rotation around a vertex, translation, or reflection across the *x*- or *y*-axis? Select all that apply.

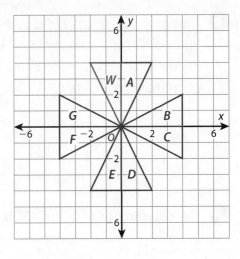

A figure *A*

B figure *B*

C figure *C*

D figure *D*

E figure *E*

F figure *F*

G figure *G*

5 Five figures are shown in the coordinate plane. Tell whether each statement is *True* or *False*.

	True	False
a. Figure *B* is a reflection of figure *A* across the *x*-axis.	○	○
b. Figure *C* is a translation of figure *B* down 4 units.	○	○
c. Figure *E* is a 180° rotation of figure *C* around the origin.	○	○
d. Figure *A* is a reflection of figure *C* across the *x*-axis.	○	○
e. Figure *D* is a 180° rotation of figure *B* around the origin.	○	○
f. Figure *E* is a reflection of figure *B* across the *y*-axis.	○	○

6 Alberto draws figure *EFGH* in the coordinate plane. He rotates figure *EFGH* 90° counterclockwise around vertex *E* to form image *EF'G'H'*. Draw the image *EF'G'H'*. What are the coordinates of figure *EF'G'H'*?

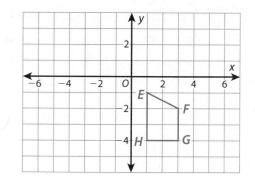

7 The coordinates of figure *ABCD* and its image *A'B'C'D'* are given below:

$A(-5, -2), B(-3, -1), C(-1, -1), D(-3, -4)$

$A'(2, -2), B'(4, -1), C'(6, -1), D'(4, -4)$

What single transformation could you use to map figure *ABCD* onto figure *A'B'C'D'*? Explain how you know.

8 **Math Journal** Draw and label a 4-sided figure in the coordinate plane. Use a single transformation to draw the image of your figure and label the vertices. Use another single transformation to draw a different image of your figure and label the vertices. Tell how you can check that each transformation was performed correctly.

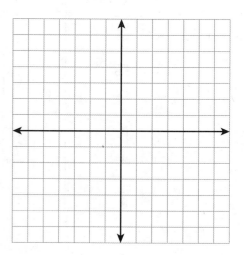

End of Lesson Checklist

☐ **INTERACTIVE GLOSSARY** Find the entry for *center of rotation*. Write the definition in your own words using the words *origin* and *vertex*.

☐ **SELF CHECK** Go back to the Unit 1 Opener and see what you can check off.

Dear Family,

This week your student is learning about sequences of transformations. When one or more transformations are performed on a figure, it is called a **sequence of transformations**.

Your student will be learning how to solve problems like the one below.

Maria and Brian each perform a reflection and a translation on figure C. Maria reflects figure C across the x-axis and then translates it 8 units down. Brian translates figure C 8 units down and then reflects it across the x-axis. Will Maria's and Brian's sequences of transformations map figure C onto the same final image C"?

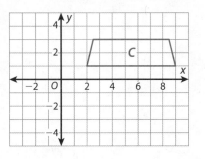

➤ **Maria's Way**

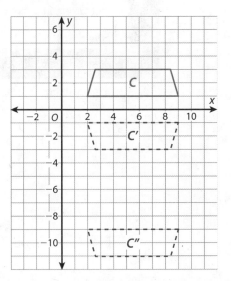

➤ **Brian's Way**

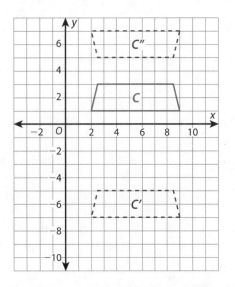

Maria and Brian mapped figure C onto different locations in the coordinate plane. In this case, performing two transformations in a different order did not map the original figure onto the same image. The order in which transformations are performed can matter.

 Use the next page to start a conversation about sequences of transformations.

Activity Thinking About Sequences of Transformations Around You

➤ **Do this activity together to describe sequences of transformations in the real world.**

Have you ever rearranged furniture in a room? When you move a chair from one side of the room to another, this can be described as a sequence of transformations!

? How many ways can you describe the movement of the furniture between the before and after pictures?

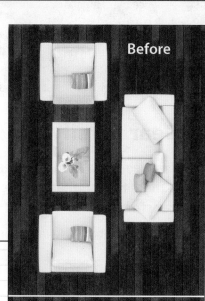

Explore Sequences of Rigid Transformations and Congruence

Previously, you learned how to perform and describe rigid transformations. In this lesson, you will learn what happens when you perform sequences of one or more rigid transformations.

➤ **Use what you know to try to solve the problem below.**

Arachne's Quilt is an Amish quilt pattern made of polygons. You can use a coordinate plane to plan a quilt. Graph a pentagon with the vertices $A(8, 0)$, $B(6, -2)$, $C(6, -6)$, $D(4, -4)$, and $E(4, 0)$. Then to graph another pentagon, follow these steps.

- Translate pentagon $ABCDE$ 4 units to the left to form pentagon $A'B'C'D'E'$.

- Rotate pentagon $A'B'C'D'E'$ 90° counterclockwise around the origin to form pentagon $A''B''C''D''E''$.

Is pentagon $A''B''C''D''E''$ the same size and shape as pentagon $ABCDE$?

TRY IT

 Math Toolkit graph paper, protractors, rulers, tracing paper

◎ **Learning Target** SMP 1, SMP 2, SMP 3, SMP 4, SMP 5, SMP 6, SMP 7
Understand that a two-dimensional figure is congruent to another if the second can be obtained from the first by a sequence of rotations, reflections, and translations; given two congruent figures, describe a sequence that exhibits the congruence between them.

CONNECT IT

1 **Look Back** Is pentagon $A''B''C''D''E''$ the same size and shape as pentagon $ABCDE$? Explain.

2 **Look Ahead** You already know that you can transform a figure. You can also transform the image of a figure. This is called performing a **sequence of transformations** on a figure.

a. You can add a prime mark to the vertex labels for each transformation you perform to name an image resulting from a sequence of transformations. How many transformations were performed to get image $X'''Y'''Z'''$? Explain.

b. Figures that are the same size and shape are **congruent**. When a figure is translated, reflected, or rotated, the image is always congruent to the original figure. That means pentagons $ABCDE$ and $A'B'C'D'E'$ are congruent.

pentagon $ABCDE \cong$ pentagon $A'B'C'D'E'$

Read $\cong$ as *is congruent to.*

Write a congruence statement for pentagons $A''B''C''D''E''$ and $A'B'C'D'E'$.

c. Enrico translates figure Q to get figure Q'. Then he rotates figure Q' to get figure Q''. Explain why figure Q and figure Q'' are congruent.

3 **Reflect** How can you use a sequence of transformations to show that one figure is congruent to another?

Name:

Prepare for Sequences of Rigid Transformations and Congruence

1 Think about what you know about transformations. Fill in each box. Use words, numbers, and pictures. Show as many ideas as you can.

Word	In My Own Words	Examples
translation		
reflection		
rotation		

2 **a.** Tell which type of transformation maps figure *A* onto figure *A'*. Then draw the line of reflection, the center of rotation, or a direction arrow to show the type of transformation on the graph.

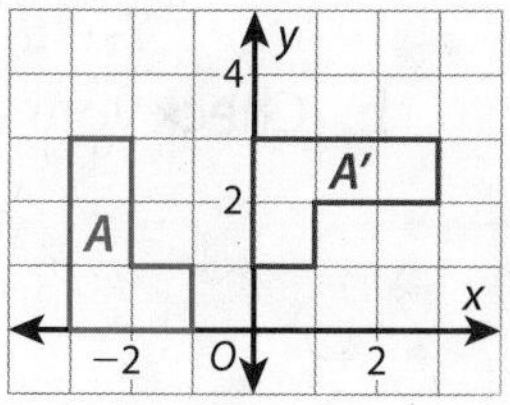

b. Describe the transformation in more detail.

LESSON 3 Work with Sequences of Transformations and Congruence   **47**

3 The quilt shown has a border made of right triangles and trapezoids.

   a. Graph one triangle with vertices at $D(-4, 0)$, $E(0, 0)$, and $F(0, -8)$. To locate another triangle, follow these steps:

      • Reflect $\triangle DEF$ across the y-axis to form $\triangle D'E'F'$.

      • Translate $\triangle D'E'F'$ 8 units up to form $\triangle D''E''F''$.

     Is $\triangle DEF$ the same size and shape as $\triangle D''E''F''$? Show your work.

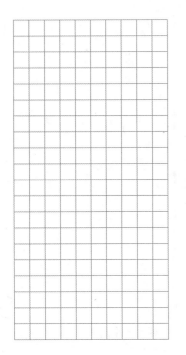

   SOLUTION _____

   b. Check your answer to problem 3a. Show your work.

Develop Performing Sequences of Rigid Transformations

➤ **Read and try to solve the problem below.**

Kimani and Jake each perform the same two transformations on figure T, but not in the same order.

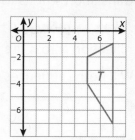

- **Kimani's sequence:** A reflection across the y-axis, followed by a translation 4 units to the left.

- **Jake's sequence:** A translation 4 units to the left, followed by a reflection across the y-axis.

Will both sequences map figure T onto the same final image?

TRY IT

Math Toolkit graph paper, tracing paper, transparency sheets

➤ **Explore different ways to perform sequences of transformations.**

Kimani and Jake each perform the same two transformations on figure *T*, but not in the same order.

Kimani's sequence: A reflection across the *y*-axis, followed by a translation 4 units to the left.

Jake's sequence: A translation 4 units to the left, followed by a reflection across the *y*-axis.

Will both sequences map figure *T* onto the same final image?

Picture It

You can draw each sequence in separate coordinate planes.

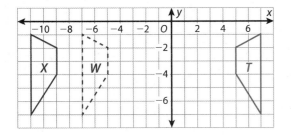
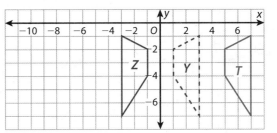

Model It

You can think about how the coordinates of each vertex change when you perform each transformation.

Kimani's Sequence		
Original coordinate	**Reflected across y-axis**	**Translated 4 units left**
(5, −2)	(−5, −2)	(−9, −2)
(7, −1)	(−7, −1)	(−11, −1)
(7, −7)	(−7, −7)	(−11, −7)
(5, −4)	(−5, −4)	(−9, −4)

Jake's Sequence		
Original coordinate	**Translated 4 units left**	**Reflected across y-axis**
(5, −2)	(1, −2)	(−1, −2)
(7, −1)	(3, −1)	(−3, −1)
(7, −7)	(3, −7)	(−3, −7)
(5, −4)	(1, −4)	(−1, −4)

➤ **Use the problem from the previous page to help you understand how an image formed by a sequence of transformations compares to the original figure.**

1 **a.** Did both sequences map figure *T* onto the same final image? How do **Picture It** and **Model It** each show this?

b. How do you know that both final images are congruent to the original figure *T*?

2 **a.** Translate figure *T* 3 units to the left. Then reflect the image across the *x*-axis. Draw the final image.

b. Then perform these same transformations in reverse order. Draw the final image.

c. Do both sequences map figure *T* onto the same final image? How do you know?

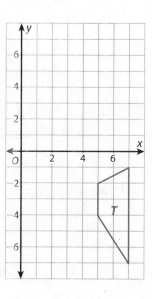

3 What can be different about a figure and any of its images after a sequence of translations, reflections, and rotations? What always stays the same? Why?

4 **Reflect** Think about all the models and strategies you have discussed today. Describe how one of them helped you better understand how to perform sequences of transformations.

Apply It

➤ **Use what you learned to solve these problems.**

5 **a.** Rotate the letter W 180° around the origin. Then translate the image up 4 units. Draw the final image. What new letter did you form?

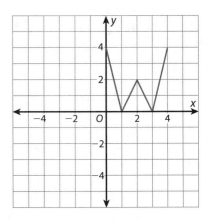

b. Is the new letter congruent to the original letter? Explain.

6 A sequence of transformations is performed on a figure. Then a different sequence is performed on the same figure. The resulting images are not in the same position. Can they be congruent? Explain.

7 **a.** Translate figure Z 3 units to the left. Then translate the image 5 units down. Draw the image after each transformation.

b. Now perform the transformations in reverse order. Draw the image after each transformation.

c. Do both sequences map figure Z onto the same final image? Explain.

Practice Performing Sequences of Rigid Transformations

➤ **Study the Example showing how to perform a sequence of transformations. Then solve problems 1–4.**

Example

Rotate figure A 90° clockwise around the origin to form figure B. Then translate figure B 6 units down to form figure C. Is figure C congruent to figure A? Explain.

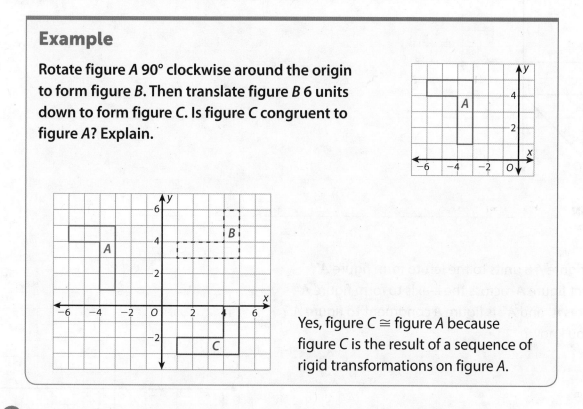

Yes, figure C ≅ figure A because figure C is the result of a sequence of rigid transformations on figure A.

1 Translate figure A from the Example 6 units down to form figure D. Then rotate figure D 90° clockwise around the origin to form figure E. Does this sequence of transformations map figure A onto figure C in the Example? Explain.

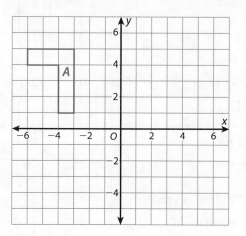

2 Reflect △*DEF* across the *y*-axis. Then rotate △*D'E'F'* 90° counterclockwise around the origin. What are the coordinates of the vertices of △*D"E"F"*? Show your work.

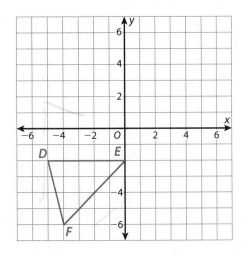

SOLUTION

3 Translate figure *A* 8 units to the left to form figure *A'*. Then reflect figure *A'* across the *x*-axis to form figure *A"*. Draw figures *A'* and *A"*. Is figure *A* congruent to figure *A"*? How do you know?

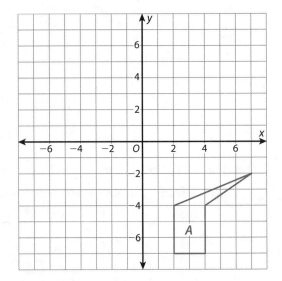

4 Perform the following sequence of transformations on figure *HJKL*:

- Rotate figure *HJKL* 180° around the origin to form figure *H'J'K'L'*.
- Reflect figure *H'J'K'L'* across the *y*-axis to form figure *H"J"K"L"*.
- Reflect figure *H"J"K"L"* across the *x*-axis to form figure *H'''J'''K'''L'''*.

What are the coordinates of the vertices of figure *H'''J'''K'''L'''*? How do the vertices of figure *H'''J'''K'''L'''* compare to the corresponding vertices of figure *HJKL*?

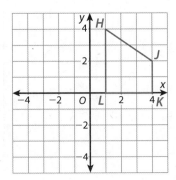

Develop Describing Sequences of Rigid Transformations

➤ **Read and try to solve the problem below.** ~ same shape size

Paula plays a game on her phone where she needs to fit shapes together. Figure *J* will fit into space *J"* only if the figure and the space are congruent. Describe a sequence of two transformations that moves the shape into its space.

TRY IT

 Math Toolkit graph paper, unit tiles, tracing paper, transparency sheets

translation
reflection
rotation

If you were to rotate figure j 90 degrees clockwise. You would then translate figure J far units down.

➤ **Explore different ways to map one figure onto another.**

Paula plays a game on her phone where she needs to fit shapes together. Figure *J* will fit into space *J″* only if the figure and the space are congruent. Describe a sequence of two transformations that moves the shape into its space.

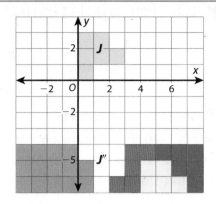

Picture It

You can start by rotating. Then you can translate.

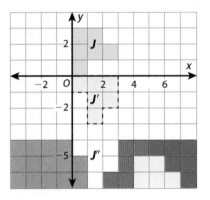

Picture It

You can start by translating. Then you can rotate around the origin.

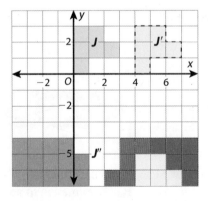

CONNECT IT

➤ **Use the problem from the previous page to help you understand how to describe sequences of transformations.**

1 Look at both **Picture Its**. Explain how the figure was transformed in each.

2 Look at the longest side of figure *J* and the corresponding side of figure *J"*. Are the sides horizontal or vertical? How could this help you decide whether or not to include a rotation in the sequence?

3 Why is one rotation around the origin not enough? What else is needed?

4 Is it possible to map figure *J* onto figure *J"* if one or both of the two transformations in the sequence is a reflection across an axis? Explain.

5 How can comparing a figure and its image help you describe a sequence of transformations that shows the two figures are congruent?

6 **Reflect** Think about all the models and strategies you have discussed today. Describe how one of them helped you better understand how to solve the **Try It** problem.

Apply It

➤ **Use what you learned to solve these problems.**

7 Figure *P* is congruent to figure *Q*. Describe a sequence of transformations that shows this. Show your work.

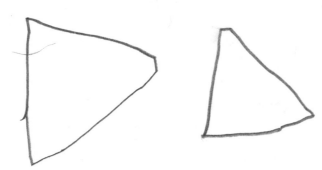 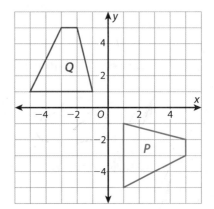

SOLUTION ___If you___

8 Figure *A* and figure *B* are congruent rectangles. Which sequences of transformations show this? Select all that apply.

A Rotate figure *A* 90° counterclockwise around the origin. Then translate the image 1 unit up.

B Translate figure *A* 4 units right. Then translate the image 1 unit up.

C Translate figure *A* 1 unit up. Then reflect the image across the *x*-axis.

D Rotate figure *A* 180° around the origin.

E Reflect figure *A* across the *x*-axis. Then reflect the image across the *y*-axis.

F Reflect figure *A* across the *y*-axis. Then translate the image 1 unit up.

9 Figure *H* is congruent to figure *H″*. Describe two different sequences of transformations you can use to show this.

Practice Describing Sequences of Rigid Transformations

➤ **Study the Example showing how to describe a sequence of transformations. Then solve problems 1–3.**

Example

Describe a sequence of transformations you could use to show that figure W is congruent to figure W″.

Rotate figure W 180° around the origin. Then translate the image 6 units to the right.

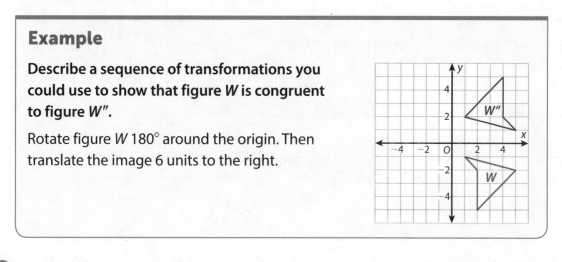

1 **a.** Look at the Example. Perform the same sequence of transformations described on figure W″. How does the image compare to figure W?

b. Describe a different sequence of transformations that you can perform on figure W to show that figure W ≅ figure W″.

2 **a.** Describe a sequence of transformations that you can perform on figure G to show that figure G ≅ figure H. Use only one type of transformation.

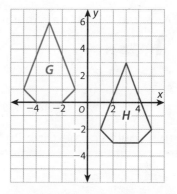

b. Describe a sequence of two different types of transformations that you can perform on figure G to show that figure G ≅ figure H.

Vocabulary

congruent
same size and shape.

sequence of transformations
one or more transformations performed in a certain order.

3 Triangles *A*, *B*, *C*, and *D* are all congruent.

a. Describe a sequence of transformations that you can perform on △*B* to show that △*B* ≅ △*D*.

b. Describe a sequence of transformations that you can perform on △*A* to show that △*A* ≅ △*C*.

c. Describe a sequence of transformations that you can perform on △*C* to show that △*C* ≅ △*D*.

d. Use your answers to problems 3b and 3c to describe a four-step sequence of transformations that you can perform on △*A* to show that △*A* ≅ △*D*.

e. Describe a sequence of two transformations that you can perform on △*A* to show that △*A* ≅ △*D*.

f. What single transformation could you perform on △*A* to show that △*A* ≅ △*D*?

Refine Working with Sequences of Transformations and Congruence

➤ **Complete the Example below. Then solve problems 1–9.**

Example

Figure *N* has vertices at $(-5, 3)$, $(0, 3)$, $(-3, 1)$, and $(-5, 1)$. Figure *N‴* has vertices at $(6, -5)$, $(6, 0)$, $(4, -3)$, and $(4, -5)$. Describe a sequence of three transformations that you can perform on figure *N* to show that figure *N* ≅ figure *N‴*.

Look at how you could show your work in the coordinate plane.

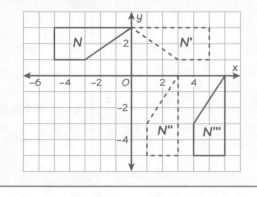

SOLUTION _____

_____

_____

CONSIDER THIS . . .
You can use triple prime notation to name the final image after three transformations.

PAIR/SHARE
Could you start with a rotation instead of a reflection?

Apply It

1 Figure *W* is congruent to figure *W″*. What sequence of transformations can you use to show this?

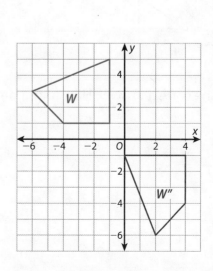

CONSIDER THIS . . .
Rotations, translations, and reflections are types of transformations.

PAIR/SHARE
Will the sequence you described map figure *W″* onto figure *W*?

LESSON 3 Work with Sequences of Transformations and Congruence   **61**

2 △*PQR* has vertices *P*(−4, 4), *Q*(−2, 3), and *R*(−5, 2). △*PQR* is reflected across the *x*-axis and rotated 180° around the origin. What are the coordinates of △*P″Q″R″*? Show your work.

> **CONSIDER THIS ...**
> You can think of the reflection as forming △*P′Q′R′*.

> **PAIR/SHARE**
> If you performed the transformations in reverse order, would the sequence map △*PQR* onto the same final image?

SOLUTION _____

3 Which graph shows the image of the triangle after a translation 6 units to the left, followed by a reflection across the *y*-axis?

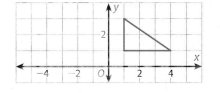

> **CONSIDER THIS ...**
> Could making a sketch help you find the answer?

A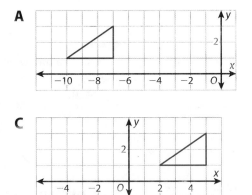

B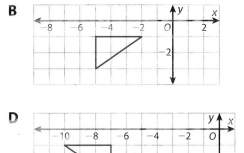

C

D

Kamal chose A as the correct answer. How might he have gotten that answer?

> **PAIR/SHARE**
> How can you tell whether all of the triangles shown are congruent to the original triangle?

4 Reflect the figure at the right across the y-axis. Then rotate the image 180° around the origin. Draw the image after each transformation. What single transformation could you perform on the figure to get the same final image?

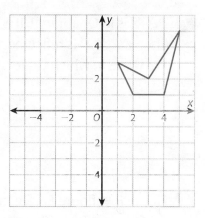

5 △ABC ≅ △DEF. Which sequences of transformations can you perform on △ABC to show this? Select all that apply.

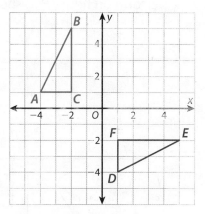

A Rotate △ABC 180° around the origin.

B Reflect △ABC across the x-axis. Then rotate the image 90° counterclockwise around the origin.

C Rotate △ABC 90° clockwise around the origin. Then reflect the image across the x-axis.

D Rotate △ABC 90° counterclockwise around the origin. Then rotate the image 90° counterclockwise around the origin.

E Reflect △ABC across the y-axis. Then rotate the image 90° clockwise around the origin.

6 Figures G and G‴ are congruent. Which sequence of transformations can you perform on figure G to show this?

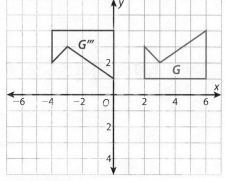

A Reflect figure G across the x-axis. Then translate figure G′ 3 units up. Then translate figure G″ 6 units to the left.

B Reflect figure G across the x-axis. Then translate figure G′ 6 units to the left. Then translate figure G″ 5 units up.

C Rotate figure G 90° counterclockwise around the origin. Then translate figure G′ 3 units up. Then translate figure G″ 2 units to the right.

D Rotate figure G 180° around the origin. Then translate figure G′ 5 units up. Then translate figure G″ 2 units to the right.

7 △*XYZ* is in Quadrant I. It is rotated 90° counterclockwise around the origin. Then △*X′Y′Z′* is reflected across the *y*-axis. Then △*X″Y″Z″* is translated 5 units to the right. In which Quadrant is △*X‴Y‴Z‴*? How do you know?

8 Figure *R* ≅ figure *R‴*. Describe a sequence of three transformations you can perform on figure *R* to show this. Show your work.

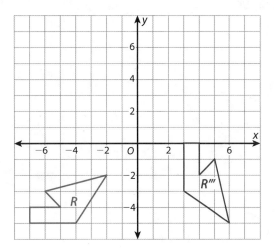

SOLUTION _____

_____

_____

9 **Math Journal** Describe two ways to use transformations to show that △*S* ≅ △*T*.

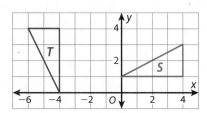

✓ End of Lesson Checklist

☐ **INTERACTIVE GLOSSARY** Find the entry for *congruent*. Draw two pairs of congruent figures. Explain how you know they are congruent.

☐ **SELF CHECK** Go back to the Unit 1 Opener and see what you can check off.

Study an Example Problem and Solution

SMP 1 Make sense of problems and persevere in solving them.

➤ **Read this problem involving rigid transformations. Then look at one student's solution to this problem on the following pages.**

Animating a Logo

Mora is an animator at a company that makes game apps for smart phones. Read this email about her next assignment for a game called Castle Gwendor.

Delete   Archive   Reply   Reply All   Forward

To: Mora
Subject: Game logo

Hi Mora,

We need you to design the initial animation sequence for the Castle Gwendor logo at the start of the game. The animation should meet these requirements:

Start: The line segments that will form the triangle in the logo should appear scattered on screen, with no overlap.

Animation: Each line segment should move to its final location in a different way, without changing shape or size.

End: The line segments should form the triangle shown.

PLEASE PROVIDE:
- coordinates for the starting locations of the endpoints of each line segment.
- a description of the transformation used to move each line segment to its final location in the logo.

Thanks!

Savanna

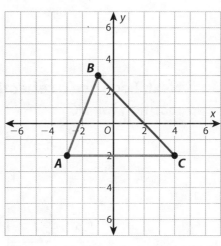

Early towers were built in the shape of rectangular prisms, but later builders favored cylindrical towers that offered better defense and visibility.

One Student's Solution

> **NOTICE THAT ...**
> Translations, reflections, and rotations result in congruent images, so they will not change the lengths of the line segments.

First, I have to decide what transformations to use.

Each line segment needs to move in a different way. Translations, rotations, and reflections move line segments in different ways, so I will use one of each.

So, I can use a translation to find a possible starting location for $\overline{AB}$.

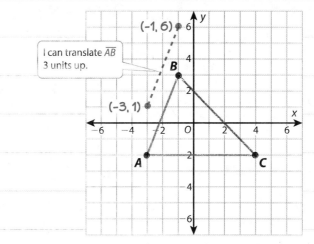

> I can translate $\overline{AB}$ 3 units up.

Next, I can use a reflection to find a possible starting location for $\overline{BC}$.

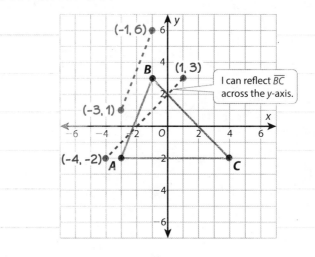

> I can reflect $\overline{BC}$ across the y-axis.

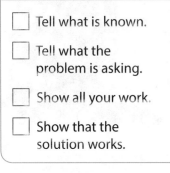

Problem-Solving Checklist

- ☐ Tell what is known.
- ☐ Tell what the problem is asking.
- ☐ Show all your work.
- ☐ Show that the solution works.

Then, I can use a rotation to find a possible starting location for $\overline{AC}$.

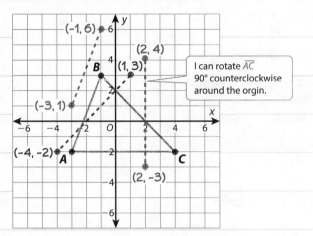

I can rotate $\overline{AC}$ 90° counterclockwise around the orgin.

NOTICE THAT...
If the starting locations of the line segments overlap, try rotating in a different direction, reflecting across the other axis, or translating a different number of units.

Now, I can check to make sure the design meets the criteria.

Each line segment moves using a different transformation. None of the segments overlap when they are in their starting locations, and each segment is congruent to its image.

Finally, I will list the starting locations and describe the transformations.

- **To form $\overline{AB}$:** Start with a line segment from $(-3, 1)$ to $(-1, 6)$. Translate the line segment 3 units down.

- **To form $\overline{BC}$:** Start with a line segment from $(1, 3)$ to $(-4, -2)$. Reflect the line segment across the y-axis.

- **To form $\overline{AC}$:** Start with a line segment from $(2, -3)$ to $(2, 4)$. Rotate the line segment 90° clockwise around the origin.

NOTICE THAT...
If you translate $\overline{AB}$ 3 units up to find its starting location, you will need to translate the segment in the starting location 3 units down to form $\overline{AB}$.

Try Another Approach

➤ **There are many ways to solve problems. Think about how you might solve the Animating a Logo problem in a different way.**

Animating a Logo

Mora is an animator at a company that makes game apps for smart phones. Read this email about her next assignment for a game called Castle Gwendor.

To: Mora
Subject: Game logo

Hi Mora,

We need you to design the initial animation sequence for the Castle Gwendor logo at the start of the game. The animation should meet these requirements:

Start: The line segments that will form the triangle in the logo should appear scattered on screen, with no overlap.

Animation: Each line segment should move to its final location in a different way, without changing shape or size.

End: The line segments should form the triangle shown.

PLEASE PROVIDE:
- coordinates for the starting locations of the endpoints of each line segment.
- a description of the transformation used to move each line segment to its final location in the logo.

Thanks!

Savanna

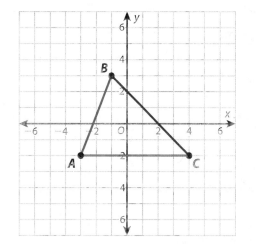

Plan It

➤ **Answer these questions to help you start thinking about a plan.**

  a. What transformations could you use to move the line segments without changing their shape or size?

  b. What are some different locations in the coordinate plane where each line segment could start?

Solve It

➤ **Find a different solution for the Animating a Logo problem. Show all your work on a separate sheet of paper. You may want to use the Problem-Solving Tips to get started.**

PROBLEM-SOLVING TIPS

Math Toolkit graph paper, tracing paper, transparency sheets

Key Terms

center of rotation	congruent	image
line of reflection	reflection	rigid transformation
rotation	transformation	translation

Sentence Starters

- To find the starting location, I . . .
- I checked my work by . . .

Reflect

Use Mathematical Practices As you work through the problem, discuss these questions with a partner.

- **Use Tools** Will a ruler or protractor be helpful for this problem? Explain how they could help, or explain why they would not be helpful.

- **Persevere** Why might you try several different locations for the starting position of each line segment before giving your final answer?

Discuss Models and Strategies

➤ **Read the problem. Write a solution on a separate sheet of paper. Remember, there can be lots of ways to solve a problem.**

Shattering a Jewel

Next, Mora works on animations for a scene in the treasure room of Castle Gwendor. Read this email about her assignment.

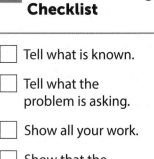

🗑 Delete   🗑 Archive | ✉ Reply   ✉ Reply All   ✉ Forward

To: Mora
Subject: Jewel of Wisdom

Hi Mora,

Today we need your help with an animation that shows the Jewel of Wisdom shattering into three pieces. The animation should meet these requirements:

Start: The three pieces form the shape of the jewel, as shown.

Animation: Each piece should move to its final location using at least two different transformations, without changing shape or size. The final location of each piece should be different from its starting location.

End: The pieces should be scattered around the screen with no overlap.

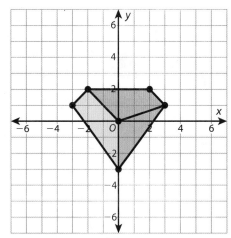

PLEASE PROVIDE:

• coordinates for the final locations of the vertices of each piece.

• a description of the transformations used to move each piece from its starting location in the jewel to its final location.

Thanks!

Savanna

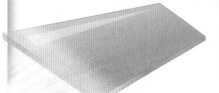

Plan It and Solve It

➤ **Find a solution to the Shattering a Jewel problem.**

Write a detailed plan and support your answer. Be sure to include:

• a coordinate plane showing the final locations of each of the three pieces.

• complete descriptions of a sequence of transformations that will move each piece from its starting location in the jewel to its final location somewhere else.

• a sketch of each piece after the first transformation in each sequence has been performed.

PROBLEM-SOLVING TIPS

Math Toolkit graph paper, tracing paper, transparency sheets

Key Terms

clockwise	counterclockwise	origin
reflection	rotation	translation
vertex	*x*-axis	*y*-axis

Questions

• What information do you need to include when you describe a translation? A reflection? A rotation?

• Why might you choose one type of transformation over another?

Reflect

Use Mathematical Practices As you work through the problem, discuss these questions with a partner.

• **Be Precise** Does the order of the transformations matter? Explain.

• **Repeated Reasoning** How do the coordinates of the vertices of a piece change when each transformation is performed?

Persevere On Your Own

➤ **Read the problem. Write a solution on a separate sheet of paper.**

Forming a Key

Mora's next animation task involves a key to a door in Castle Gwendor. Read this email about her assignment.

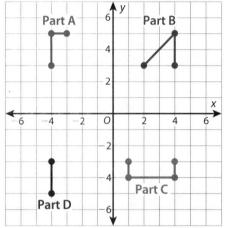

● ● ●

🗑 Delete   🗑 Archive   ✉ Reply   ✉ Reply All   ✉ Forward

To: Mora
Subject: Key to the tower door

Hi Mora,

Next, we need you to work on the key for the tower door. This key is broken into the four parts shown. Once a player collects all four parts, we need an animation showing the parts moving and joining to form a closed shape. The animation should meet these requirements:

Start: The parts begin in the locations shown.

Animation: Each part should move to its final location without changing shape or size. Use at least one reflection, one rotation, and one translation to make the key.

End: All parts should connect to form a closed shape. The closed shape does not have to look like a typical door key.

PLEASE PROVIDE:
• a drawing of the final design of the key.
• descriptions of the transformation or sequence of transformations that will move each part to its final location in the design.

Thanks!

Savanna

Solve It

➤ **Find a solution to the Forming a Key problem.**

- Draw the final design of the key on a coordinate plane, and make sure it is a closed shape. Label the vertices with their coordinates.

- Describe the transformation or sequence of transformations that moves each part of the key to its final location.

Reflect

Use Mathematical Practices After you complete the problem, choose one of these questions to discuss with a partner.

- **Use Structure** How could you transform the four parts a different way to form a key with a different closed shape?

- **Critique Reasoning** Do the transformations your partner described result in the formation of a closed shape? Explain.

Self Reflection

In this unit you learned to . . .

Skill	Lesson(s)
Recognize translations, reflections, and rotations as rigid transformations.	**1, 2**
Understand that rigid transformations do not change the size and shape of a figure.	**1, 2**
Perform translations, reflections, and rotations in the coordinate plane.	**2**
Describe a rigid transformation that maps a figure onto an image.	**2, 3**
Understand that two figures are congruent if one can be mapped exactly onto the other by a sequence of one or more rigid transformations.	**3**
Perform sequences of translations, rotations, and reflections in the coordinate plane.	**3**
Describe a sequence of translations, rotations, and reflections that maps a figure onto an image.	**3**
Use math vocabulary and precise language to describe the effects of rigid transformations on a figure.	**1–3**

Think about what you have learned.

➤ **Use words, numbers, and drawings.**

1 Three examples of what I learned are . . .

2 The hardest thing I learned to do is _____ because . . .

3 One thing I am still confused about is . . .

➤ Review the unit vocabulary. Put a check mark by terms you can use in speaking and writing. Look up the meaning of any terms you do not know.

Math Vocabulary

☐ center of rotation   ☐ line of reflection

☐ congruent   ☐ reflection

☐ corresponding sides   ☐ rigid transformation

☐ image   ☐ rotation

Academic Vocabulary

☐ clockwise

☐ counterclockwise

☐ original

☐ perform

➤ Use the unit vocabulary to complete the problems.

1 Describe a possible sequence of transformations that maps Figure *ABCDE* onto figure *A′B′C′D′E′*. Use at least two math or academic vocabulary terms in your answer. Underline each term you use.

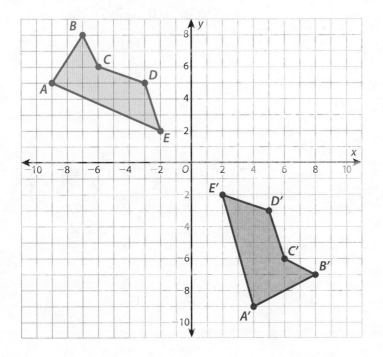

2 Describe the relationship between Figures *ABCDE* and *A′B′C′D′E′* using at least three math or academic vocabulary terms from the unit in your answer. Underline each term you use.

➤ **Use what you have learned to complete these problems.**

1 Figure *F* is a rotation of figure *C*.

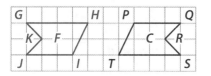

Choose the corresponding line segment of figure *C* for each given line segment of figure *F*.

	Corresponding Line Segment			
	$\overline{QP}$	$\overline{ST}$	$\overline{SR}$	$\overline{TP}$
a. $\overline{GH}$	○	○	○	○
b. $\overline{HI}$	○	○	○	○
c. $\overline{JI}$	○	○	○	○
d. $\overline{GK}$	○	○	○	○

2 Which angles have the same measure as $\angle E$? Choose all the correct answers.

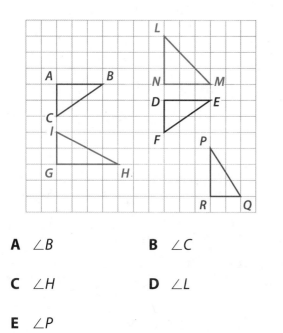

A $\angle B$　　　　**B** $\angle C$

C $\angle H$　　　　**D** $\angle L$

E $\angle P$

3 Does figure *B* appear to be a rigid transformation of figure *A*? Use parallel sides to explain your reasoning.

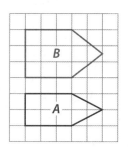

SOLUTION _____

_____

_____

_____

4 Figure $R \cong R'''$. Describe a sequence of three transformations that can be performed on figure *R* to show this. Show your work.

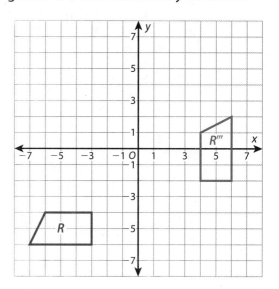

SOLUTION _____

_____

_____

_____

5 △DEF ≅ △LMN. Which sequence of transformations can be performed on △DEF to show this?

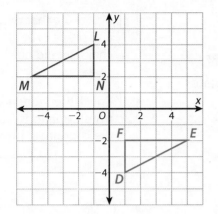

A Reflect △DEF across the y-axis. Then translate the image 6 units up.

B Translate △DEF 6 units up. Then rotate the image 90° counterclockwise around the origin.

C Rotate △DEF 90° clockwise around the origin. Then rotate the image 90° clockwise around the origin.

D Translate △DEF 6 units to the left. Then rotate the image 90° clockwise around the origin.

6 Sarah draws figure EFGH in the coordinate plane. She rotates figure EFGH 90° clockwise around vertex E to form image EF'G'H'. Draw the image EF'G'H' on the coordinate plane.

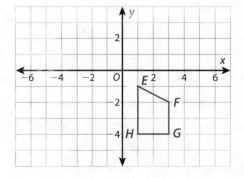

7 △PQR has vertices P(−4, 4), Q(−2, 3), and R(−5, 2). △PQR is rotated 90° clockwise around the origin. Then the image is translated 5 units down and reflected across the y-axis. What are the coordinates of △P‴Q‴R‴? Show your work.

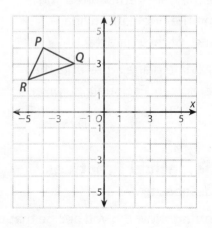

SOLUTION _____

_____

Performance Task

➤ **Answer the questions and show all your work on separate paper.**

A computer software company asks you to design a program that can be used to create a video game character. The character moves, but its size and shape do not change. The company gives you a list of program requirements.

- Create a character by graphing a geometric figure composed of straight-line segments in the coordinate plane. List the coordinates of the character.

- Use each of the rigid transformations to describe a movement that the character makes when players press a certain key on the keypad. Identify the key and the transformation the character undergoes when the key is pressed.

- List a sequence of keys pressed and transformations that will take place. Graph the sequence of transformations in the coordinate plane. List the coordinates of the final location of the character.

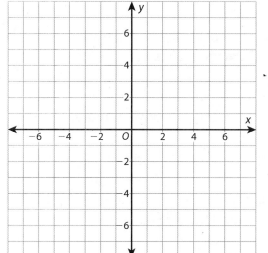

Describe the transformations using words and the original and final coordinates of the character.

The coordinate plane represents the computer screen. Each unit is a pixel.

Checklist

Did you . . .

☐ Create at least one rotation, reflection, and translation?

☐ Make sure that the size and shape of your character did not change?

☐ Check the sequence of transformations and the coordinate points?

Reflect

Use Mathematical Practices After you complete the task, choose one of the following questions to answer.

- **Use Reasoning** How did you decide that the transformations would move your character to its final location?

- **Model** How did you make sure you accurately showed each transformation in the sequence?

Unit 2

Geometric Figures

Transformations, Similarity, and Angle Relationships

☑ **Self Check**

Before starting this unit, check off the skills you know below.
As you complete each lesson, see how many more skills you can check off!

I can ...	Before	After
Understand that a dilation is a transformation in which the shape of a figure stays the same, but its size can change.	☐	☐
Understand that if a figure can be obtained by transforming a different figure, they are similar.	☐	☐
Perform and describe a sequence of transformations that shows two figures are similar.	☐	☐
Identify pairs of angles that are formed when two lines are cut by a transversal.	☐	☐
Use angle relationships to find unknown angle measurements given a pair of parallel lines cut by a transversal.	☐	☐
Find unknown angle measurements by using the interior and exterior angle relationships of a triangle.	☐	☐
Show that if two triangles have two pairs of corresponding angles that are congruent, then the triangles are similar.	☐	☐
Agree or disagree with ideas in discussions about geometric figures and explain why.	☐	☐

Prepare for Transformations and Similarity

➤ **Write what you know about sequences of transformations in the boxes.**
Share your ideas with a partner and add any new information you think of together.

What It Is

What I Know About It

sequences of transformations

Related Terms

Examples

Dear Family,

This week your student is exploring dilations and similarity.

A **dilation** is a transformation that makes a scale copy of a figure. When you dilate a figure, you start from a point called the **center of dilation**. Each point on the image is on a ray that starts at the center of dilation and passes through the corresponding point on the original figure. Dilating a figure usually reduces or enlarges it. The dilated image is **similar** to the original figure. This means it has the same shape as the original figure. The length of each side on the image is the same scale factor times the length of the corresponding side on the original figure.

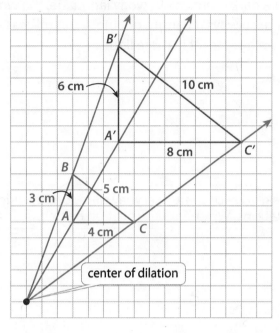

For example, $\triangle A'B'C'$ is a dilation of $\triangle ABC$, with the side lengths of $\triangle ABC$ multiplied by the scale factor 2:

   3 cm $\times$ 2 = 6 cm, 4 cm $\times$ 2 = 8 cm, and 5 cm $\times$ 2 = 10 cm

Students will be exploring what happens to a figure when it is dilated.

➤ **ONE WAY** to dilate a figure is to enlarge it. Multiply the side lengths by a scale factor greater than 1. Figure *E* is a dilation of figure *D*.

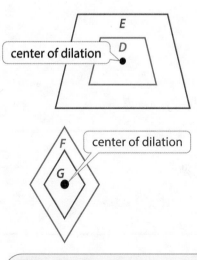

➤ **ANOTHER WAY** to dilate a figure is to reduce it. Multiply the side lengths by a scale factor less than 1 but greater than 0. Figure *G* is a dilation of figure *F*.

▶ Use the next page to start a conversation about dilations and similarity.

Activity Thinking About Dilations and Similarity

Bright Light

Dim Light

➤ **Do this activity together to investigate dilations in the real world.**

You can see examples of dilations in technology and science! For example, the pupil in your eye dilates when you enter a dark room. In everyday language, the word *dilate* almost always means to get bigger. In this case, your pupil gets bigger to let in more light.

? Make a list of some everyday situations in which you might see dilations. Why might the dilation be helpful in each situation?

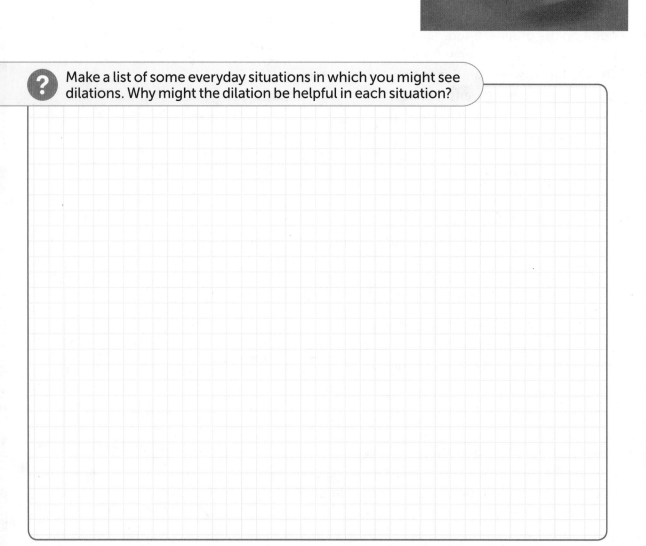

Explore Dilations and Similarity

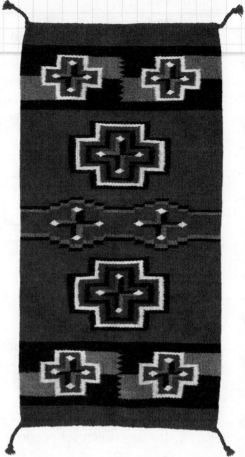

Model It

➤ **Complete the problems about enlarging and reducing a figure.**

1 In art class, Kennedy draws scale copies of figure *A* to make a rug pattern. She uses a scale factor of $\frac{3}{2}$ to draw figure *B*. Complete figure *B* by drawing the missing sides.

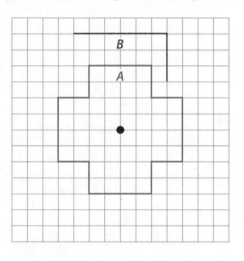

2 Kennedy uses a scale factor of $\frac{1}{2}$ to draw figure *C*. Complete figure *C* by drawing the missing sides.

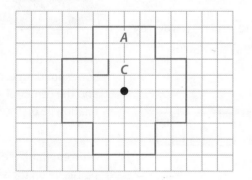

A transformation that makes a scale copy of a figure is called a **dilation**. Figures *B* and *C* in problems 1 and 2 are dilations of figure *A*.

DISCUSS IT

Ask: How did you decide how long to make the sides in figure *B*? In figure *C*?

Share: I noticed . . . so I decided . . .

◎ **Learning Target** SMP 2, SMP 3, SMP 6, SMP 7
Understand that a two-dimensional figure is similar to another if the second can be obtained from the first by a sequence of rotations, reflections, translations, and dilations; given two similar two-dimensional figures, describe a sequence that exhibits the similarity between them.

Model It

➤ **Complete the problems about dilating a figure.**

3 A dilation may change a figure's size. In a dilation, corresponding angles are congruent and corresponding side lengths are related by the same scale factor. Complete the table to determine whether figures *Q, R,* and *S* are dilations of figure *P*.

Figure	Corresponding angles are congruent	Corresponding sides are multiplied by the same scale factor	Dilation of *P*?
Q			
R			
S			

4 The point from which a figure is dilated is called the **center of dilation**. A center of dilation can be inside, on, or outside a figure.

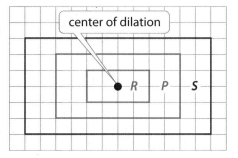

a. Use a straightedge to draw rays from the center of dilation through each set of corresponding vertices of figures *R, P,* and *S*.

For two figures,

- If the figures are dilations of each other, then you can draw rays from the center of dilation through each pair of corresponding vertices.

- If at least one pair of corresponding vertices do not lie on the same ray drawn from the center of dilation, then neither figure is a dilation of the other.

b. Can you draw rays from the point shown through each pair of corresponding vertices of figures *R* and *Q*?

5 **Reflect** Does a dilation change a figure's shape? How is a dilation different from a translation, rotation, or reflection?

> ## DISCUSS IT
>
> *Ask:* Why do corresponding vertices and the center of dilation lie on the same ray?
>
> *Share:* I think these points lie on the same ray because . . .

Prepare for Dilations and Similarity

1   Think about what you know about scale factors and scale drawings. Fill in each box. Use words, numbers, and pictures. Show as many ideas as you can.

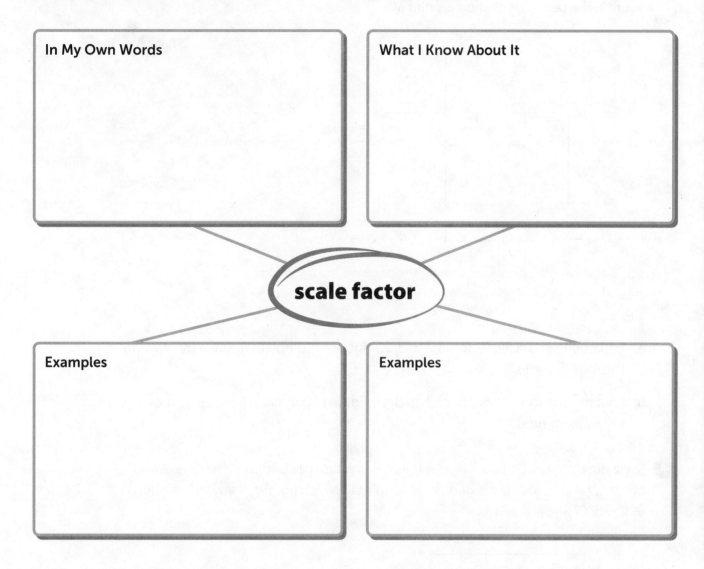

In My Own Words	What I Know About It

scale factor

Examples	Examples

2   Figure *B* is a scale copy of figure *A*. Circle the scale factor that was used to draw figure *B*.

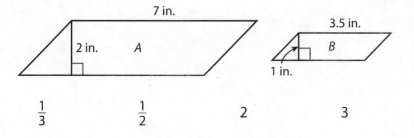

$\dfrac{1}{3}$ $\dfrac{1}{2}$ 2   3

➤ **Complete problems 3 and 4.**

3 In woodworking class, Eduardo makes a pattern for the top of a wooden box. He uses scale copies of figure *J*. The center of dilation is point *M*.

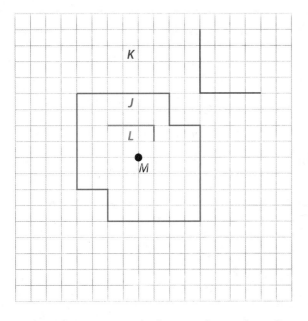

a. Eduardo uses a scale factor of 2 to draw figure *K*. Complete figure *K* by drawing the missing sides.

b. Eduardo uses a scale factor of $\frac{1}{2}$ to draw figure *L*. Complete figure *L* by drawing the missing sides.

4 Layla draws figure *C* as the original figure in a wallpaper pattern. Then she draws figures *D* and *E*. The center of dilation is point *F*. Which figures, if any, are dilations of figure *C*? Show your work.

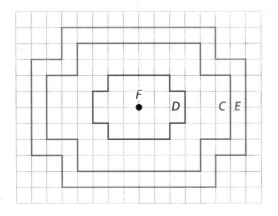

SOLUTION _____

©Curriculum Associates, LLC   Copying is not permitted.

Develop Understanding of Dilations and Similarity

Model It: Look at Size and Shape

 Try these three problems involving dilations.

1 Figure *S* is dilated to form figure *T*. The scale factor is 1.5 and the center of dilation is point *A*.

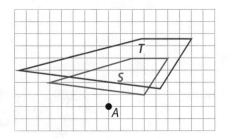

   a. How are figures *S* and *T* the same?

   b. How are figures *S* and *T* different?

2 Figures that are the same shape are **similar**. Two figures are similar if you can map one figure onto the other by a sequence of one or more transformations.

   Figures *S* and *T* in problem 1 are similar because you can map figure *S* onto figure *T* using a dilation. You can write the similarity statement:

     figure *S* ~ figure *T*

     | Read ~ as *is similar to.* |

   Is figure *T* similar to figure *S*? How do you know?

3 Choose two figures below that appear to be similar and write a similarity statement for them.

 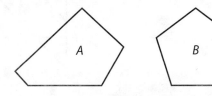 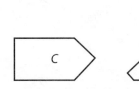

DISCUSS IT

Ask: How did you decide which two figures of *A*, *B*, *C*, and *D* are similar?

Share: I noticed . . . so I decided . . .

Model It: Look at Corresponding Parts

➤ **Try these two problems involving dilations.**

1 Figure *DEFGHI* is dilated to form similar figure *D'E'F'G'H'I'*. The scale factor is $\frac{1}{3}$ and the center of dilation is point *X*.

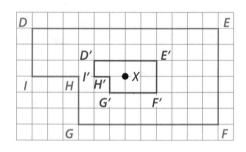

a. Side $\overline{D'E'}$ corresponds to side $\overline{DE}$. The quotient of their lengths can be written as a fraction: $\frac{D'E'}{DE} = \frac{4}{12}$. Write a fraction for each of the other five pairs of corresponding side lengths.

$\frac{E'F'}{EF} =$ _____ $\frac{F'G'}{FG} =$ _____ $\frac{G'H'}{GH} =$ _____ $\frac{H'I'}{HI} =$ _____ $\frac{D'I'}{DI} =$ _____

b. What is the relationship between the quotients of corresponding side lengths? How does this compare to the scale factor?

c. How do the measures of the corresponding angles compare?

2 What is the relationship between the corresponding side lengths and corresponding angles in similar figures *DEFGHI* and *D'E'F'G'H'I'*?

> **DISCUSS IT**
>
> *Ask:* Why does the relationship between the scale factor and the quotients of corresponding side lengths make sense?
>
> *Share:* I think the relationship makes sense because . . .

CONNECT IT

➤ **Complete the problems below.**

3 Describe two ways you can tell that two figures are similar.

4 Label the center of dilation for triangles *XYZ* and *XY'Z'*. Then write a similarity statement for the triangles.

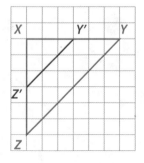

©Curriculum Associates, LLC   Copying is not permitted.

Practice Dilations and Similarity

➤ **Study how the Example shows how to determine if figures are similar. Then solve problems 1–4.**

Example

Jia draws figures *A*, *B*, *C*, and *D* on the grid. The center of dilation is point *E*. Which figures, if any, are similar to figure *A*? Explain how you know.

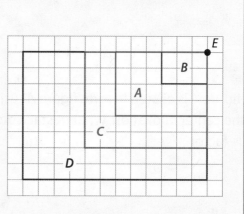

Figures *B* and *D* are similar to figure *A* because corresponding angles are congruent and the quotients of corresponding side lengths are equivalent. Figure *C* is not similar to figure *A*. Corresponding angles of figures *A* and *C* are congruent, but the quotients of corresponding side lengths are not equivalent.

1 Christopher draws figures *W*, *X*, *Y*, and *Z*. The center of dilation is *V*. Which figures, if any, are dilations of figure *W*? Explain.

2 Ms. Romano draws figures *A* and *A'* on the board.

   a. Are figures *A* and *A'* similar? Explain.

   b. Nadia says figure *A* is dilated to form figure *A'* using a scale factor of 2 and point *B* as the center of dilation. What mistake did Nadia make? What is the correct scale factor?

3 Adnan wants a larger garden. He draws △*PQR* to show his original garden. He wants to enlarge the garden, so he uses a dilation to form the image △*PQ'R'*. He uses vertex *P* as the center of dilation.

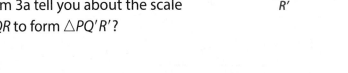

   a. Write a fraction for each quotient of corresponding side lengths.

$$\frac{PQ'}{PQ} = \underline{\quad\quad} \qquad \frac{Q'R'}{QR} = \underline{\quad\quad} \qquad \frac{PR'}{PR} = \underline{\quad\quad}$$

   b. What do your answers to problem 3a tell you about the scale factor Adnan used to dilate △*PQR* to form △*PQ'R'*?

   c. How do you know that the corresponding angles of △*PQR* and △*PQ'R'* are congruent?

4 Figure *WX'Y'Z'* is a dilation of figure *WXYZ*. Label the center of dilation. Then write a similarity statement.

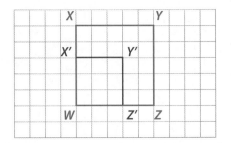

Refine Ideas About Dilations and Similarity

Apply It

➤ **Complete problems 1–5.**

1 **Analyze** Veda draws figures *A* and *B* and their dilations. Then she uses quotients to compare the area of each image with the area of its original figure. Veda says the quotient of the areas is equal to the scale factor. Is Veda correct? Explain.

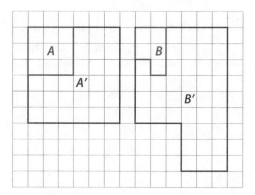

2 **Solve** Tyrone draws trapezoid *K* and its dilation, trapezoid *K′*. Draw the center of dilation. What is the scale factor? Show your work.

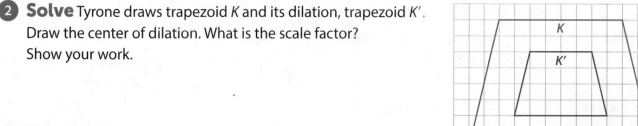

SOLUTION _____

3 **Determine** Mr. Lin draws triangles *STU* and *XYZ* on the board. Then he writes the quotients of the corresponding side lengths as fractions.

$$\frac{XY}{ST} = \frac{2}{8} \qquad \frac{YZ}{TU} = \frac{3}{12} \qquad \frac{XZ}{SU} = \frac{4}{15}$$

Mr. Lin says that △*XYZ* is not a dilation of △*STU*. Is Mr. Lin correct? How do you know?

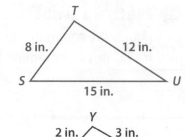

4 Aiyana draws figures *JKLM* and *PQRS* on the grid.

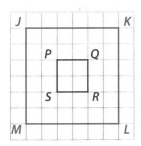

PART A Aiyana dilates figure *JKLM* to form image *JK'L'M'*. She uses a scale factor of 1 and point *J* as the center of dilation. How are the original figure and its image related?

PART B Draw and label figure *JK'L'M'* on the grid. Are figures *JK'L'M'* and *PQRS* similar to figure *JKLM*? Are they congruent to figure *JKLM*? Explain.

PART C Are all squares similar? Are all squares congruent? Explain.

5 **Math Journal** Mrs. Aba says: *All congruent figures are similar, but not all similar figures are congruent.* Use the definition of congruent figures and what it means for figures to be similar to explain whether this statement is correct.

✓ **End of Lesson Checklist**

☐ **INTERACTIVE GLOSSARY** Find the entry for *center of dilation*. Write a definition that would make sense to a younger student. Show an example and label the center of dilation.

Dear Family,

This week your student is learning how to perform and describe dilations in the coordinate plane. For example, the coordinate grid to the right shows △A dilated by a scale factor of 0.5. The center of dilation is at the origin. △A′ is the resulting image.

Students will use their understanding of dilations from the previous lesson to enlarge and reduce figures in the coordinate plane. They will identify the coordinates of the vertices of the figure's image, as in the problem below.

Rectangle *ABCD* is dilated by a scale factor of 2. The center of dilation is at the origin. What are the coordinates of the vertices of the image rectangle *A′B′C′D′*?

➤ **ONE WAY** to find the coordinates of the vertices of the image is to use a table.

ABCD	A(2, 2)	B(2, 3)	C(4, 3)	D(4, 2)
A′B′C′D′	A′(4, 4)	B′(4, 6)	C′(8, 6)	D′(8, 4)

Since the center of dilation is at the origin, you can multiply the original coordinates by the scale factor to find the coordinates of the vertices of the image.

➤ **ANOTHER WAY** is to graph the image and identify the coordinates of its vertices from the coordinate plane.

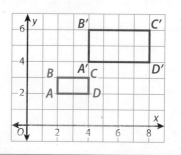

Using either method, the coordinates of the vertices of the image are the same: *A′*(4, 4); *B′*(4, 6); *C′*(8, 6); *D′*(8, 4).

 Use the next page to start a conversation about dilations in the real world.

Activity Thinking About Dilations Around You

➤ **Do this activity together to investigate performing and describing dilations.**

Dilations are important in many aspects of technology! For example, zooming in on an image using a digital camera dilates the real-world image and makes it look larger. Zooming out on the image dilates it to make it look smaller.

? What are other examples of dilations you have seen in the real world?

Explore Dilations in the Coordinate Plane

Previously, you learned about rigid transformations and dilations. In this lesson, you will learn about sequences of transformations in the coordinate plane involving both rigid transformations and dilations.

➤ **Use what you know to try to solve the problem below.**

Malcolm uses a program on his computer to resize photos for the yearbook. He drags the top right corner of the photo, represented by rectangle *ABCD*, along the dashed line. This forms the image rectangle *A'B'C'D'*. Malcolm uses a scale factor of 2. The center of dilation is at the origin. What are the coordinates of the vertices of image rectangle *A'B'C'D'*?

TRY IT   **Math Toolkit** graph paper, tracing paper, transparency sheets

DISCUSS IT

Ask: How did you get started finding the coordinates of rectangle *A'B'C'D'*?

Share: At first I thought . . .

◎ Learning Target   SMP 1, SMP 2, SMP 3, SMP 4, SMP 5, SMP 6, SMP 7, SMP 8
Describe the effect of dilations, translations, rotations, and reflections on two-dimensional figures using coordinates.

CONNECT IT

1 **Look Back** What are the coordinates of the vertices of rectangle $A'B'C'D'$? Describe your strategy for finding them.

2 **Look Ahead** You know that when you dilate a figure, the image is similar to the original figure. In similar figures, corresponding angle measures are congruent and corresponding side lengths are proportional. When the center of dilation is at the origin, the coordinates of the corresponding vertices of a figure and its image are also proportional.

a. Compare the coordinates of the vertices of rectangles $ABCD$ and $A'B'C'D'$ in the **Try It**. What can you multiply each vertex coordinate of figure $ABCD$ by to get the corresponding vertex coordinate of figure $A'B'C'D'$?

b. How could you use the scale factor to find the coordinates of the vertices of rectangle $A'B'C'D'$?

c. The table shows the coordinates of the vertices of $\triangle DEF$ and its dilated image $\triangle D'E'F'$. The center of dilation is the origin. What is the scale factor? How do you know?

DEF	$D(2, 3)$	$E(6, 4)$	$F(4, 8)$
D'E'F'	$D'(1, \frac{3}{2})$	$E'(3, 2)$	$F'(2, 4)$

3 **Reflect** You have the coordinates of a figure and a scale factor for a dilation. How can you find the coordinates of the image if the center of dilation is at the origin?

Name:

Prepare for Transformations Involving Dilations

1 Think about what you know about ratios and proportional relationships. Fill in each box. Use words, numbers, and pictures. Show as many ideas as you can.

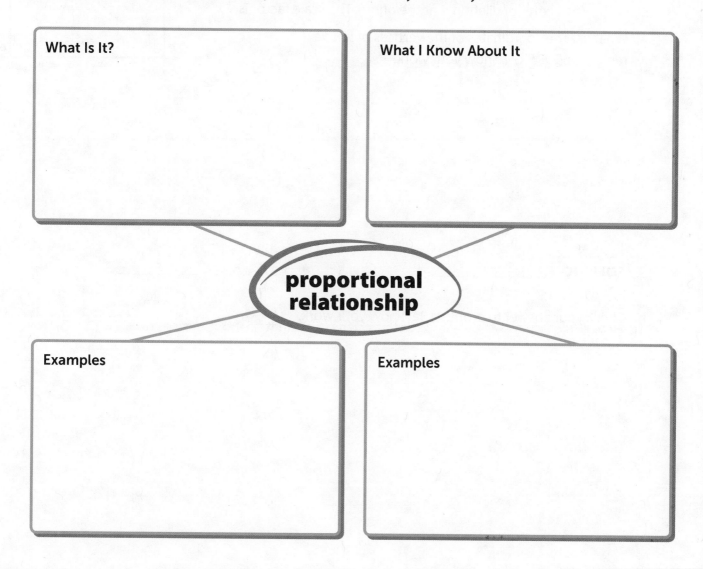

What Is It?

What I Know About It

proportional relationship

Examples

Examples

2 Is there a proportional relationship between the corresponding sides of each pair of rectangles?

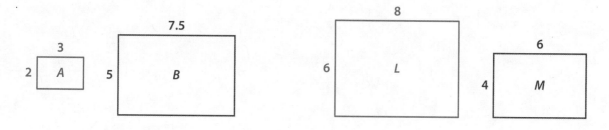

3 Cai uses a computer program to resize photos for the school newspaper. She drags the top right corner of the photo, represented by rectangle *DEFG*, along the dashed line to form the image rectangle *D'E'F'G'*. The center of dilation is at the origin. The scale factor is $\frac{1}{2}$.

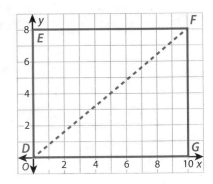

a. What are the coordinates of the vertices of image rectangle *D'E'F'G'*? Show your work.

SOLUTION _____

b. Check your answer to problem 3a. Show your work.

Develop Performing Sequences of Transformations Involving Dilations

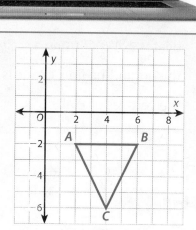

➤ **Read and try to solve the problem below.**

Abran is learning to program graphics on a computer. He draws $\triangle ABC$ and reflects it across the x-axis to form $\triangle A'B'C'$. Then he dilates $\triangle A'B'C'$ using a scale factor of $\frac{1}{2}$ with the center of dilation at the origin. The final image is $\triangle A''B''C''$. What are the coordinates of the vertices of $\triangle A''B''C''$?

TRY IT

Math Toolkit graph paper, tracing paper, transparency sheets

DISCUSS IT

Ask: Why did you choose that strategy to find the coordinates of $\triangle A''B''C''$?

Share: I knew . . . so I . . .

➤ **Explore different ways to perform a sequence of transformations involving dilations.**

Abran is learning to program graphics on a computer. He draws △ABC and reflects it across the x-axis to form △A'B'C'. Then he dilates △A'B'C' using a scale factor of $\frac{1}{2}$ with the center of dilation at the origin. The final image is △A"B"C". What are the coordinates of the vertices of △A"B"C"?

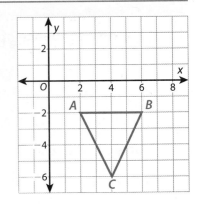

Model It

You can use what you know about how coordinates change for different transformations.

Original	After reflection	After dilation
(2, −2)	(2, 2)	(1, 1)
(6, −2)	(6, 2)	(3, 1)
(4, −6)	(4, 6)	(2, 3)

Picture It

You can show both transformations in the coordinate plane.

Use the coordinates from your table to draw each transformation.

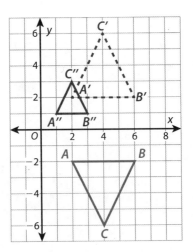

➤ **Use the problem from the previous page to help you understand how to perform a sequence of transformations involving dilations.**

1 **a.** Look at **Model It**. Describe how the coordinates of the vertices change from △ABC to the reflected figure △A′B′C′.

b. Describe how the coordinates of the vertices change from △A′B′C′ to the dilated figure △A″B″C″. What are the coordinates of the vertices of △A″B″C″?

2 **a.** Is △A′B′C′ similar to △ABC? Is △A″B″C″ similar to △A′B′C′? Explain.

b. Is △A″B″C″ similar to △ABC? Explain.

3 **Reflect** Think about all the models and strategies you have discussed today. Describe how one of them helped you better understand how to perform sequences of transformations involving dilations.

Apply It

➤ **Use what you learned to solve these problems.**

4 Grace wants to rotate *PQRS* 90° clockwise around the origin to form figure *P'Q'R'S'*. Then she wants to dilate the image using a scale factor of 2 and the origin as the center of dilation to form figure *P"Q"R"S"*. Grace's graph is shown. What mistake did Grace make? What are the correct coordinates of the vertices of figure *P"Q"R"S"*?

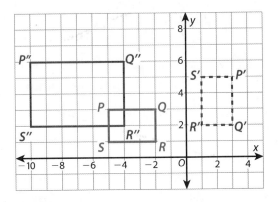

5 Two transformations are performed on △*X* in the coordinate plane. First, △*X* is rotated 90° counterclockwise around the origin to form image △*X'*. Then △*X'* is dilated using a scale factor of $\frac{3}{4}$ with the center of dilation at the origin to form image △*X"*. Which statement about △*X* and △*X"* is true?

A △*X* is similar to △*X"*.

B △*X* is congruent to △*X"*.

C △*X* is both congruent and similar to △*X"*.

D △*X* is neither congruent nor similar to △*X"*.

6 Dario dilates △*JKL* in the coordinate plane using a scale factor of 0.5 and a center of dilation at the origin. He labels the image △*J'K'L'*. Then he translates the image 3 units up to form △*J"K"L"*. What are the coordinates of the vertices of △*J"K"L"*? Show your work.

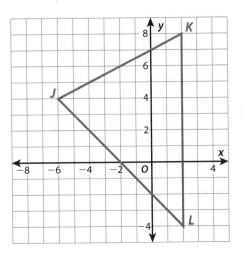

SOLUTION _____

Practice Performing Sequences of Transformations Involving Dilations

➤ **Study the Example showing how to perform a sequence of transformations involving dilations. Then solve problems 1–4.**

Example

Lamont designs obstacles for a skate park. He draws trapezoid *WXYZ* in the coordinate plane. Then he reflects trapezoid *WXYZ* across the *y*-axis to form image *W'X'Y'Z'*. Then he dilates the image to form trapezoid *W"X"Y"Z"*. He uses a scale factor of 1.5 and a center of dilation at the origin. What are the coordinates of the vertices of trapezoid *W"X"Y"Z"*?

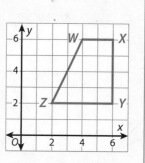

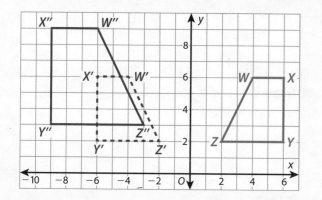

The coordinates are *W"*(−6, 9); *X"*(−9, 9); *Y"*(−9, 3); *Z"*(−3, 3).

1 Rani dilates figure *ABCD* to form figure *A'B'C'D'*. She uses a scale factor of $\frac{3}{4}$ and a center of dilation at the origin. Then she translates the image up 7 units to form figure *A"B"C"D"*.

What are the coordinates of the vertices of figure *A"B"C"D"*?

Show your work.

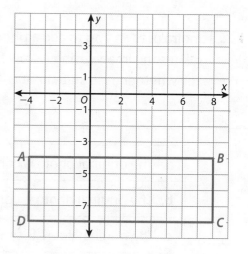

SOLUTION _____

2 Cyrus plans a design to paint on his bass drum. He starts with figure *P* and translates it 3 units to the right to form figure *P'*. Then he reflects figure *P'* across the *y*-axis to form figure *P''*. Then Cyrus dilates figure *P''* using a scale factor of 2 to form figure *P'''*. The center of dilation is at the origin. Draw figures *P'*, *P''*, and *P'''* in the coordinate plane.

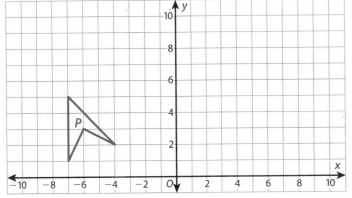

3 △*EFG* is translated 3 units to the left. Then the image is dilated by a scale factor of 0.5 to form △*E"F"G"*. The center of dilation is the origin. Vertex *E* is located at (5, −6). What are the coordinates of vertex *E"*? Show your work.

SOLUTION _____

4 Indira uses an app to add a photo to a poster. She rotates the photo. Then she dilates the image using a scale factor of 3 and a center of dilation at the origin. Tell whether each statement is *True* or *False*.

	True	False
a. The original photo is congruent to the final image.	○	○
b. The original photo is congruent to the rotated photo.	○	○
c. The original figure is similar to the rotated photo.	○	○
d. The original photo is similar to the final image.	○	○

Develop Describing Sequences of Transformations Involving Dilations

➤ **Read and try to solve the problem below.**

For the Challenge of the Week, Ryan's teacher draws figures *ABCD* and *EFGH* in the coordinate plane. The challenge is to show that the two figures are similar using three or fewer transformations. What is one sequence of transformations that Ryan could use?

1) Dilation by a scale factor of 1/2

2) Reflection across x-axis

3) Reflection across y-axis

TRY IT

Math Toolkit graph paper, tracing paper, transparency sheets

LESSON 5 Perform and Describe Transformations Involving Dilations **105**

➤ **Explore different ways to map one figure onto another.**

For the Challenge of the Week, Ryan's teacher draws figures *ABCD* and *EFGH* in the coordinate plane. The challenge is to show that the two figures are similar using three or fewer transformations. What is one sequence of transformations that Ryan could use?

Picture It

You can graph the possible transformations.

You can map figure *ABCD* onto figure *EFGH* using three transformations.

- reflection
- **reflection**
- dilation

Model It

You can use what you know about coordinates of transformations.

You can map figure *ABCD* onto figure *EFGH* using two transformations.

A rotation faces figure *ABCD* in the same direction as figure *EFGH*. A dilation reduces the image.

ABCD	After rotation	EFGH
$A(-2, 2)$	$(2, -2)$	$E(1, -1)$
$B(-2, 4)$	$(2, -4)$	$F(1, -2)$
$C(4, 4)$	$(-4, -4)$	$G(-2, -2)$
$D(2, 2)$	$(-2, -2)$	$H(-1, -1)$

➤ **Use the problem from the previous page to help you understand how to describe sequences of transformations involving dilations.**

1 Look at **Picture It** and **Model It**. Give the details of the transformations used in each sequence.

2 Look at **Model It**. Does it matter whether figure *ABCD* is dilated or rotated first in the sequence? Explain.

3 What is another way you could map figure *ABCD* onto figure *EFGH*?

4 Suppose figure *EFGH* is the original figure and figure *ABCD* is the final image. What two transformations could you perform to map figure *EFGH* onto figure *ABCD*?

5 **Reflect** Think about all the models and strategies you have discussed today. Describe how one of them helped you better understand how to solve the **Try It** problem.

Apply It

➤ **Use what you learned to solve these problems.**

6 The vertices of △ABC are located at A(4, 8), B(8, 0), and C(−8, 4). Which sequence of transformations of triangle △ABC results in △A″B″C″? *eliminate*

A Rotate △ABC 90° clockwise around the origin. Dilate the image by a scale factor of 4 with a center of dilation at the origin.

B Rotate △ABC 90° counterclockwise around the origin. Then dilate the image by a scale factor of 4 with a center of dilation at the origin.

(not clockwise eliminate)

C Rotate △ABC 90° clockwise around the origin. Then dilate the image by a scale factor of $\frac{1}{4}$ with a center of dilation at the origin.

D Rotate △ABC 90° counterclockwise around the origin. Then dilate the image by a scale factor of $\frac{1}{4}$ with a center of dilation at the origin.

1) Rotation
2) Dilation

7 Pilar draws rectangle JKLM in the coordinate plane. She performs two transformations on rectangle JKLM to form rectangle J″K″L″M″.

a. What sequence of transformations could Pilar have performed?

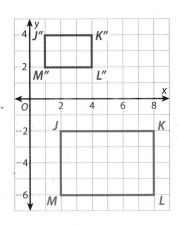

b. Could Pilar have performed the same two transformations in the reverse order to form rectangle J″K″L″M″? Explain.

Practice Describing Sequences of Transformations Involving Dilations

➤ **Study the Example showing how to describe a sequence of transformations involving dilations. Then solve problems 1–5.**

Example

What is one possible sequence of transformations that shows that △ABC ~ △DEF?

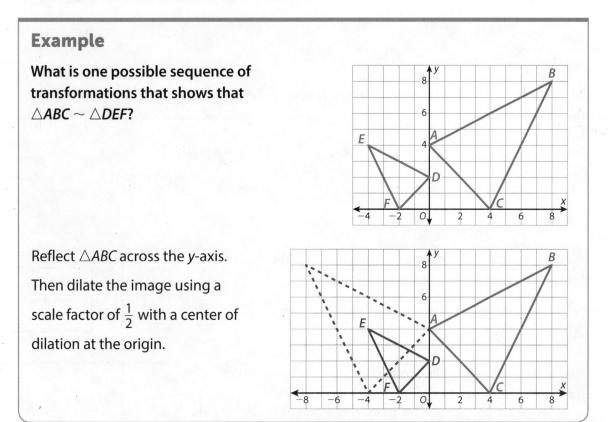

Reflect △ABC across the y-axis.

Then dilate the image using a scale factor of $\frac{1}{2}$ with a center of dilation at the origin.

---

1 Look at the Example. What is one possible sequence of transformations you could perform to map △DEF onto △ABC?

 2 Describe a sequence of transformations that maps △PQR onto △LMN.

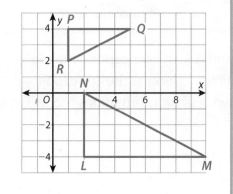

Vocabulary

dilation
a transformation that makes a scale copy of a figure.

sequence of transformations
one or more transformations performed in a certain order.

3 Notah draws figure *X* in the coordinate plane. Then he performs a sequence of transformations on figure *X* to form figure *Y*.

    a. What sequence of transformations could Notah have performed to map figure *X* onto figure *Y*?

    b. What is another sequence of transformations Notah could have performed to map figure *X* onto figure *Y*?

4 Which sequences of transformations could map rectangle *A* onto rectangle *B*? Select all that apply.

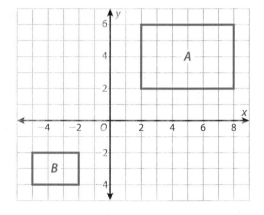

    A A 90° clockwise rotation around the origin, followed by a translation to the left

    B A dilation with a center of dilation at the origin, followed by a translation down and a translation to the left

    C A reflection across the *x*-axis, followed by a dilation with a center of dilation at the origin and a translation to the left

    D A reflection across the *y*-axis, followed by a translation down and a dilation with a center of dilation at the origin

    E A 180° rotation around the origin, followed by a dilation with a center of dilation at the origin, a translation down, and a translation to the left

5 Chantel graphs △*S* and △*T*. The corresponding angles are congruent. The side lengths of △*T* are 5 times as long as the corresponding side lengths of △*S*. Can you give a sequence of transformations that will map △*S* onto △*T*? Explain.

Refine Performing and Describing Transformations Involving Dilations

➤ **Complete the Example below. Then solve problems 1−8.**

Example

Dylan dilates figure *HIJK* to form figure *H′I′J′K′*. He uses a scale factor of 3 with a center of dilation at vertex *H*. What are the coordinates of figure *H′I′J′K′*?

Look at how you could use the coordinate plane.

Find the length of each side of figure *HIJK*. Multiply each side by 3 to find the corresponding lengths of figure *H′I′J′K′*. Count from *H* to find the corresponding vertices *I′*, *J′*, and *K′*.

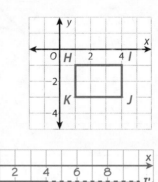

SOLUTION _____

Apply It

1 Khadija draws △*ABC* in the coordinate plane. She dilates △*ABC* using a scale factor of $\frac{2}{3}$ with the center of dilation at the origin to form △*A′B′C′*. Then she dilates △*A′B′C′* using a scale factor of $\frac{1}{2}$ with a center of dilation at the origin to form △*A″B″C″*.

What are the coordinates of △*A″B″C″*? Show your work.

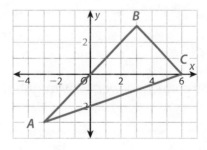

SOLUTION _____

2 Caleb wants to prove that figures *A* and *B* are similar. What sequence of transformations could Caleb perform to prove that the figures are similar? Show your work.

SOLUTION _____

_____

_____

3 Yolanda designs a holiday card that measures 3 inches by 5 inches. The card is represented by figure *ABCD*. She enlarges the card to form image *A′B′C′D′*. She uses a scale factor of 2 with a center of dilation at the origin. What are the coordinates of *B′*?

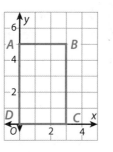

A (3, 5)

B (5, 7)

C (6, 5)

D (6, 10)

Wyatt chose B as the correct answer. How might he have gotten that answer?

4 $\triangle ABC$ was rotated 90° counterclockwise around the origin to form $\triangle A'B'C'$. $\triangle A'B'C'$ was dilated using a scale factor of $\frac{1}{3}$ with a center of dilation at the origin. The result is $\triangle A''B''C''$, shown in the coordinate plane. What are the coordinates of $\triangle ABC$? Show your work.

SOLUTION _____

5 Gabe is designing a greenhouse. The original plan for the floor is represented by figure *GHIJ*. Gabe dilates the floor by a scale factor of $\frac{2}{3}$ with a center of dilation at the origin to form figure $G'H'I'J'$. Then he translates figure $G'H'I'J'$ 3 units to the right and 3 units up. The final figure is labeled $G''H''I''J''$.

a. Draw Gabe's transformations in the coordinate plane.

b. What single transformation could map figure *GHIJ* onto figure $G''H''I''J''$?

c. Why do you think the parallel sides in figure *GHIJ* remain parallel to the corresponding sides of figure $G'H'I'J'$ after the dilation?

6 Leon designs a fabric pattern using figure *STUVW*. He dilates figure *STUVW* using a scale factor of 2 with a center of dilation at vertex *V* to form figure *S′T′U′V′W′*. Then Leon rotates this image 90° clockwise around the origin to form figure *S″T″U″V″W″*. What are the coordinates of figure *S″T″U″V″W″*?

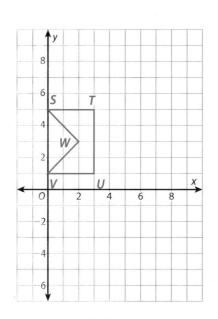

7 Maya performs three transformations on figure *WXYZ* to show that figures *WXYZ* and *W‴X‴Y‴Z‴* are similar. She dilates the figure by a scale factor of 2 with center of dilation at the origin, rotates the image 90° counterclockwise around the origin, and then reflects that image across the *x*-axis. Does the order of transformations matter? Explain.

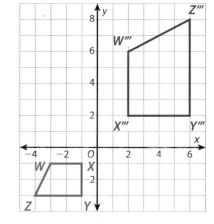

8 **Math Journal** Draw a triangle in the coordinate plane and label it △*ABC*. Transform △*ABC* using one rigid transformation and one dilation. Draw and label the final image △*A″B″C″*.

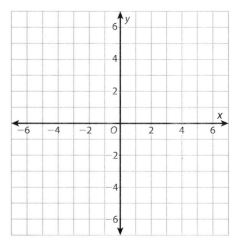

✓ End of Lesson Checklist

☐ **INTERACTIVE GLOSSARY** Find the entry for *dilation*. Add two important things you learned about dilations in this lesson.

☐ **SELF CHECK** Go back to the Unit 2 Opener and see what you can check off.

Dear Family,

This week your student is learning about angle relationships. Angles are formed when two lines are intersected, or cut, by a third line. The third line is called a **transversal**. When the two lines are parallel, some of the angles formed by the transversal are congruent.

In the figure below, $\overleftrightarrow{AB}$ is parallel to $\overleftrightarrow{CD}$. $\overleftrightarrow{EF}$ is the transversal. Three types of congruent angles are formed when parallel lines are cut by a transversal:

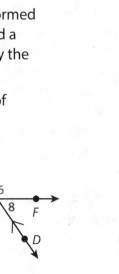

- ∠4 and ∠5 are **alternate interior angles**. Alternate interior angles are on opposite sides of the transversal and between the two lines cut by the transversal.

- ∠1 and ∠8 are **alternate exterior angles**. Alternate exterior angles are on the opposite sides of the transversal and outside the two lines cut by the transversal.

- ∠2 and ∠6 are **corresponding angles**. Corresponding angles are in the same relative position when two lines are cut by a transversal.

Your student will learn to use angle relationships to identify angle measurements. In the figure below, $\overleftrightarrow{UV}$ is parallel to $\overleftrightarrow{WX}$. Can you name a pair of angles that have the same measure?

➤ **ONE WAY** to use angle relationships is to identify alternate interior angles.

∠3 and ∠6 are alternate interior angles.
$m\angle 3$ and $m\angle 6$ are equal.

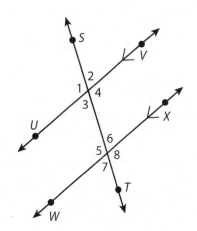

➤ **ANOTHER WAY** to use angle relationships is to identify alternate exterior angles.

∠1 and ∠8 are alternate exterior angles.
$m\angle 1$ and $m\angle 8$ are equal.

Use the next page to start a conversation about angle relationships.

Activity Thinking About Angle Relationships

➤ **Do this activity together to investigate angle relationships in real life.**

There are many places in the world around you where angles and their relationships are important. One example is a truss bridge. Part of the structure of a truss bridge is shown. These bridges are built using a design involving parallel lines cut by transversals. The angles formed by this structure meet the required safety standards for strength and stability!

? What angle relationships do you see in the picture of the truss bridge? What are other real-world examples of angle relationships?

Explore Angle Relationships

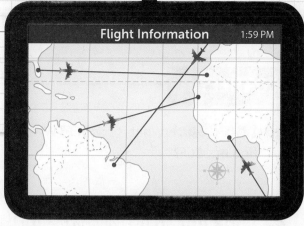

Flight Information   1:59 PM

Previously, you learned about pairs of angles formed when two lines intersect. In this lesson, you will learn about pairs of angles formed when one line intersects two other lines.

➤ **Use what you know to try to solve the problem below.**

Zahara says she can use angle relationships to find all the angle measures in the figure. What is $m\angle BCF$?

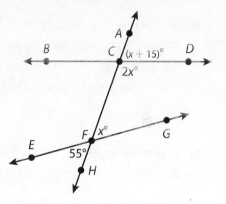

TRY IT

DISCUSS IT

Ask: How did you decide which angle measure to find first?

Share: The first angle measure I found was . . .

◎ **Learning Target**   SMP 1, SMP 2, SMP 3, SMP 4, SMP 5, SMP 6
Use informal arguments to establish facts about the angle sum and exterior angle of triangles, about the angles created when parallel lines are cut by a transversal, and the angle-angle criterion for similarity of triangles.

CONNECT IT

1 **Look Back** What is $m\angle BCF$? What types of angle relationships did you use to find $m\angle BCF$?

2 **Look Ahead** The figure in the **Try It** problem shows pairs of angles you know, such as adjacent angles, supplementary angles, and vertical angles. The figure also shows pairs of angles that are new to you.

a. You know that supplementary angles are two angles whose measures have a sum of 180°. A **linear pair** is a pair of supplementary angles that are adjacent. What two angles form the linear pair shown? What is the value of x?

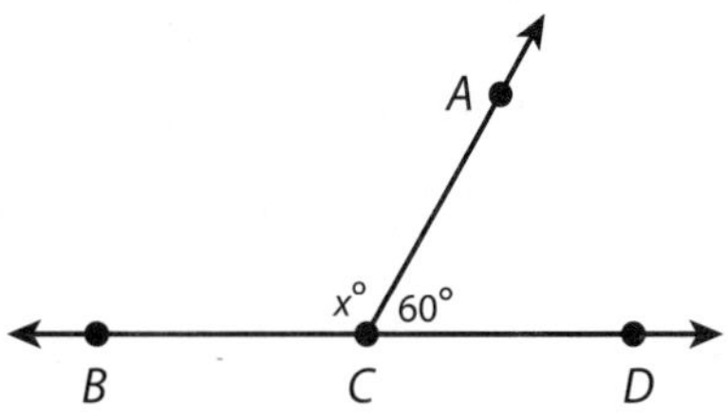

b. A **transversal** is a line that intersects or cuts two or more lines. Which line is the transversal in the figure at the right?

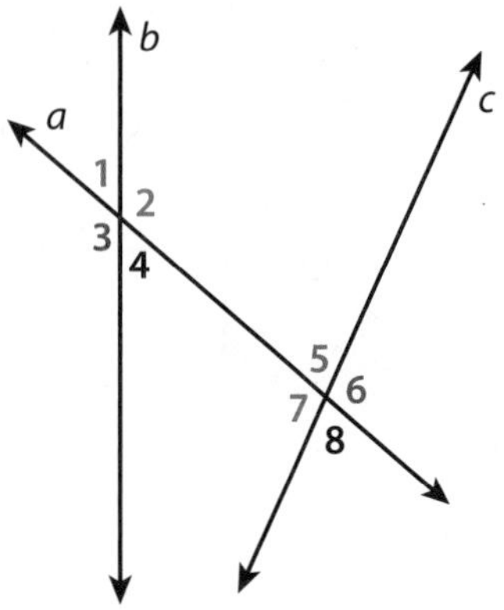

c. In the figure, $\angle 2$ and $\angle 7$ are **alternate interior angles**. These angles are on opposite sides of the transversal, and they are inside, or between, the other two lines. What is the other pair of alternate interior angles?

d. $\angle 3$ and $\angle 6$ are **alternate exterior angles**. These angles are on opposite sides of the transversal, but are on the outside of the other two lines. What is the other pair of alternate exterior angles?

e. $\angle 1$ and $\angle 5$ are **corresponding angles**. These angles are in the same position relative to the lines and the transversal. $\angle 2$ and $\angle 6$ are also corresponding angles. What are the other two pairs of corresponding angles?

3 **Reflect** Is it possible for a pair of angles to be both corresponding angles and alternate interior angles? Explain.

Prepare for Describing Angle Relationships

1️⃣ Think about what you know about angles. Fill in each box. Use words, numbers, and pictures. Show as many ideas as you can.

Word	In My Own Words	Example
adjacent angles		
supplementary angles		
vertical angles		

2️⃣ For each figure, are ∠1 and ∠2 *adjacent angles* or *vertical angles*? Explain.

a.

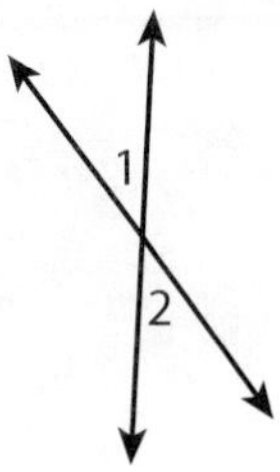

1
2

b.

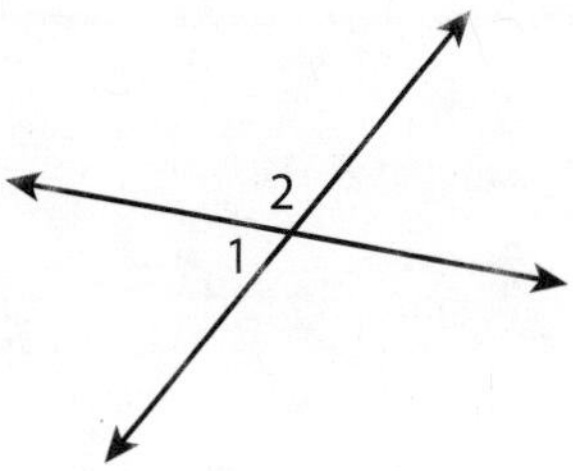

2
1

3 **a.** What is $m\angle TVZ$? Show your work.

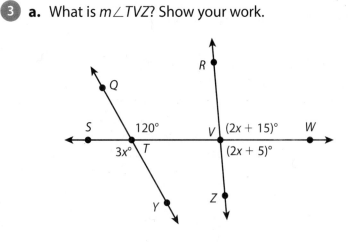

SOLUTION _____

b. Check your answer to problem 3a. Show your work.

Develop Describing Congruent Angle Relationships

➤ **Read and try to solve the problem below.**

The design on this Native American wedding vase contains many angles. Part of the design is shown in the coordinate plane to help show that some angles are congruent. What sequence of transformations can be used to show that ∠WXO and ∠ZYO are congruent?

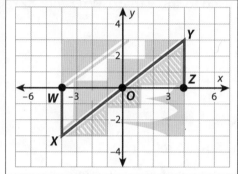

 TRY IT

Math Toolkit graph paper, tracing paper, transparencies

DISCUSS IT

Ask: How did you choose which transformation to use?

Share: I noticed that . . .

➤ **Explore different ways to find and describe congruent angle relationships.**

The design on this Native American wedding vase contains many angles. Part of the design is shown in the coordinate plane to help show that some angles are congruent. What sequence of transformations can be used to show that ∠WXO and ∠ZYO are congruent?

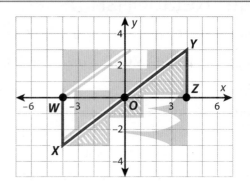

Model It

You can use reflections.

A sequence of two reflections maps ∠WXO onto ∠ZYO.

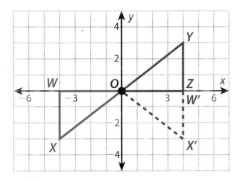

Model It

You can use a rotation.

Rotate the entire figure 180° around the origin to map ∠WXO onto ∠W'X'O'.

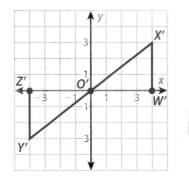

©Curriculum Associates, LLC   Copying is not permitted.

➤ **Use the problem from the previous page to help you understand how to find and describe congruent angle relationships.**

1 ∠*WXO* and ∠*ZYO* in the **Try It** problem are alternate interior angles. How can you tell? How do you know these angles are congruent?

2 Can you use a sequence of transformations to show that the pairs of alternate interior angles in this figure are congruent? Explain.

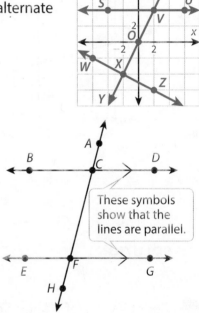

3 **a.** Alternate interior angles formed by parallel lines cut by a transversal are congruent. Mark the two pairs of alternate interior angles that are congruent. Then mark the vertical angles that are congruent.

b. Name the pairs of alternate exterior angles in the figure. How are alternate exterior angles related when formed by parallel lines cut by a transversal?

These symbols show that the lines are parallel.

c. Name the pairs of corresponding angles in the figure. How are corresponding angles related when formed by parallel lines cut by a transversal?

4 **Reflect** Think about all the models and strategies you have discussed today. Describe how one of them helped you better understand the congruent angles formed by parallel lines cut by a transversal.

Apply It

➤ **Use what you learned to solve these problems.**

5 Name a pair of corresponding angles in the figure. What sequence of transformations could you use to show that the angles are congruent?

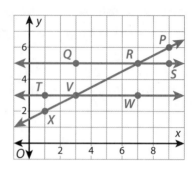

6 Find the value of *x*. Show your work.

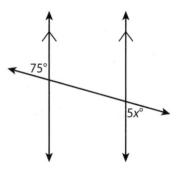

SOLUTION _____

7 Find the value of *x*. Show your work.

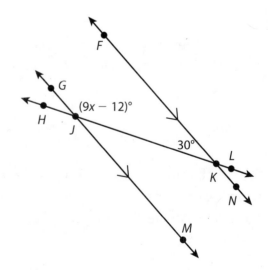

SOLUTION _____

Practice Describing Congruent Angle Relationships

➤ **Study the Example showing how to use angle relationships to find unknown angle measures. Then solve problems 1–6.**

Example

What is the value of *x*?

$\overline{BD}$ and $\overline{EG}$ are parallel, so corresponding angles are congruent.

$$25x - 2 = 148$$
$$25x = 150$$
$$x = 6$$

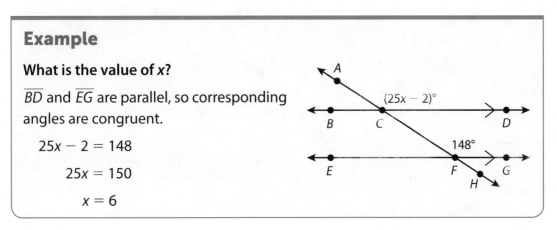

1. **a.** In the Example, what angle forms a pair of alternate interior angles with $\angle CFG$?

   b. What is the measure of the angle you named in problem 1a?

2. What is the value of *x*? Show your work.

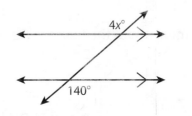

SOLUTION _____

3. Describe a sequence of transformations you can use to show $\angle JLK \cong \angle QNR$.

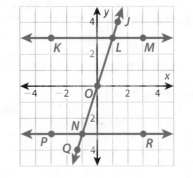

④ In which figures is $\angle 1 \cong \angle 2$? Select all that apply.

A

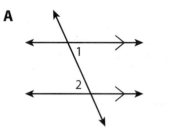

B

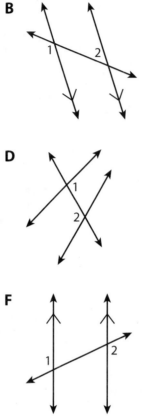

C

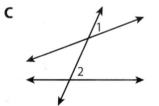

D

E

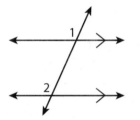

F

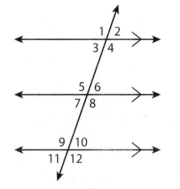

⑤ Tell whether each statement about the figure is *True* or *False*.

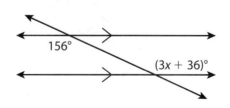

	True	False
a. $\angle 1$ and $\angle 9$ are corresponding angles.	○	○
b. $\angle 2$ and $\angle 7$ are alternate exterior angles.	○	○
c. $\angle 3$ and $\angle 10$ are alternate interior angles.	○	○
d. $\angle 4$ and $\angle 7$ are alternate interior angles.	○	○

⑥ What is the value of *x*? Show your work.

156°

$(3x + 36)°$

SOLUTION _____

Develop Describing Supplementary Angle Relationships

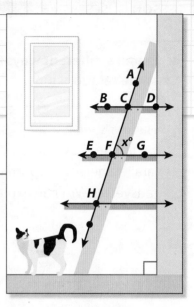

➤ **Read and try to solve the problem below.**

A ladder shelf is a shelf that leans against a wall like a ladder. The image shows a side view of a ladder shelf. There are three parallel shelves supported by a brace. The brace acts like a transversal. Write an expression for $m\angle DCF$ in terms of x.

TRY IT

► **Explore different ways to find and describe supplementary angle relationships.**

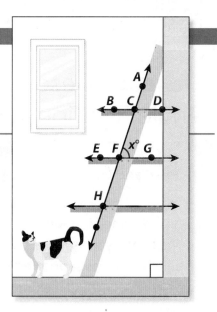

A ladder shelf is a shelf that leans against a wall like a ladder. The image shows a side view of a ladder shelf. There are three parallel shelves supported by a brace. The brace acts like a transversal. Write an expression for $m\angle DCF$ in terms of x.

Model It

You can use what you know about alternate interior angles.

$\overleftrightarrow{BD} \parallel \overleftrightarrow{EG}$, so $\angle EFC$ and $\angle DCF$ are congruent alternate interior angles.

$\angle EFC$ and $\angle CFG$ form a linear pair, so $m\angle EFC + m\angle CFG = 180°$.

$m\angle EFC = m\angle DCF$, so you can substitute $m\angle DCF$ for $m\angle EFC$:

$m\angle DCF + m\angle CFG = 180°$

Model It

You can use what you know about corresponding angles.

$\overleftrightarrow{BD} \parallel \overleftrightarrow{EG}$, so $\angle ACD$ and $\angle CFG$ are congruent corresponding angles.

$\angle ACD$ and $\angle DCF$ form a linear pair, so $m\angle ACD + m\angle DCF = 180°$.

$m\angle ACD = m\angle CFG$, so you can substitute $m\angle CFG$ for $m\angle ACD$:

$m\angle CFG + m\angle DCF = 180°$

➤ **Use the problem from the previous page to help you understand how to find and describe supplementary angle relationships.**

1 Look at both **Model Its**. What is $m\angle CFG$? What is an expression for $m\angle DCF$ in terms of x?

2 Would this relationship be true if the lines cut by the transversal were not parallel? Explain.

3 **a.** In **Try It**, $\angle DCF$ and $\angle CFG$ are **same-side interior angles**. These angles are on the same side of the transversal, between $\overleftrightarrow{BD}$ and $\overleftrightarrow{EG}$. How are the measures of same-side interior angles related when when they are formed by parallel lines cut by a transversal?

b. In **Try It**, $\angle ACD$ and $\angle HFG$ are **same-side exterior angles**. These angles are on the same side of the transversal, not between $\overleftrightarrow{BD}$ and $\overleftrightarrow{EG}$. How are their measures related? Explain.

4 You can use the angles formed by two lines cut by a transversal to conclude that the two lines are parallel. For example, the lines are parallel if corresponding angles are congruent. Use similar reasoning to explain how to show two lines are parallel using same-side interior or same-side exterior angles.

5 **Reflect** Think about all the models and strategies you have discussed today. Describe how one of them helped you better understand the supplementary angles formed by parallel lines and angle relationships.

Apply It

➤ **Use what you learned to solve these problems.**

6 What is $m\angle LPR$? Show your work.

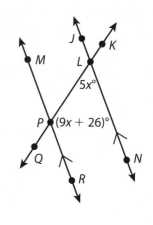

SOLUTION _____

7 Which of these situations show that the lines cut by a transversal are parallel? Select all that apply.

A alternate exterior angles are supplementary

B alternate interior angles are supplementary

C corresponding angles are congruent

D same-side exterior angles are congruent

E same-side interior angles are supplementary

8 The figure shows a picnic table. The top is represented by $\overleftrightarrow{BD}$. The ground is represented by $\overleftrightarrow{EG}$. The table leg represented by $\overleftrightarrow{AH}$ acts like a transversal. What value of x will show that the table top is parallel to the ground? Show your work.

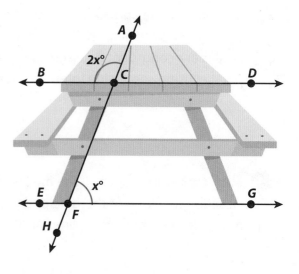

SOLUTION _____

©Curriculum Associates, LLC   Copying is not permitted.

Practice Describing Supplementary Angle Relationships

➤ **Study the Example showing how to use angle relationships to solve problems. Then solve problems 1–5.**

Example

What is the value of x?

∠ACD and ∠HFG are same-side exterior angles. $\overleftrightarrow{BD}$ and $\overleftrightarrow{EG}$ are parallel, so m∠ACD + m∠HFG = 180°.

$3x + 6x + 81 = 180$

$9x = 99$

$x = 11$

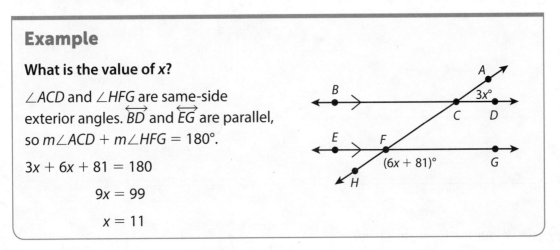

1 What is the angle relationship between ∠DCF and ∠CFG in the Example? What are the measures of these angles? Show your work.

SOLUTION _____

2 Find the value of x. Show your work.

Vocabulary

same-side exterior angles
when two lines are cut by a transversal, a pair of angles on the same side of the transversal and outside the two lines.

same-side interior angles
when two lines are cut by a transversal, a pair of angles on the same side of the transversal and between the two lines.

transversal
a line that cuts two or more lines.

SOLUTION _____

③ The figure shows two lines cut by a transversal. What value of x shows that the lines are parallel? Show your work.

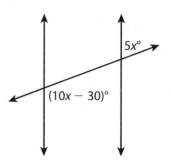

SOLUTION _____

④ Which statements about the figure are true? Select all that apply.

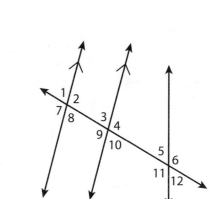

A $\angle 2 \cong \angle 3$

B $\angle 10$ and $\angle 11$ are supplementary angles.

C $\angle 2$ are $\angle 5$ are same-side interior angles.

D $\angle 8$ and $\angle 9$ are supplementary angles.

E $\angle 9$ and $\angle 12$ are same-side exterior angles.

F $m\angle 3 + m\angle 6 = 180°$

⑤ The figure shows two lines cut by a transversal. What value of x shows that the lines parallel? Show your work.

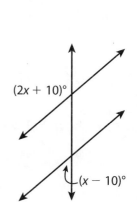

SOLUTION _____

Refine Describing Angle Relationships

➤ **Complete the Example below. Then solve problems 1–10.**

CONSIDER THIS . . .
Each line in the figure is also a transversal.

Example

The figure shows a pair of parallel lines intersected by another pair of parallel lines. How are the measures of ∠6 and ∠12 related?

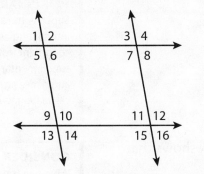

Look at how you could use angle relationships.

∠6 ≅ ∠8 ← Corresponding angles are congruent.

m∠8 + m∠12 = 180° ← Same-side interior angles are supplementary.

m∠6 + m∠12 = 180° ← Substitute m∠6 for m∠8.

SOLUTION _____

PAIR/SHARE
What is another way to solve the problem?

Apply It

1 What is the value of *x*? Show your work.

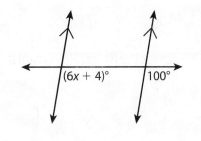

(6x + 4)°   100°

CONSIDER THIS . . .
How are the labeled angles related?

PAIR/SHARE
Explain how to check if your answer is reasonable.

SOLUTION _____

2 Draw the lines described. Then label any angle measures that you can determine.

Two parallel lines are cut by a transversal. The alternate interior angles are supplementary.

CONSIDER THIS . . .
How are alternate interior angles related when formed by parallel lines cut by a transversal?

PAIR/SHARE
Suppose the alternate interior angles were congruent instead of supplementary. What angle measures can you calculate now?

3 The figure shows two lines cut by a transversal. Which value of x shows that the lines are parallel?

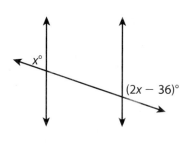

CONSIDER THIS . . .
What needs to be true about the angles labeled for the lines to be parallel?

A $x = 36$

B $x = 42$

C $x = 48$

D $x = 72$

Noah chose A as the correct answer. How might he have gotten that answer?

PAIR/SHARE
If the lines are parallel, what are the measures of the eight angles formed where the transversal crosses?

4 Which figures show parallel lines? Select all that apply.

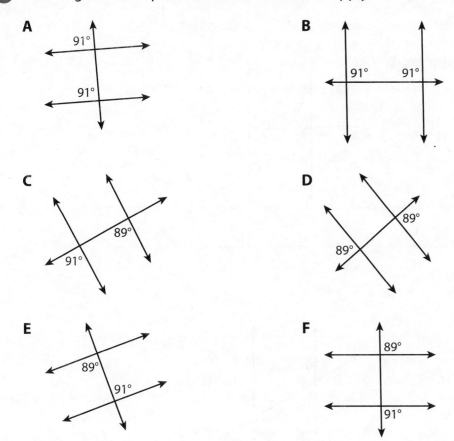

A
91°
91°

B
91°   91°

C
89°
91°

D
89°
89°

E
89°
91°

F
89°
91°

5 Which angles are congruent to ∠5? How do you know?

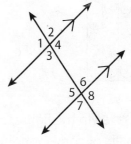

2
1 4
3

6
5 8
7

6 The figure shows two lines cut by a transversal. Are the lines parallel if $x = 9$? Explain.

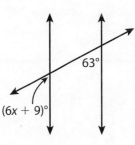

63°

$(6x + 9)°$

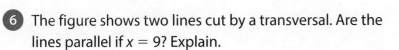

7　Two lines cut by a transversal are parallel if the alternate exterior angles

formed are ＿＿＿＿＿ .

8　What is the value of x? Show your work.

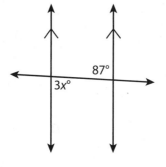

SOLUTION ＿＿＿＿＿＿＿＿＿＿＿＿＿＿＿＿＿＿＿＿＿＿＿＿＿＿＿

9　What is the value of x?

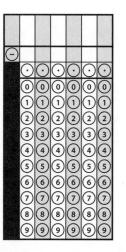

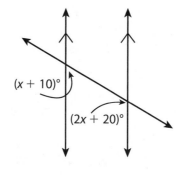

10　**Math Journal** In the figure, $\angle 3 \cong \angle 6$. Explain how you know that all four pairs of corresponding angles are congruent.

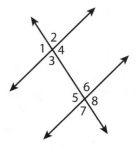

✓ End of Lesson Checklist

☐ **INTERACTIVE GLOSSARY** Find the entries for *corresponding angles*, *alternate interior angles*, and *same-side interior angles*. Sketch an example for each term.

☐ **SELF CHECK** Go back to the Unit 2 Opener and see what you can check off.

©Curriculum Associates, LLC　Copying is not permitted.

Dear Family,

This week your student is learning about angle relationships in triangles. Students will learn that the sum of the three angle measures in a triangle is 180°. They will use this new knowledge and what they know about angle relationships to solve problems, like the one below.

Use what you know about angle relationships to find the measures of ∠1 and ∠2 in the figure below.

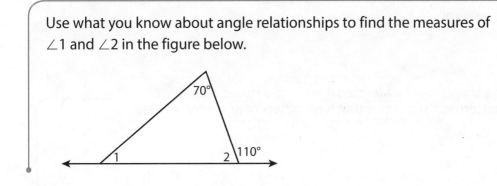

➤ **ONE WAY** to find the unknown angle measures is to use the properties of linear pairs of angles.

∠2 and the angle labeled 110° form a linear pair. A linear pair is two adjacent angles that together measure 180°.

$$m\angle 2 + 110° = 180°$$
$$m\angle 2 = 180° - 110°$$
$$m\angle 2 = 70°$$

➤ **ANOTHER WAY** is to use the properties of angle measures in a triangle.

The sum of the three angle measures in a triangle is 180°.

$$m\angle 1 + m\angle 2 + 70° = 180°$$
$$m\angle 1 + 70° + 70° = 180° \quad \longleftarrow m\angle 2 = 70°$$
$$m\angle 1 = 180° - 140°$$
$$m\angle 1 = 40°$$

 Use the next page to start a conversation about angle relationships in triangles.

LESSON 7 Describe Angle Relationships in Triangles   **137**

Activity Thinking About Angle Relationships in Triangles

➤ **Do this activity together to investigate angle measures in triangles in the real world.**

Triangles are common in many patterns, such as in the tile pattern shown. It is important to know the relationships of the angles when making the triangular tiles. For example, should the angles have the same measure? Should they sum to 180°? If the angles are not measured correctly, there will be spaces or overlapping tiles in the finished pattern!

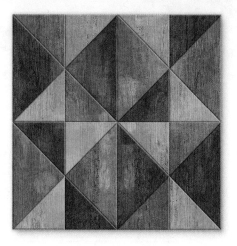

? How might the tile pattern be affected if angle measures changed? Draw a new pattern with triangles that have different angle measures.

Explore The Sum of the Angle Measures in a Triangle

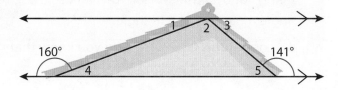

Previously, you learned about the measures of angles formed by parallel lines and transversals. In this lesson, you will learn about angle measures of triangles.

➤ **Use what you know to try to solve the problem below.**

An architect needs to know the angle measures of the roof shown in the photo. The triangle to the right models the shape of the roof. What is the sum of the angle measures of the triangle?

TRY IT

Math Toolkit grid paper, straightedges

DISCUSS IT

Ask: What did you do first to find the sum of the angle measures?

Share: First, I found the angle measures by . . .

◎ **Learning Target** SMP 1, SMP 2, SMP 3, SMP 4, SMP 5, SMP 6
Use informal arguments to establish facts about the angle sum and exterior angle of triangles, about the angles created when parallel lines are cut by a transversal, and the angle-angle criterion for similarity of triangles.

CONNECT IT

1 **Look Back** Write an equation to show the sum of the angle measures of the triangle in the **Try It**.

2 **Look Ahead** You know several angle relationships related to parallel lines being cut by a transversal. You can use these relationships to find the sum of the angle measures of a triangle.

a. Look at this figure. How do you know that $m\angle 1 = m\angle 4$ and $m\angle 3 = m\angle 5$?

b. Write an equation for the sum of the measures of $\angle 1$, $\angle 2$, and $\angle 3$. How do you know the sum of these angle measures?

c. Use your answers to problems 2a and 2b to find the sum of the measures of the angles of the triangle, $m\angle 2 + m\angle 4 + m\angle 5$.

3 **Reflect** Is the sum you found in problem 2c the same as the sum you found in the **Try It**? Do you think you would get this result for any triangle? Explain.

Prepare for Angle Relationships in Triangles

1 Think about what you know about similarity and similar triangles. Fill in each box.
Use words, numbers, and pictures. Show as many ideas as you can.

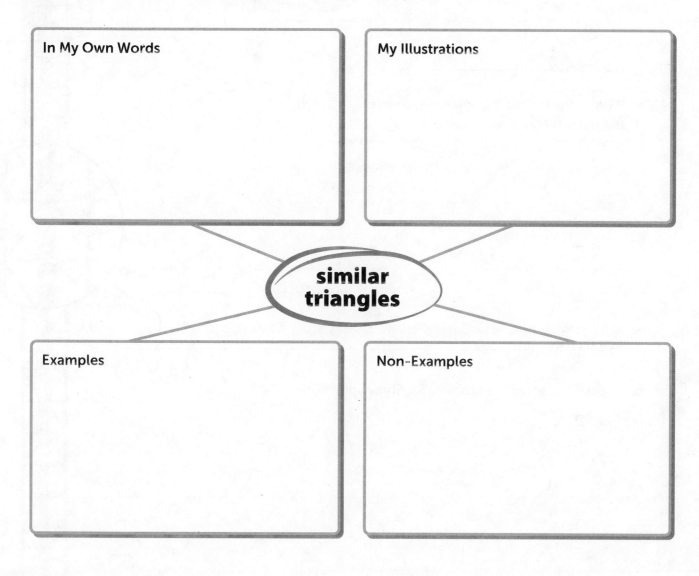

In My Own Words	My Illustrations

similar triangles

Examples	Non-Examples

2 Are the triangles similar? Explain.

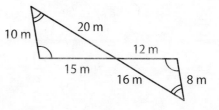

3 The triangle below models a section of the supports you might see in a construction crane.

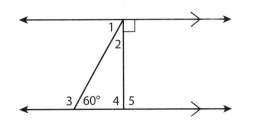

a. What is the sum of the angle measures of the triangle? Show your work.

SOLUTION _____

b. Check your answer to problem 3a. Show your work.

Develop Describing the Exterior Angles of a Triangle

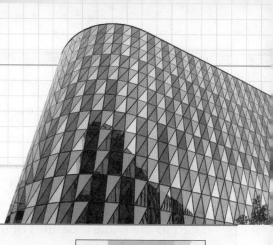

➤ **Read and try to solve the problem below.**

The triangular windows of the Aula Medica conference center in Sweden are formed by three sets of parallel lines going in different directions.

A close-up of the window design shows a triangle. The measure of ∠4 is related to the angle measures of the triangle. How can you use the measures of ∠1 and ∠2 to write an expression for the measure of ∠4?

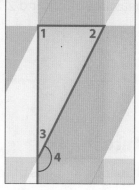

TRY IT

➤ **Explore different ways to describe angle relationships in triangles.**

The triangular windows of the Aula Medica conference center in Sweden are formed by three sets of parallel lines going in different directions.

A close-up of the window design shows a triangle. The measure of ∠4 is related to the angle measures of the triangle. How can you use the measures of ∠1 and ∠2 to write an expression for the measure of ∠4?

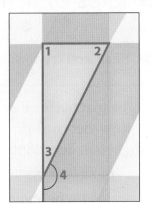

Picture It

You can look for pairs of congruent angles.

$m\angle 4 = m\angle 5 + m\angle 6$

$m\angle 5 = m\angle 2$ ⟵ ∠2 and ∠5 are alternate interior angles.

$m\angle 6 = m\angle 1$ ⟵ ∠1 and ∠6 are corresponding angles.

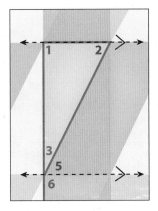

Model It

You can use angle relationships.

$m\angle 1 + m\angle 2 + m\angle 3 = 180°$ ⟵ The sum of the angle measures of a triangle is 180°.

$m\angle 3 + m\angle 4 = 180°$ ⟵ ∠3 and ∠4 form a linear pair.

$m\angle 1 + m\angle 2 + m\angle 3 = m\angle 3 + m\angle 4$

➤ **Use the problem from the previous page to help you understand angle relationships in triangles.**

1 An **exterior angle** of a triangle is formed by extending one side of a triangle. There are two exterior angles at each vertex of a triangle, as shown for ∠ZXY in the figures at the right. Why are the two exterior angles at the same vertex congruent?

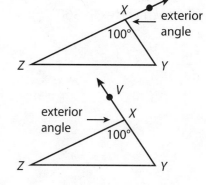

2 Look at **Model It**. Simplify the last equation. What is the relationship between an exterior angle of a triangle and its nonadjacent interior angles?

3 Look at the triangle to the right. Use the measures of the interior angles to write an equation for the measure of each exterior angle.

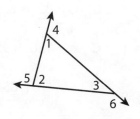

4 Use the equations you wrote in problem 3 to find the sum of the measures of the exterior angles of a triangle, one at each vertex.

5 Do you think your answers to problems 2 and 4 are true for all triangles? Explain.

6 **Reflect** Think about all the models and strategies you have discussed today. Describe how one of them helped you better understand how to solve the **Try It** problem.

Apply It

➤ **Use what you learned to solve these problems.**

7 Use linear pairs to find the sum of all the angles labeled in the triangle. Then use what you know about the interior angles of a triangle to show that the sum of the measures of the exterior angles of a triangle, one at each vertex, is 360°.

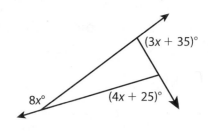

8 Which equations can you use to find the value of x? Select all that apply.

A $x + 120 + 85 = 180$

B $x + 85 = 120$

C $x + 120 + 95 = 360$

D $x = 60 + 85$

E $x + 60 + 85 = 180$

F $x + 35 = 180$

9 What is the value of x? Show your work.

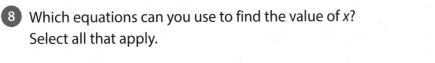

SOLUTION _____

Name:

Practice Describing the Exterior Angles of a Triangle

➤ **Study the Example showing how to use the relationship between exterior and interior angles of a triangle. Then solve problems 1–6.**

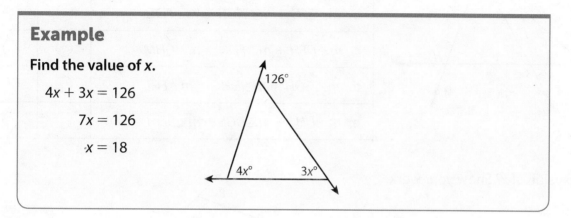

Example

Find the value of x.

$$4x + 3x = 126$$
$$7x = 126$$
$$x = 18$$

126°

$4x°$ $3x°$

1 What are the three exterior angle measures of the triangle in the Example?

2 What is $m\angle CAB$? Show your work.

115°   C   D

A

80°

B

SOLUTION _____

3 Can a triangle have an exterior angle that measures 90° at two different vertices? Explain.

Vocabulary

exterior angle
when you extend one side of a polygon, the angle between the extended side and the adjacent side.

4 Tell whether each statement about the diagram is *True* or *False*.

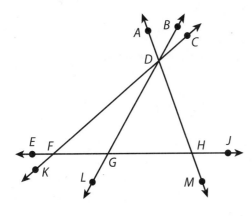

	True	False
a. ∠FGD is an exterior angle of △DHG.	○	○
b. m∠EFD + m∠HGD = m∠FDG	○	○
c. m∠DFH + m∠FDH = m∠GHM	○	○
d. m∠GDH + m∠DHG = m∠EGL	○	○
e. m∠DHJ + m∠DGE + m∠BDH = 360°	○	○

5 What is the value of *x*? Show your work.

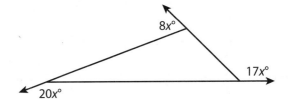

SOLUTION _____

6 **a.** What is *m*∠QTR? Show your work.

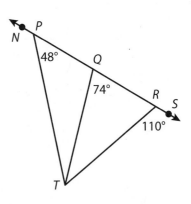

SOLUTION _____

b. What is *m*∠PTR? Show your work.

SOLUTION _____

Develop Using Angles to Determine Similar Triangles

➤ **Read and try to solve the problem below.**

Jorge wants to draw two triangles that have the same angle measures and are not similar. Carlos says that is not possible to do.

Make or draw two triangles that have the same three angle measures but different side lengths. Are the triangles similar?

 TRY IT

Math Toolkit grid paper, protractors, rulers

DISCUSS IT

Ask: How did you make sure that the angles of your triangles had the same measures?

Share: After I made the first triangle . . .

➤ **Explore different ways to make triangles with the same angle measures.**

Jorge wants to draw two triangles that have the same angle measures and are not similar. Carlos says that is not possible to do.

Make or draw two triangles that have the same three angle measures but different side lengths. Are the triangles similar?

Model It

You can cut out a triangle and trace its angles to make a second triangle.

Draw one side of the second triangle so that it is longer than a side of the first triangle. Trace two angles of the first triangle at either end of the new side.

Extend the two sides to complete the triangle. Be sure the third angle matches the third angle of the first triangle.

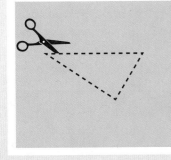

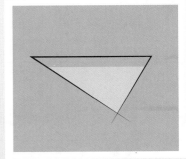

Model It

You can choose angle measures and one pair of corresponding side lengths.

For example, draw triangles with angles of 26°, 40°, and 114° such that there is one pair of corresponding sides with lengths 10 cm and 5 cm. Measure and compare the other corresponding side lengths.

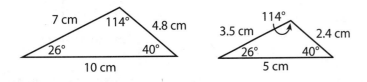

©Curriculum Associates, LLC Copying is not permitted.

➤ **Use the problem from the previous page to help you understand how to use angle measures to tell whether two triangles are similar.**

1 Look at the pairs of triangles you and your classmates accurately made or drew as you worked on the **Try It** problem. Are the triangles in each pair similar? Explain.

2 Look at the triangles in the second **Model It**. Are the triangles similar? Explain.

3 Will all possible triangles with the same three angle measures be similar? Explain.

4 Suppose two angle measures of one triangle are equal to two angle measures of another triangle. Must the third angle measures also be equal? Explain.

5 Suppose two triangles have two pairs of corresponding angles that are congruent. Are the triangles similar? Explain.

6 **Reflect** Think about all the models and strategies you have discussed today. Describe how one of them helped you better understand how to solve the **Try It** problem.

Apply It

➤ **Use what you learned to solve these problems.**

7 Are the triangles similar? How do you know? Show your work.

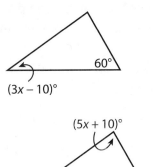

(3x − 10)°   60°

(5x + 10)°

35°   4x°

SOLUTION _____

8 Find *DE*. Show your work.

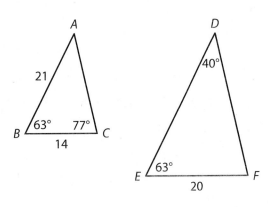

A

21

B 63°   77° C
   14

D

40°

E 63°
   20   F

SOLUTION _____

9 An ironing board, its legs, and the floor form two triangles as shown in the figure. The top of the board, $\overline{PQ}$, is parallel to the floor, $\overline{ST}$. Write a similarity statement for the two triangles. Explain how you know that they are similar.

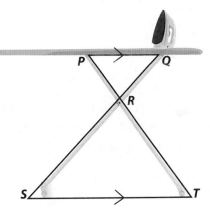

P   Q

R

S   T

Practice Using Angles to Determine Similar Triangles

➤ **Study the Example showing how to use angle measures to identify similar triangles. Then solve problems 1–6.**

Example

Which triangles are similar?

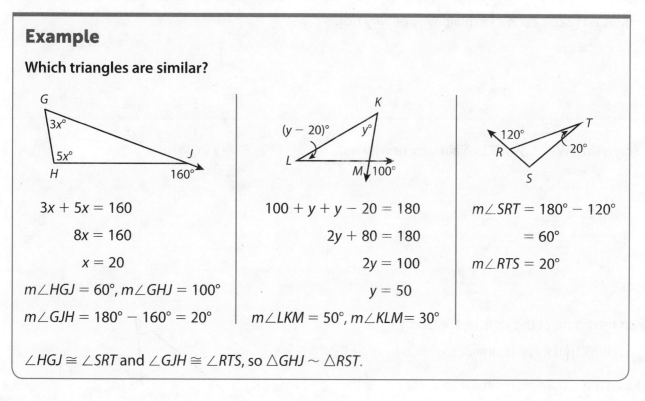

$3x + 5x = 160$

$8x = 160$

$x = 20$

$m\angle HGJ = 60°, m\angle GHJ = 100°$

$m\angle GJH = 180° - 160° = 20°$

$100 + y + y - 20 = 180$

$2y + 80 = 180$

$2y = 100$

$y = 50$

$m\angle LKM = 50°, m\angle KLM = 30°$

$m\angle SRT = 180° - 120°$

$= 60°$

$m\angle RTS = 20°$

$\angle HGJ \cong \angle SRT$ and $\angle GJH \cong \angle RTS$, so $\triangle GHJ \sim \triangle RST$.

1 Is $\triangle ABC$ similar to any of the triangles in the Example? Explain.

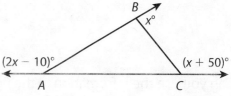

2 Triangle X has two angles that measure 80° and 30°. Triangle Y has two angles that measure 80° and 70°. Hannah says that triangles X and Y are not similar. Jasmine says they are similar. Who is correct? Explain.

3 **a.** Is △XYW ~ △XWZ? Explain why or why not.

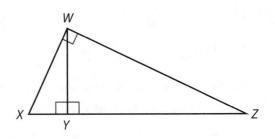

b. Is △WYZ ~ △XWZ? Explain why or why not.

c. Is △XYW ~ △WYZ? Explain why or why not.

4 In the figure at the right, ∠C ≅ ∠F.

a. Which triangle is similar to △BCD?

b. Which triangle is similar to △ACE?

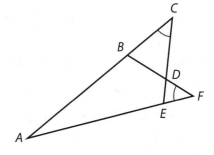

5 Can you use the information in the figure to show that the triangles are similar? Explain. If so, find the value of x.

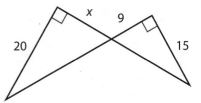

6 Can you use the information in the figure to show that the triangles are similar? Explain. If so, find the value of x.

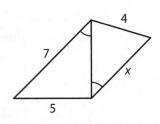

Refine Describing Angle Relationships in Triangles

➤ **Complete the Example below. Then solve problems 1 – 10.**

Example

What is the sum of the angle measures of a pentagon?

Look at how you could use the sum of the angle measures of a triangle.

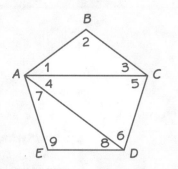

$m\angle EAB + m\angle ABC + m\angle BCD + m\angle CDE + m\angle DEA =$

$(m\angle 7 + m\angle 4 + m\angle 1) + m\angle 2 + (m\angle 3 + m\angle 5) +$
$(m\angle 6 + m\angle 8) + m\angle 9 =$

$(m\angle 1 + m\angle 2 + m\angle 3) + (m\angle 4 + m\angle 5 + m\angle 6) +$
$(m\angle 7 + m\angle 8 + m\angle 9) = 180° + 180° + 180°$

SOLUTION _____

CONSIDER THIS . . .
How can you draw triangles so that the angles of the triangles make up the angles of the pentagon?

PAIR/SHARE
Can you use the same strategy to find the sum of the angle measures of a hexagon? Explain.

Apply It

1 What is the value of *x*? Show your work.

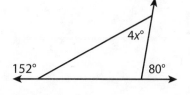

CONSIDER THIS . . .
How is each exterior angle measure related to the interior angle measures?

PAIR/SHARE
How could you use a different angle relationship to solve this problem?

SOLUTION _____

2 Explain how you know that △*MJK* ~ △*NLK*.

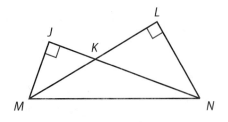

CONSIDER THIS . . .
Look at each pair of
corresponding angles.

PAIR/SHARE
Is △*MJN* ~ △*NLM*?
How do you know?

3 A triangle has exterior angles, one at each vertex, that measure 90°, 3*x*°, and 3*x*°. What is the value of *x*?

A 15

B 45

C 90

D 135

Zhen chose D as the correct answer. How might she have gotten that answer?

CONSIDER THIS . . .
What do you know
about the exterior angle
measures of a triangle?

PAIR/SHARE
Can you explain to a
partner how you solved
this problem?

4 The angles of a mountain bike frame are shown.

a. What is $m\angle WXZ$? Show your work.

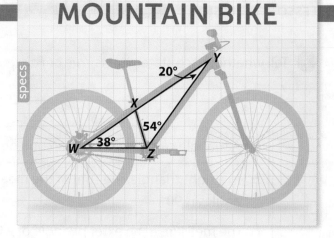

MOUNTAIN BIKE

SOLUTION _____

b. What is $m\angle XZW$? Show your work.

SOLUTION _____

5 Which triangles are similar to the triangle at the right? Select all that apply.

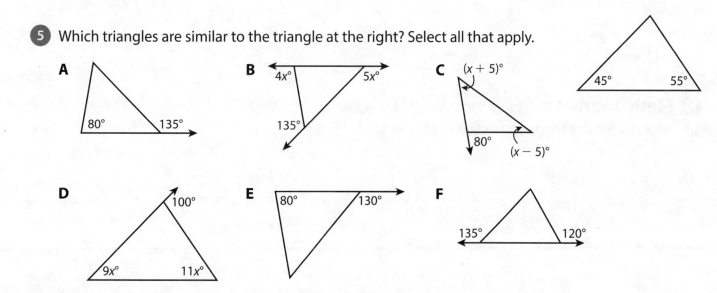

A

80°   135°

B

4x°   5x°

135°

C

(x + 5)°

80°

(x − 5)°

45°   55°

D

100°

9x°   11x°

E

80°   130°

F

135°   120°

6 Can a triangle have an exterior angle that is obtuse at two vertices? Explain.

7 Tell whether each statement is *True* or *False*.

	True	False
a. A triangle can have more than one obtuse angle.	○	○
b. In a right triangle, the sum of the measures of the acute angles is 90°.	○	○
c. The measure of an exterior angle of a triangle is equal to the sum of the two nonadjacent interior angles.	○	○
d. The sum of the measures of the exterior angles of a triangle, one at each vertex, is 180°.	○	○

8 If all three angles of a triangle are congruent, what is each angle measure? Explain.

9 What is the value of *x*?

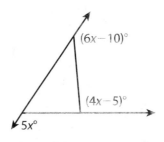

$(6x - 10)°$

$(4x - 5)°$

$5x°$

10 **Math Journal** The figure shows one triangle inside another. Are the two triangles similar? Explain.

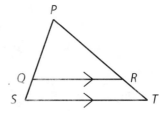

End of Lesson Checklist

☐ **INTERACTIVE GLOSSARY** Find the entry for *exterior angle*. Sketch an example of an exterior angle of a triangle.

☐ **SELF CHECK** Go back to the Unit 2 Opener and see what you can check off.

Study an Example Problem and Solution

➤ **Read this problem involving transformations. Then look at one student's solution to this problem on the following pages.**

Building Nesting Boxes

In Technology class, Isabella is building bird nesting boxes. She will use a computer program to provide directions to the laser cutter to cut out the pieces of the nesting boxes. Read the requirements, and help Isabella complete her project.

Nesting Box Project

For this project, you will build two nesting boxes. One should be for a chickadee, and the other should be for a different bird of your choice.

• Here is a scale drawing of the pieces needed for a chickadee nesting box. The distance between grid lines represents 2 inches. Pieces may be arranged differently than shown, but there must be at least 1 inch between pieces.

Chickadee Nesting Box Pieces

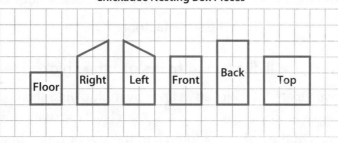

Floor | Right | Left | Front | Back | Top

• The table shows the floor dimensions required for nesting boxes for a few different types of birds.

• The pieces for your second nesting box should be similar in shape to the pieces for your chickadee box.

• All pieces for both boxes must fit on one 50-inch by 28-inch piece of plywood.

Bird Type	Floor Dimensions
Bluebird	5-inch square
Flycatcher	6-inch square
Pileated Woodpecker	8-inch square

YOUR TASK: Make a sketch on grid paper showing how you will arrange the pieces for the laser cutter.

The pileated woodpecker is the largest North American woodpecker. Its wingspan can be up to 28 inches, and it can peck 20 times in a second.

One Student's Solution

NOTICE THAT...
You could start with any piece, or place all of the pieces for the first box, and then find the locations for all of the pieces for the second box.

First, I need to choose which additional box I want to build.

In addition to the chickadee box, I will build a flycatcher box.

Next, I will sketch the floor of the chickadee box.

I plan to use a sequence of transformations so that the floor for the flycatcher box is similar to the floor for the chickadee box. I will place the chickadee floor piece on a coordinate plane so that one vertex is at the origin, and I will use a scale of 2 on each axis.

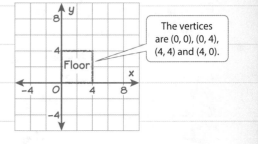

The vertices are (0, 0), (0, 4), (4, 4) and (4, 0).

NOTICE THAT...
The scale factor will be the same for all lengths of all pieces.

Now, I can find a scale factor to make the flycatcher floor.

I know the floor of the chickadee box is a square with 4-inch sides, and the flycatcher box needs to have a square floor with 6-inch sides.

$6 \div 4 = 1.5$, so the scale factor is 1.5.

Next, I will dilate and translate the chickadee floor.

I will dilate the chickadee floor by multiplying the coordinates of each vertex by the scale factor, 1.5. Then I will translate the dilated image 8 units to the right by adding 8 to the x-coordinate of each vertex.

Problem-Solving Checklist

- ☐ Tell what is known.
- ☐ Tell what the problem is asking.
- ☐ Show all your work.
- ☐ Show that the solution works.

Original Coordinates	Coordinates After Dilation	Coordinates After Translation
(0, 0)	(0, 0)	(8, 0)
(0, 4)	(0, 6)	(8, 6)
(4, 4)	(6, 6)	(14, 6)
(4, 0)	(6, 0)	(14, 0)

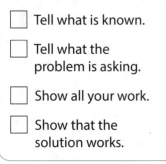

Chickadee

Flycatcher

Then, I will transform the remaining pieces.

I will place the other pieces of the chickadee box on the coordinate plane. I will dilate each piece by a scale factor of 1.5 with the center at the origin. That will make the piece the right size for the flycatcher box. Then, I will use other transformations to move it to a new location.

- **Front:** Rotate 90° counterclockwise around the origin and translate left 8 units and up 9 units.

- **Back:** Rotate 90° counterclockwise around the origin and translate left 35 units and up 4 units.

- **Top:** Translate 6 units right and 2 units up.

- **Right side:** Reflect across the y-axis and then across the x-axis. Then, translate right 20 units and up 26 units.

- **Left side:** Translate left 2 units and up 20 units.

> **NOTICE THAT . . .**
> It is easier to perform the dilation on each piece first. That way you know how much space it takes up.

> **NOTICE THAT . . .**
> Because the scale on both axes is 2, some vertices of these figures fall halfway between gridlines.

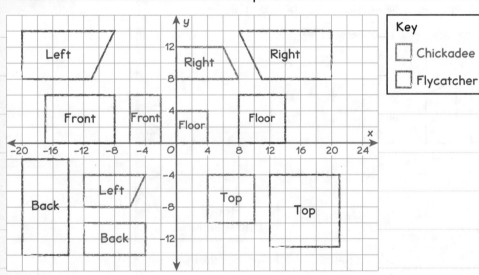

Finally, I will check my work.

The dimensions of each flycatcher piece are 1.5 times the dimensions of the corresponding chickadee piece and the angles are the same size. So, I know that the pieces are similar. The pieces will all fit on a 50-inch by 28-inch piece of plywood.

Try Another Approach

➤ **There are many ways to solve problems. Think about how you might solve the Building Nesting Boxes problem in a different way.**

Building Nesting Boxes

In Technology class, Isabella is building bird nesting boxes. She will use a computer program to provide directions to the laser cutter to cut out the pieces of the nesting boxes. Read the requirements, and help Isabella complete her project.

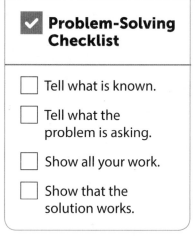

✓	**Problem-Solving Checklist**
☐	Tell what is known.
☐	Tell what the problem is asking.
☐	Show all your work.
☐	Show that the solution works.

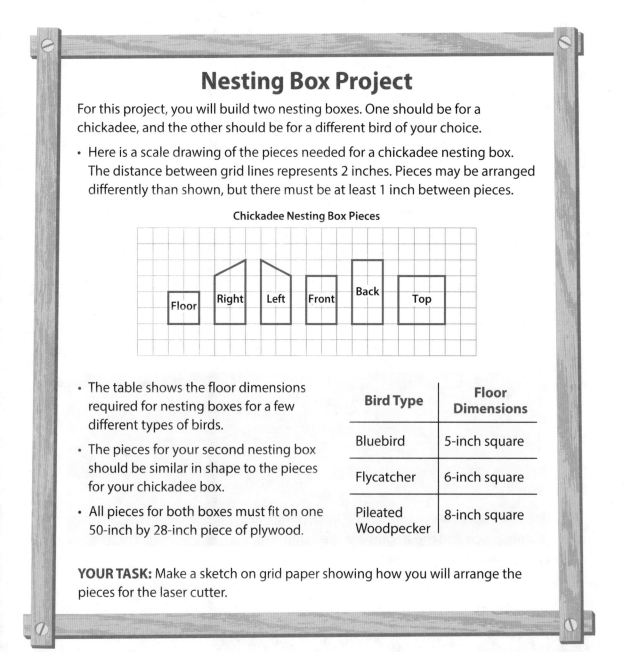

Nesting Box Project

For this project, you will build two nesting boxes. One should be for a chickadee, and the other should be for a different bird of your choice.

- Here is a scale drawing of the pieces needed for a chickadee nesting box. The distance between grid lines represents 2 inches. Pieces may be arranged differently than shown, but there must be at least 1 inch between pieces.

Chickadee Nesting Box Pieces

Floor | Right | Left | Front | Back | Top

- The table shows the floor dimensions required for nesting boxes for a few different types of birds.
- The pieces for your second nesting box should be similar in shape to the pieces for your chickadee box.
- All pieces for both boxes must fit on one 50-inch by 28-inch piece of plywood.

Bird Type	Floor Dimensions
Bluebird	5-inch square
Flycatcher	6-inch square
Pileated Woodpecker	8-inch square

YOUR TASK: Make a sketch on grid paper showing how you will arrange the pieces for the laser cutter.

©Curriculum Associates, LLC   Copying is not permitted.

Plan It

➤ **Answer these questions to help you start thinking about a plan.**

a. What scale factor could you use to dilate the pieces for the chickadee nesting box to build a bluebird nesting box? A pileated woodpecker nesting box?

b. How can you be sure you are sketching pairs of shapes that are similar?

Solve It

➤ **Find a different solution for the Building Nesting Boxes problem. Show all your work on a separate sheet of paper. You may want to use the Problem-Solving Tips to get started.**

PROBLEM-SOLVING TIPS

Math Toolkit grid paper, protractor, ruler, tracing paper, transparency sheets

Key Terms

similar	translation	dilation
congruent	rotation	reflection

Models You may want to use . . .

• a scale factor to enlarge or reduce each piece.

• a sequence of transformations for each piece to ensure that corresponding pieces are similar in shape.

• a table to organize your work.

Reflect

Use Mathematical Practices As you work through the problem, discuss these questions with a partner.

• **Persevere** What is your first step? What will you do next?

• **Critique Reasoning** Choose a pair of similar shapes in your partner's sketch. What is a sequence of transformations that proves these two shapes are similar?

Discuss Models and Strategies

➤ **Read the problem. Write a solution on a separate sheet of paper.**
Remember, there can be lots of ways to solve a problem.

Toolboxes

Isabella and Hugo are working together to plan and then build a toolbox. Read an email from Hugo about their toolbox design, and help Isabella come up with a response.

Delete   Archive   Reply   Reply All   Forward

To: Isabella
Subject: Toolbox Project

Hi Isabella,

I think we should make our toolbox a bigger size than the plans we have.

I copied the plan for the end piece onto a coordinate plane, using 1 square for each square centimeter. We should make the end piece for our toolbox similar to the one in the plan. The area of the end piece should be no greater than 400 square centimeters.

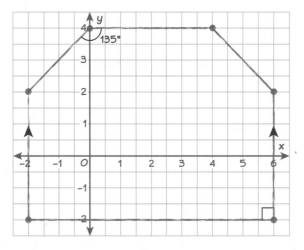

WE NEED TO DECIDE:
- What scale factor will we use?
- What will be the new vertex coordinates for our end piece?
- What will be the angle measures for our end piece?
- What will be the area of our end piece?

Thanks!

Hugo

Plan It and Solve It

➤ **Find a solution to the Toolboxes problem.**

Write a detailed plan and support your answer. Be sure to include:

- the scale factor you will use to dilate the shape.
- vertex coordinates that Isabella and Hugo could use to draw the new end piece.
- a drawing showing the angle measures of the end piece.
- any calculations or drawings you used to find the area of the end piece.

PROBLEM-SOLVING TIPS

Math Toolkit graph paper, ruler, tracing paper

Key Terms

dilation	scale factor	coordinate plane
parallel	transversal	alternate interior angle
exterior angle	corresponding angles	linear pair

Questions

- What is a scale factor that would be too big? What is a scale factor that would be too small?

- What angle relationships could you use to find the unmarked angle measures?

Reflect

Use Mathematical Practices As you work through the problem, discuss these questions with a partner.

- **Use Models** What models can you use to help you determine the coordinates of the vertices of the new end piece? What models can you use to help you determine the unmarked angle measures?

- **Make an Argument** How could you justify the scale factor you chose?

Persevere On Your Own

➤ **Read the problem. Write a solution on a separate sheet of paper.**

Designing Shelves

For another project, Isabella will be building a set of ladder shelves. Read Isabella's design idea. Then draw a diagram to show how Isabella could build the set of shelves. What total length of 12-inch-wide planks will Isabella need to buy for all of the shelves?

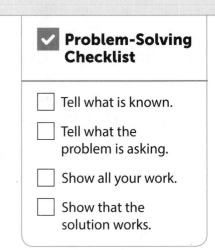

Problem-Solving Checklist

☐ Tell what is known.

☐ Tell what the problem is asking.

☐ Show all your work.

☐ Show that the solution works.

Ladder Shelves Design

I will build two ladders to support the shelves.

Both ladders will share the top rung.

39°

Rungs support the shelves. Both ladders have the same number of rungs.

I want to have between 4 and 6 shelves.
- The shelves do not need to be spaced evenly.
- Each shelf will be parallel to the floor.
- Each shelf will be exactly one foot longer than the distance between its rungs.

12 in.

← Rails

I need to decide how long to make the ladders. I have four identical boards to use for the rails and rungs of the ladders. Each of these boards is 12 feet long. I know that I do not have enough to make the rails 12 feet long, but when I set up two of the boards with a 39° angle at the top, it looked like this:

39°

12 feet

◁- - - - 8 feet - - - -▷

Solve It

➤ **Find a solution to the Designing Shelves problem.**

- Use what you know about similar triangles, transformations, and angle relationships to help Isabella with her design.

- Make a sketch that shows the length of the rails, the lengths and locations of the shelves, and the angle measures.

- Determine the total length of all the shelves.

Reflect

Use Mathematical Practices After you complete the problem, choose one of these questions to discuss with a partner.

- **Reason Mathematically** How did you choose the number of shelves? How did you choose the length of the rails?

- **Use Structure** How did you use similar shapes, transformations, and angle relationships to help you find a solution?

In this unit you learned to . . .

Skill	Lesson(s)
Understand that a dilation is a transformation in which the shape of a figure stays the same, but its size can change.	**4, 5**
Understand that if a figure can be obtained by transforming a different figure, they are similar.	**4, 5**
Perform and describe a sequence of transformations that shows two figures are similar.	**5**
Identify pairs of angles that are formed when two lines are cut by a transversal.	**6**
Use angle relationships to find unknown angle measurements given a pair of parallel lines cut by a transversal.	**6, 7**
Find unknown angle measurements by using the interior and exterior angle relationships of a triangle.	**7**
Show that if two triangles have two pairs of corresponding angles that are congruent, then the triangles are similar.	**7**
Agree or disagree with ideas in discussions about geometric figures and explain why.	**4–7**

Think about what you have learned.

➤ **Use words, numbers, and drawings.**

1 Two things I learned in math are . . .

2 I am proud that I can . . .

3 A question I still have is . . .

➤ **Review the unit vocabulary. Put a check mark by terms you can use in speaking and writing. Look up the meaning of any terms you do not know.**

Math Vocabulary		**Academic Vocabulary**
☐ alternate exterior angles	☐ dilation	☐ adjacent
☐ alternate interior angles	☐ linear pair	☐ enlarge
☐ center of dilation	☐ similar	☐ intersect
☐ corresponding angles	☐ transversal	☐ reduce

➤ **Use the unit vocabulary to complete the problems.**

1 Lines *g* and *h* are parallel lines cut by a transversal. $m\angle 7 = 135°$. Write the measure of angles 1–8 in the figure.

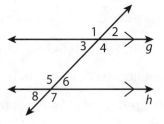

a. What is $m\angle 6$? Explain how you know.

b. What is $m\angle 4$? Explain how you know.

c. What is $m\angle 3$? Explain how you know.

d. What is $m\angle 1$? Explain how you know.

2 Use what you know about transformations to describe the relationship between figure *PQRS* and figure *P′Q′R′S′*. Use at least three math or academic vocabulary terms from this unit in your answer. Underline each term you use.

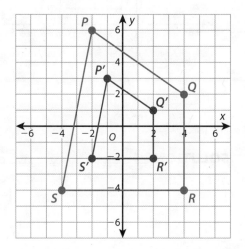

➤ **Use what you have learned to complete these problems.**

1 Which angle is congruent to ∠8?

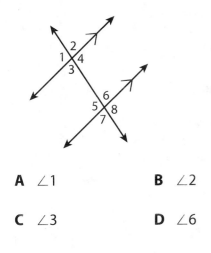

A ∠1   **B** ∠2

C ∠3   **D** ∠6

2 Figure *DEFG* is dilated using a scale factor of $\frac{1}{2}$ with a center of dilation at vertex *E* to form figure *D′E′F′G′*. Then the image is reflected across the *x*-axis to form figure *D″E″F″G″*. What are the coordinates of figure *D″E″F″G″*? Show your work.

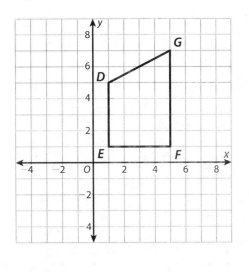

SOLUTION _____

_____

3 Figure *B′* is a dilation of figure *B*. Which statements about the dilation are true? Choose all the correct answers.

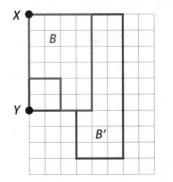

A The center of dilation is at point *X*.

B The center of dilation is at point *Y*.

C The scale factor must be less than 1.

D The scale factor must be greater than 1.

E The scale factor is $\frac{3}{2}$.

F The scale factor is $\frac{2}{3}$.

4 Hannah adjusts photos in her digital scrapbook. She translates the photo to the left. Then she dilates the image using a scale factor of 2 and a center of dilation at the origin. Hannah thinks the original photo is congruent and similar to the final image. Is she correct? Explain your reasoning.

SOLUTION _____

_____

_____

_____

_____

5 Figure *ABCD* is dilated by a scale factor of 3 with a center of dilation at the origin to form figure *A′B′C′D′*. What are the coordinates of *B′*?

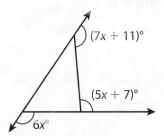

A (1, 2)

B (3, 6)

C (9, 6)

D (9, 18)

6 What is the value of *x*? Record your answer on the grid. Then fill in the bubbles.

$(7x + 11)°$

$(5x + 7)°$

$6x°$

7 The figure shows a pair of parallel lines intersected by another pair of parallel lines. Are the measures of ∠4 and ∠14 related in the same way as the measures of ∠9 and ∠7? Show your work.

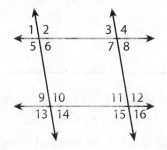

SOLUTION _____

_____

_____

Performance Task

➤ **Answer the questions and show all your work on separate paper.**

City Council plans to add walkways and flower corners to a small park. The upper and lower boundaries of the park are fences that form parallel sides. Right now, the park looks like this:

——————————————————

——————————————————

City Council asks you to plan two diagonal walkways that intersect with each other and form transversals with the fences. They also ask you to identify at least three pairs of congruent angles formed by the walkways that can be used as flower corners.

Be sure to include the following in your plan and description:

- A drawing to show where the diagonal, intersecting walkways will be located

- Labels at vertices, so you can name the angles formed

- At least three pairs of angles that you prove are congruent

Reflect

Use Mathematical Practices After you complete the task, choose one of the following questions to answer.

- **Model** Where do you see the requirements of the task in your drawing?

- **Use Reasoning** How are the walkways and flower corners related to transversals and congruent angles?

Unit 3

Linear Relationships

Slope, Linear Equations, and Systems

Self Check

Before starting this unit, check off the skills you know below. As you complete each lesson, see how many more skills you can check off!

I can . . .	Before	After
Define *slope* and show that the slope of a line is the same between any two points on the line.	☐	☐
Find the slope of a line and graph linear equations given in any form.	☐	☐
Derive the linear equations $y = mx$ and $y = mx + b$.	☐	☐
Represent and solve one-variable linear equations with the variable on both sides of the equation.	☐	☐
Determine whether one-variable linear equations have one solution, infinitely many solutions, or no solutions, and give examples.	☐	☐
Solve systems of linear equations graphically and algebraically.	☐	☐
Represent and solve systems of linear equations to solve real-world and mathematical problems.	☐	☐
Justify solutions to problems about linear equations by telling what I noticed and what I decided to do as a result.	☐	☐

UNIT 3

Prepare for Slope, Linear Equations, and Systems

➤ **Think about what you know about rates, proportional relationships, and plotting points in a coordinate plane. Write what you know about proportional relationships in the boxes. Share your ideas with a partner and add any new information to the organizer.**

Equations

Descriptions

Proportional Relationships

Related Terms

Examples

Dear Family,

This week your student is learning about slope. Students have learned previously about proportional relationships and unit rate. The graph of a proportional relationship is a line. When talking about a line, the unit rate is called the **slope**. Slope can be found by taking two points on the line and dividing the vertical change by the horizontal change. Students will learn to solve problems like the one below.

A local coffeeshop sells coffee beans by weight. The graph shows the relationship between weight in ounces and cost. Find the slope of the line. How much does 1 ounce of coffee beans cost?

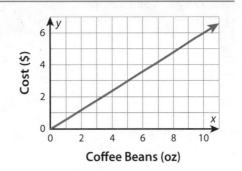

➤ **ONE WAY** to find the slope of a line is to divide the vertical change by the horizontal change between two points on the line.

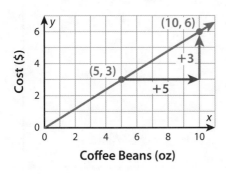

$3 \div 5 = 0.6$

➤ **ANOTHER WAY** to find the slope of a line is to choose two points on the line and use the slope formula,

$$\text{slope} = \frac{\text{change in } y\text{-coordinates}}{\text{change in } x\text{-coordinates}} \text{ or}$$

$$m = \frac{y_2 - y_1}{x_2 - x_1}.$$

Choose points $(0, 0)$ and $(5, 3)$.

$$m = \frac{y_2 - y_1}{x_2 - x_1} = \frac{3 - 0}{5 - 0} = \frac{3}{5}$$

Using either method, the slope is $\frac{3}{5}$, or 0.6. One ounce of coffee beans costs $0.60.

 Use the next page to start a conversation about slope.

Activity Thinking About Slope

➤ **Do this activity together to investigate slope in the real world.**

When a proportional relationship is modeled by a straight line, the unit rate is the same as the slope of the line. For example, when someone drives at a rate of 60 miles per hour on the highway, the unit rate of this proportional relationship is 60. The slope of the line modeling this relationship is also 60.

? Where else do you see examples of unit rate and slope in the world around you?

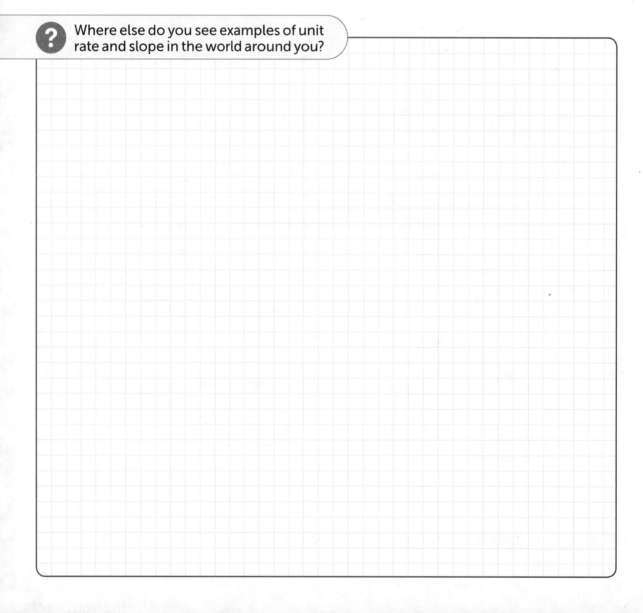

Explore Proportional Relationships and Slope

2.5 mi : 5 min

Previously, you learned about proportional relationships. In this lesson, you will learn about slope.

➤ **Use what you know to try to solve the problem below.**

A scientist is using a tracking device to measure how fast a blue whale swims. Data from the device show that the whale swam at a constant rate for 5 minutes and covered 2.5 miles in that time. Make a graph showing the change in the whale's distance over time. How far does the blue whale swim in 1 minute?

TRY IT

 Math Toolkit graph paper, straightedges

 **DISCUSS IT**

Ask: How did you get started making your graph?

Share: I knew . . . so I . . .

Learning Targets SMP 1, SMP 2, SMP 3, SMP 4, SMP 5, SMP 6, SMP 7
• Graph proportional relationships, interpreting the unit rate as the slope of the graph.
• Use similar triangles to explain why the slope *m* is the same between any two distinct points on a non-vertical line in the coordinate plane.

CONNECT IT

1 **Look Back** How far does the blue whale swim in 1 minute? How did you get your answer?

2 **Look Ahead** This table and graph represent the speed of a different blue whale over a period of 5 minutes.

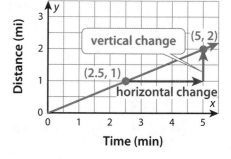

Time (min)	0	1	2	3	4	5
Distance (mi)	0	0.4	0.8	1.2	1.6	2

a. What is the unit rate for this proportional relationship? What does the unit rate mean in this situation?

b. The point (2.5, 1) is also on the line. What is the **vertical change** between (2.5, 1) and (5, 2)? What is the **horizontal change**?

c. The unit rate for a proportional relationship describes the **rate of change** between the variables. The rate of change is the quotient of the vertical change, or change in the *y*-variable, to the corresponding horizontal change, or change in the *x*-variable. On a graph, the rate of change is called the **slope**.

Use your answers to problem 2b to find the slope of the line between (2.5, 1) and (5, 2).

d. Compare your answers to problems 2a and 2c. How does the slope compare to the unit rate?

3 **Reflect** How can you find the slope of a line on a graph?

Prepare for Graphing Proportional Relationships and Defining Slope

1 Think about what you know about rates. Fill in each box. Use words, numbers, and pictures. Show as many ideas as you can.

Word	In My Own Words	Examples
constant of proportionality		
proportional relationship		
unit rate		

2 The graph shows the relationship between time and distance for Mason's training run.

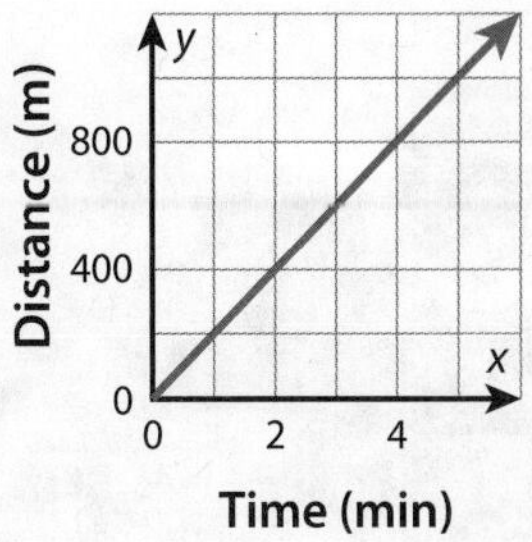

a. Does the graph show a proportional relationship? How do you know?

b. What is the unit rate for Mason's run?

c. What does the unit rate mean in this situation?

3 A marine biologist is studying how fast a dolphin swims. The dolphin swims at a constant speed for 5 seconds. The distance it swims is 55 meters. The relationship between time and distance for the trip is proportional.

a. Make a graph showing the change in the dolphin's distance over time. How far does the dolphin swim in 1 second?
Show your work.

SOLUTION _____

b. Check your answer to problem 3a. Show your work.

Develop Showing That the Slope of a Line Is Constant

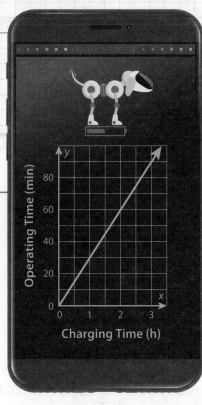

➤ **Read and try to solve the problem below.**

A delivery company uses robot dogs to deliver packages in an office building. The graph shows how long a robot dog can operate for each hour its battery is charged.

Pick any two points on the line. Find the slope of the line between these two points. Can you find another pair of points on the line that gives you a different slope?

TRY IT

Math Toolkit graph paper, straightedges

DISCUSS IT

Ask: What did you do first to find the slope? Why?

Share: I started by . . .

➤ **Explore different ways to show that the slope of a line is constant.**

A delivery company uses robot dogs to deliver packages in an office building. The graph shows how long a robot dog can operate for each hour its battery is charged.

Pick any two points on the line. Find the slope of the line between these two points. Can you find another pair of points on the line that gives you a different slope value?

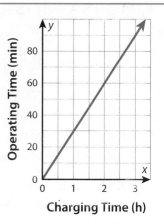

Model It

You can use translations of right triangles.

Choose any two points, *A* and *B*, on the line. Draw segments for the vertical and horizontal distances between the two points to find the slope between these two points.

Translate this *slope triangle* along the line to compare the slope between different pairs of points on the line.

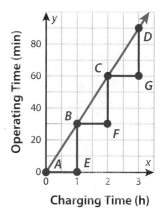

Model It

You can use dilations of right triangles.

Again, choose any two points, *A* and *B*, on the line and draw a slope triangle.

Dilate this triangle along the line using different scale factors to determine if the slope between any two points changes along the line.

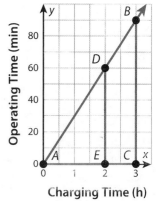

➤ **Use the problem from the previous page to help you understand how to determine if the slope of a line is constant.**

1 Look at the first **Model It**.

    a. Are $\triangle ABE$, $\triangle BCF$, and $\triangle CDG$ congruent? How do you know?

    b. How can you use $\triangle ABE$ to determine the slope of the line between points A and B? What is the slope?

    c. Is the slope of the line between points A and B the same as the slope between points B and C? Between points C and D? Explain.

2 Look at the second **Model It**. What is the slope of the line between points A and B? What is the slope of the line between points A and D?

3 Both models started by choosing points A and B. How do you know the slope of a line is the same between any two points on the line?

4 **Reflect** Think about all the models and strategies you have discussed today. Describe how one of them helped you better understand how to solve the **Try It** problem.

Apply It

➤ **Use what you learned to solve these problems.**

5 Jamila sells honey. She posts this sign for her customers. Then she makes a graph that shows the price of each size jar. Is Jamila's price the same per ounce for any size jar? Explain.

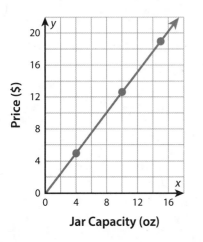

6 Akio draws a graph to record the distance he rides on a long bike ride. What is the slope of the line for the first two hours? What is the slope of the line for all five hours? What does the slope mean in this situation?

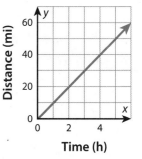

7 Lupita drew a graph to describe her airplane trip. Is the slope constant for the entire trip? Explain.

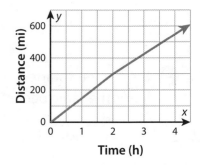

Practice Showing That the Slope of a Line Is Constant

➤ **Study the Example showing that the slope of a line is constant. Then solve problems 1–5.**

Example

Cece draws a graph representing her family's car trip to the beach. She wants to show her father that their gas mileage in miles per gallon was the same for the entire trip. Cece chose three points on the line and drew vertical line segments from the points to the x-axis. How can she use these segments to prove that the gas mileage was constant for the trip?

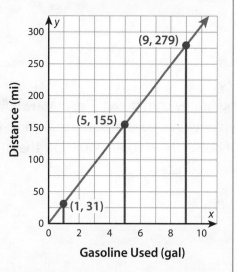

The vertical line segments create three similar right triangles. Because the triangles are similar, the quotient of the length of the vertical side to the length of the horizontal side is the same for each triangle. These quotients are slopes between (0, 0) and the points Cece chose. Because Cece could have chosen *any* points on the line to make the similar triangles, the slope is constant for the whole line. So, the gas mileage is constant for the whole trip.

1 For the graph in the Example, find the slope between the origin and each of the points Cece chose.

2 What was the gas mileage for the trip in the Example?

3. The graph shows how the number of gallons of water in a bathtub changes as the tub is being filled.

   a. What is the slope of the line?

   b. How can you show that the slope of the line is constant?

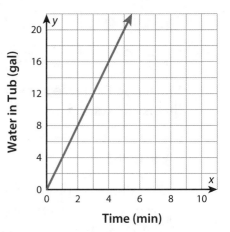

Time (min)

4. Estela is making honey corn bread. The graph shows the relationship between cups of corn meal and tablespoons of honey. How could you show that the slope of the line is constant?

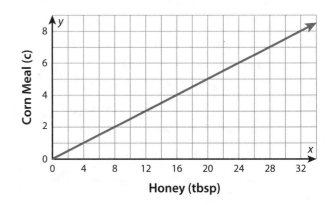

Honey (tbsp)

5. Ummi sees an advertisement for her favorite cereal. Then she writes these quotients:

   $$\frac{2.90}{10} = \frac{0.29}{1} \qquad \frac{3.48}{12} = \frac{0.29}{1} \qquad \frac{4.48}{16} = \frac{0.28}{1}$$

   a. What do Ummi's quotients represent in this situation?

   b. If you were to graph the (weight, cost) pairs for each box, would you be able to draw a straight line through the points? Explain.

Develop Finding the Slope of a Line

➤ **Read and try to solve the problem below.**

Holi Festival–a Hindu festival of color to welcome spring.

Ashwini's family is getting ready for the local Holi festival. Ashwini mixes yellow and red food coloring to make orange according to the graph. What is the slope of the line? What does the slope represent?

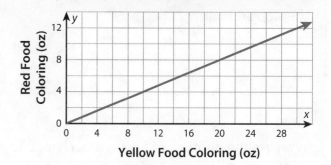

TRY IT

Math Toolkit graph paper, straightedges

DISCUSS IT

Ask: How do you know your slope is reasonable?

Share: In my solution . . . represents . . .

➤ **Explore different ways to find the slope of a line.**

Ashwini's family is getting ready for the local Holi festival. Ashwini mixes yellow and red food coloring to make orange according to the graph. What is the slope of the line? What does the slope represent?

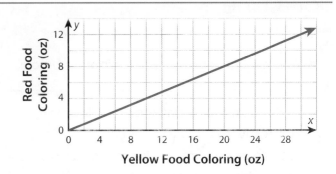

Model It

You can use the quotient of the vertical change to the horizontal change between any two points on the line to find the slope of a line.

This quotient representing slope, $\frac{\text{vertical change}}{\text{horizontal change}}$, is also called $\frac{\text{rise}}{\text{run}}$.

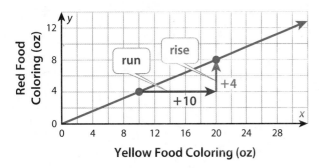

Model It

You can choose any two points on the line and use the slope formula to find the slope of a line.

For any two points on a line, (x_1, y_1) and (x_2, y_2), the slope between these points can be found using the formula $m = \frac{y_2 - y_1}{x_2 - x_1}$. In this formula, the letter m means slope.

$(10, 4)$ and $(20, 8)$ are two points on the line.

$$m = \frac{y_2 - y_1}{x_2 - x_1} = \frac{8 - 4}{20 - 10}$$

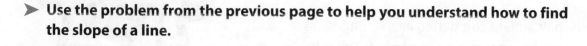

CONNECT IT

➤ **Use the problem from the previous page to help you understand how to find the slope of a line.**

1 What is the slope of the line in the **Try It** problem? Why is it helpful to know the slope in this situation?

2 Look at both **Model Its**. Use the quotient representing slope to explain why the slope formula makes sense.

3 Find the slope of the line using two other pairs of points. Why does it make sense that you get the same value for slope no matter which points you choose on the line?

4 How do you decide which points to use to find the slope of a line?

5 **Reflect** Think about all the models and strategies you have discussed today. Describe how one of them helped you better understand how to find the slope of a line.

Apply It

➤ **Use what you learned to solve these problems.**

6 Oren is a wheelchair athlete competing in a 100-meter race. His coach tracks his progress in the table below. The coach plans to make a graph using these points. What will be the slope of the line? What does the slope represent? Show your work.

Time (s)	0	5	10	15
Distance (m)	0	31.25	62.5	93.75

SOLUTION _____

7 This graph shows the relationship between cups of yogurt and cups of berries in Kaley's smoothie recipe.

a. What is the slope of the line? What does the slope represent in this situation?

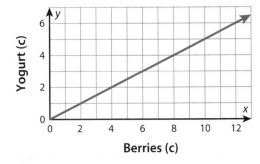

b. Kaley uses 9 cups of yogurt. How many cups of berries should she use? Show your work.

SOLUTION _____

8 This graph shows how fast Heidi ran on a track. Heidi says she was running 1.5 laps per minute because $\frac{3}{2} = 1.5$. What mistake did she make? How fast was Heidi running?

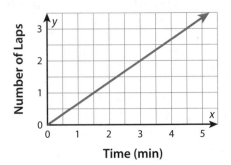

Practice Finding the Slope of a Line

➤ **Study the Example showing how to find the slope of a line. Then solve problems 1–5.**

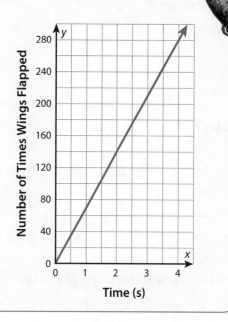

Example

A scientist made this graph showing the number of times a hummingbird flaps its wings for different lengths of time. What is the slope of the line? What does the slope mean in this situation?

Find two points on the line: (2, 140), (4, 280)

Find the slope: $m = \dfrac{280 - 140}{4 - 2} = \dfrac{140}{2} = \dfrac{70}{1}$

The slope is $\dfrac{70}{1}$, or 70. The hummingbird flaps its wings 70 times per second.

---

1 Alejandro said that the slope of the line in the Example is $\dfrac{140}{2}$ because for points (2, 140) and (0, 0), the rise is 140 and the run is 2. Is Alejandro correct? Explain.

2 Safara wants to rent a bicycle. The graph shows the cost for renting a bicycle for different lengths of time.

a. What is the slope of the line? Show your work.

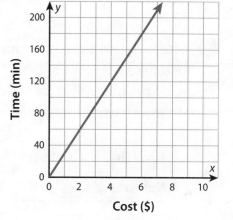

SOLUTION _____

b. What does the slope represent in this situation?

3 Colin wants to make purple paint. He finds a graph online that shows how much red and blue paint he should use to make the shade of purple he wants.

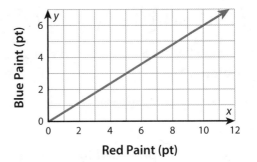

Red Paint (pt)

a. What is the slope of the line?
Show your work.

SOLUTION _____

b. What does the slope represent in this situation?

4 Rafael wants to find the slope of the line.

a. This is Rafael's work. What mistake did he make?

$$m = \frac{4 - 2}{100 - 50} = \frac{2}{50} = \frac{1}{25}$$

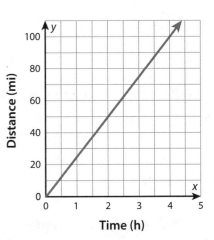

Time (h)

b. What is the slope of the line?

5 A factory makes cars at a constant rate. The table shows the number of cars made for different lengths of time. A manager draws a graph of the number of cars made per hour. What is the slope of the line? What does the slope represent? Show your work.

Time (h)	0	5	8	12	24
Number of Cars	0	130	208	312	624

SOLUTION _____

Refine Graphing Proportional Relationships and Defining Slope

➤ **Complete the Example below. Then solve problems 1–8.**

Example

Mr. Aba drew this graph on the board. What is the slope of the line?

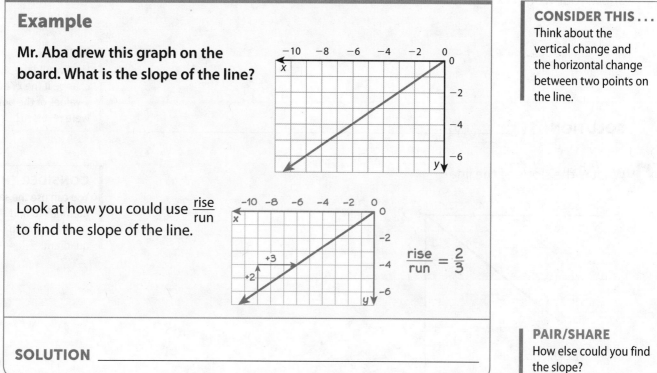

Look at how you could use $\frac{rise}{run}$ to find the slope of the line.

$$\frac{rise}{run} = \frac{2}{3}$$

SOLUTION _____

Apply It

1 The graph shows how many skateboards a company made over a period of time. How can you show that the slope is constant?

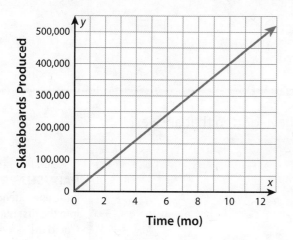

2 Gavin makes bracelets by stringing beads on a cord. The cost of a cord is proportional to the length of the cord. Gavin graphs a line that shows the cost per yard of cord. Two points on the line are $\left(\frac{3}{4}, 3\right)$ and $\left(7\frac{1}{2}, 30\right)$. What is the slope of the line? What does the slope mean in this situation?

Show your work.

CONSIDER THIS . . .
How can you use the coordinates of the two points to find the slope of the line?

PAIR/SHARE
How would the slope change if the *x*- and *y*-values of the points were reversed?

SOLUTION

3 What is the slope of the line?

CONSIDER THIS . . .
You can use the same methods to find the slope of a line in any quadrant.

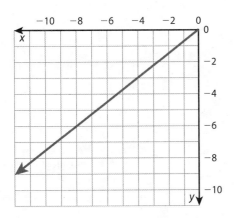

A $\frac{3}{4}$

B $\frac{4}{3}$

C $-\frac{3}{4}$

D $-\frac{4}{3}$

Elon chose D as the correct answer. How might he have gotten that answer?

PAIR/SHARE
If the line extended into the first quadrant, would the slope change?

4 A dairy farmer sells milk at a farmer's market. The graph shows what she charges for different quantities of milk.

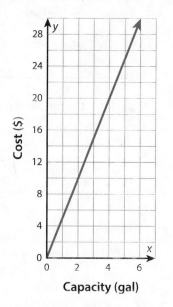

a. What is the slope of the line?

b. How much will the farmer charge for half a gallon of milk? Show your work.

SOLUTION _____

5 The graph shows the walking speeds for Khalid, represented by line *A*, and his daughter, represented by line *B*.

a. Who walks faster? How can you tell who walks faster just by looking at the graph?

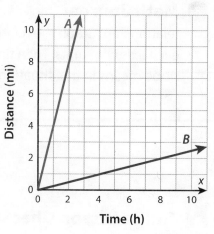

b. The slope of line *A* is _____ , so Khalid's walking speed is _____ miles per hour.

c. The slope of line *B* is _____ , so his daughter's walking speed is _____ mile per hour.

6 Querida makes this graph of the amounts of water and lemon juice to mix to make lemonade. Tell whether each statement about the line is *True* or *False*.

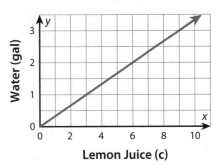

Lemon Juice (c)

	True	False
a. The $\frac{rise}{run}$ is $\frac{3}{1}$.	○	○
b. The unit rate is the same as the slope.	○	○
c. The line shows a proportional relationship.	○	○
d. The slope is less than 1.	○	○
e. The slope tells how many cups of water for each gallon of lemonade.	○	○

7 Troy makes green slime for his brother. He uses this graph to add the correct amount of blue and yellow food coloring to white slime. What is the slope of the line? Show your work.

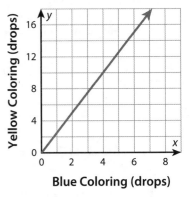

Blue Coloring (drops)

SOLUTION _____

8 **Math Journal** Think of a situation that is a proportional relationship. Graph the relationship in the coordinate plane. Label each axis with units. Then find the slope of the line. Tell what the slope means in this situation.

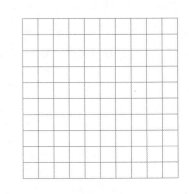

✔ End of Lesson Checklist

☐ **INTERACTIVE GLOSSARY** Find the entry for *slope*. Add two important things you learned about slope in this lesson.

☐ **SELF CHECK** Go back to the Unit 3 Opener and see what you can check off.

Dear Family,

This week your student is learning about equations of lines and their graphs. Students will learn that a **linear equation**, or an equation that describes a straight line, can be written in **slope-intercept form**.

The slope-intercept form of a linear equation is $y = mx + b$, where m is the slope and b is the **y-intercept**, or the y-coordinate of the point where the line crosses the y-axis. When $b = 0$, a linear equation is written in the form $y = mx$. Students can graph a linear equation written in slope-intercept form, like in the example below.

Graph the line for the linear equation $y = 2x + 1$.

➤ **ONE WAY** to graph the line is to use the equation to find points on the line.

    If $x = 0$, then $y = 2(0) + 1$, or 1.

    If $x = 2$, then $y = 2(2) + 1$, or 5.

    If $x = 4$, then $y = 2(4) + 1$, or 9.

    (0, 1), (2, 5), and (4, 9) are points on the line.

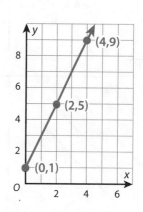

➤ **ANOTHER WAY** is to use the y-intercept and the slope to find points on the line.

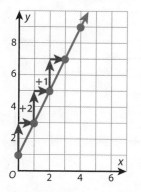

The y-intercept is 1, so the point (0, 1) is on the line. The slope is 2, or $\frac{2}{1}$, so move up 2 units and right 1 unit from (0, 1) to plot the next point. You can continue moving up 2 units and right 1 unit to plot more points.

Using either method, the graph is a line with a slope of 2 and a y-intercept of 1.

 Use the next page to start a conversation about slope-intercept form.

Activity Thinking About Slope-Intercept Form

➤ **Do this activity together to investigate slope-intercept form.**

Slope-intercept form of an equation can be used to model many real-world situations that involve a starting value and a consistent change in value. Some examples include the height of a plant that grows at a constant rate and the distance covered by a car traveling at a constant speed.

? What patterns do you see between the equations written in slope-intercept form and their lines in each graph?

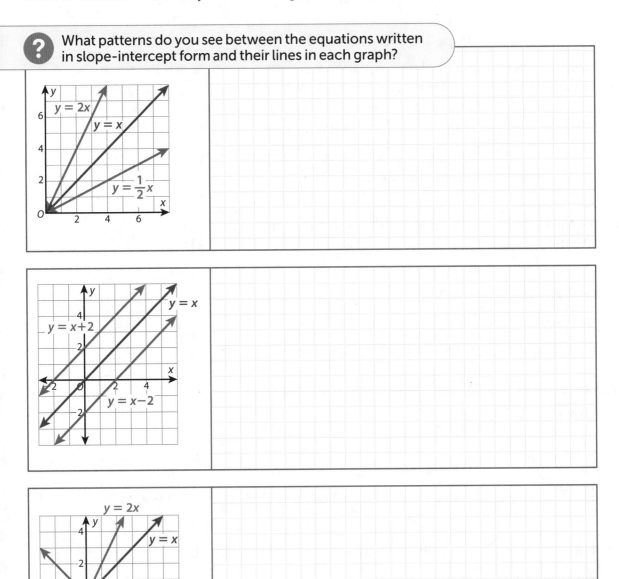

©Curriculum Associates, LLC Copying is not permitted.

Explore Deriving $y = mx$

Previously, you learned about slope. In this lesson, you will learn about writing the equation of a line.

➤ **Use what you know to try to solve the problem below.**

Kendra is a blind marathon runner training for the Junior Paralympics. Kendra's coach graphs a line representing Kendra's distance from the start over the first 10 minutes of a practice 5K race. What is the slope of the line? What equation could you use to find y, Kendra's distance from the start after x minutes?

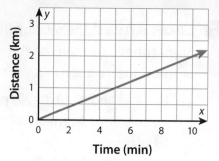

TRY IT

Math Toolkit graph paper, straightedges

◎ **Learning Target** SMP 1, SMP 2, SMP 3, SMP 4, SMP 5, SMP 6, SMP 7
Use similar triangles to explain why the slope m is the same between any two distinct points on a non-vertical line in the coordinate plane; **derive the equation** $y = mx$ for a line through the origin and the equation $y = mx + b$ for a line intercepting the vertical axis at b.

CONNECT IT

1 **Look Back** What is the slope and what is equation of the line representing Kendra's distance from the start in terms of time? Explain how you found each.

2 **Look Ahead** The relationship between distance and time in **Try It** is proportional. You can use the slope formula to derive the general equation for a proportional relationship.

    a. Use (x, y) and $(0, 0)$ as two points on the graph of a proportional relationship. Use the slope formula to find the slope between these two points. Fill in the blanks.

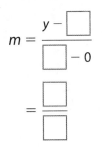

    b. What can you do to get y alone on one side of the equation? Fill in the blanks.

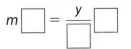

    c. Simplify the equation and rewrite it with y on the left side. This is the general equation for all proportional relationships.

$$y = \boxed{}$$

3 **Reflect** In problem 2a, how do you know that the point $(0, 0)$ is on the graph of any proportional relationship?

Prepare for Deriving and Graphing Linear Equations of the Form $y = mx + b$

1) Think about what you know about slope and lines. Fill in each box.
Use words, numbers, and pictures. Show as many ideas as you can.

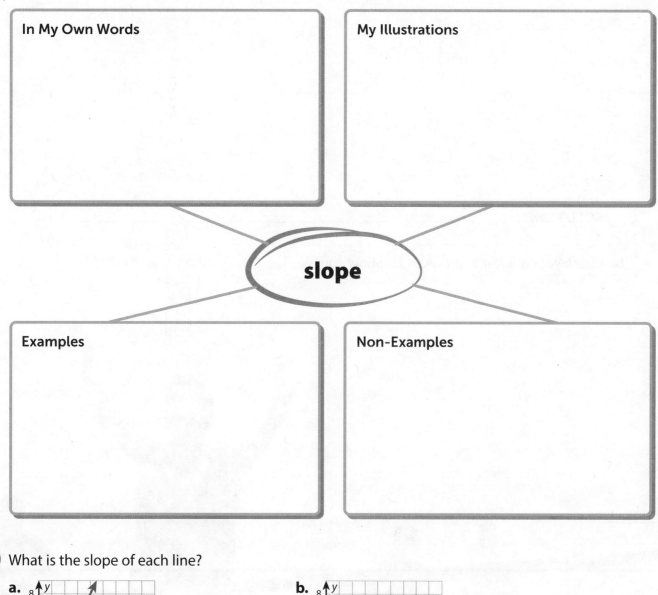

In My Own Words	My Illustrations

slope

Examples	Non-Examples

2) What is the slope of each line?

a.

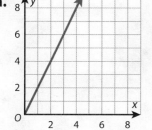

b.

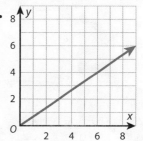

3 Ethan's coach graphs a line representing the first 5 minutes of Ethan's 5K race.

    a. What is the slope of the line? What equation could you write to find Ethan's distance, *y*, for any number of minutes, *x*, during this first part of the race? Show your work.

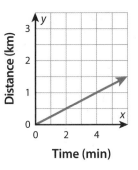

SOLUTION _____

    b. Check your answer to problem 3a. Show your work.

Develop Deriving $y = mx + b$

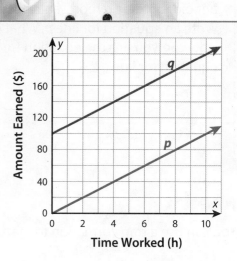

➤ **Read and try to solve the problem below.**

Ramona has a new job as a chef. She earns the same amount per hour as she did in her old job, plus she got a $100 sign-on bonus. Line p represents Ramona's earnings in her old job. Line q represents her earnings in her new job. Write an equation for line p. What does the slope mean? How can you use the equation for line p to write an equation for line q?

TRY IT

Math Toolkit graph paper, straightedges

DISCUSS IT

Ask: How did you use the old job's equation to find the new job's equation?

Share: At first, I thought . . .

➤ **Explore different ways to derive $y = mx + b$.**

Ramona has a new job as a chef. She earns the same amount per hour as she did in her old job, plus she got a $100 sign-on bonus. Line p represents Ramona's earnings in her old job. Line q represents her earnings in her new job. Write an equation for line p. What does the slope mean? How can you use the equation for line p to write an equation for line q?

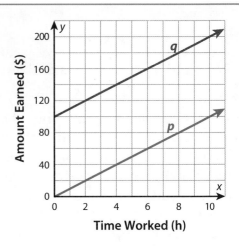

Model It

You can use a transformation to map **line p** onto **line q**.

The slopes of the lines are equal since the earnings per hour at each job are the same. The lines are parallel.

The y-coordinate of the point where a line meets or crosses the y-axis is called the **y-intercept**.

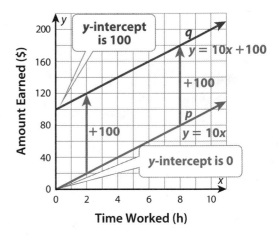

Analyze It

You can write the equation for line p in the form $y = mx$.

Line p represents earnings at the **old job**. (0, 0) and (2, 20) are on line p.

$$m = \frac{y_2 - y_1}{x_2 - x_1} = \frac{20 - 0}{2 - 0} = 10$$

The equation for line p is $y = 10x$ where y is the amount earned and x is the number of hours worked.

The equation for **line q** should include the hourly earnings at the **new job** plus the sign-on bonus. The equation is $y = 10x + 100$.

➤ **Use the problem from the previous page to help you understand how to derive** $y = mx + b$.

1 Look at **Model It**.

   a. Describe how to map line p onto line q.

   b. What does the y-intercept of line q represent?

2 Look at **Analyze It**. How are the equations for Ramona's earnings at the old job and the new job alike? How are they different? Explain.

3 A **linear equation** describes a straight line. It can be written in **slope-intercept form**, $y = mx + b$, where m is the slope and b is the y-intercept. The equation for line q is shown in slope-intercept form. Write the equation for line p in slope-intercept form. Circle the slope and underline the y-intercept.

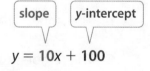

4 You can use the slope formula to also derive the slope-intercept form of a linear equation. Use the slope formula to find the slope between (x, y), any point on a line, and $(0, b)$, the point at the y-intercept. Then solve for y.

5 **Reflect** Think about all the models and strategies you have discussed today. Describe how one of them helped you better understand how to solve the **Try It** problem.

Apply It

➤ **Use what you learned to solve these problems.**

6 Liam's class is planting bamboo seedlings in the school garden. The line represents the average height of a bamboo plant after it has been planted. Write an equation in slope-intercept form that Liam could use to predict the height y of his bamboo after x days. Explain what the slope and the y-intercept mean in this situation.

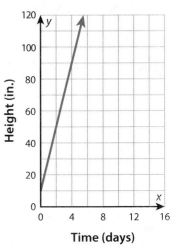

Height (in.) / Time (days)

7 Jennifer's weather app has a graph that shows the predicted outside temperature starting at 7 AM. Which statements are true about the graph? Select all that apply.

A The line is the graph of a linear equation.

B The slope of the line is $\frac{1}{2}$.

C The temperature increases throughout the morning at a steady rate.

D The equation of the line is $y = -3x + 2$ where y is the temperature in degrees Fahrenheit and x is the time in hours after 7 AM.

E The y-intercept means it was $-3°F$ at 7 AM.

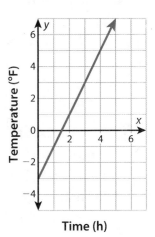

Temperature (°F) / Time (h)

8 Julio sells hand-painted skateboards. The graph shows how the price of a skateboard is related to the amount of time Julio spends painting it. Julio says the equation of the line is $y = 10x + 15$. Explain what mistake Julio made. Write the correct equation for Julio's line.

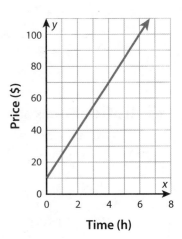

Price ($) / Time (h)

Practice Deriving $y = mx + b$

> **Study the Example showing how to write the equation of a line in slope-intercept form from a graph. Then solve problems 1–5.**

Example

An oceanographer is studying the growth of giant kelp. She selects one giant kelp plant and records its height each day. Then she draws this graph. What is the equation of the line in slope-intercept form? Define your variables.

(0, 10) and (2, 60) are two points on the line.

$$m = \frac{60 - 10}{2 - 0}$$

$$= \frac{50}{2}, \text{ or } 25 \qquad \text{The slope is 25.}$$

The line intersects the y-axis at (0, 10).
The y-intercept is 10.

The equation $y = 25x + 10$ shows the height, y, of the giant kelp plant after x days.

1. What do the slope and y-intercept in the Example represent in this situation?

2. A meteorologist tracks the amount of snowfall over a 5-hour period. She graphs her measurements. What is the equation of the meteorologist's line in slope-intercept form? Define your variables.

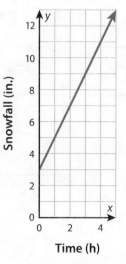

3 The growth in earnings for a digital music service is shown in the graph. What is the equation of the line? Show your work. Define your variables.

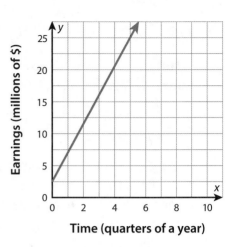

Earnings (millions of $)

Time (quarters of a year)

SOLUTION _____

_____

4 Daria and her brother want to make 100 bracelets to sell at a craft fair. They have made some already. Daria made this graph to show how they can reach their goal. The equation of Daria's line is $y = 14x + 30$ where y is the number of bracelets and x is the time in hours.

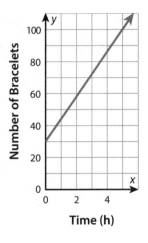

Number of Bracelets

Time (h)

a. What is the slope of the line?

b. What is the y-intercept?

5 Write each linear equation under the graph of its line.

$y = 4x - 2$ $y = \frac{1}{4}x + 2$ $y = 2x + \frac{1}{4}$

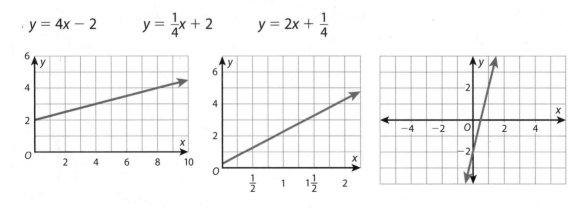

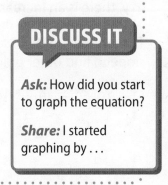

Develop Graphing a Linear Equation of the Form $y = mx + b$

➤ **Read and try to solve the problem below.**

A 60-gallon rain barrel is filled to capacity. Elena opens the stopper to let water drain out to water her garden.

The equation $y = -3x + 60$ can be used to find y, the number of gallons of water left after the barrel drains for x minutes. Graph the equation.

TRY IT

Math Toolkit graph paper, straightedges

DISCUSS IT

Ask: How did you start to graph the equation?

Share: I started graphing by . . .

➤ **Explore different ways to graph a linear equation of the form $y = mx + b$.**

A 60-gallon rain barrel is filled to capacity. Elena opens the stopper to let water drain out to water her garden.

The equation $y = -3x + 60$ can be used to find y, the number of gallons of water left after the barrel drains for x minutes. Graph the equation.

Analyze It

You can look at the equation in slope-intercept form.

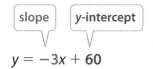

The y-intercept tells you where one point on the line is located. The slope tells you how the line slants.

Lines with positive slope slant up from left to right.

Lines with negative slope slant down from left to right.

Graph It

You can use the slope and the y-intercept to plot points.

A slope of -3 can be written as $\frac{-3}{1}$ in $\frac{\text{rise}}{\text{run}}$ form. So, for every **decrease of 3 in y**, there is an **increase of 1 in x**.

Because of the scale of this graph, it is easier to use the equivalent $\frac{\text{rise}}{\text{run}}$ quotient $\frac{-30}{10}$. So, for every **decrease of 30 in y**, there is an **increase of 10 in x**.

The y-intercept is 60, so one point on the line is (0, 60). Use the slope to find other points on the line.

$(0 + 10, 60 - 30) = (10, 30)$ $\qquad$ $(10 + 10, 30 - 30) = (20, 0)$

➤ **Use the problem from the previous page to help you understand how to graph linear equations of the form $y = mx + b$.**

1 Look at **Graph It**. Do all the points on the line make sense for the situation? Explain.

2 **a.** Look at **Analyze It** and **Graph It**. Why does it make sense that the slope is negative? Why does it make sense that the y-intercept is positive?

3 **a.** Explain why a horizontal line has a slope of 0.

b. Explain why we use the term *undefined* to describe the slope of a vertical line.

4 How can you use the slope and y-intercept to graph a linear equation of the form $y = mx + b$?

5 **Reflect** Think about all the models and strategies you have discussed today. Describe how one of them helped you better understand graphing a linear equation of the form $y = mx + b$.

Apply It

➤ **Use what you learned to solve these problems.**

6 Describe what the graph of the equation $y = 50x + 125$ will look like.

7 Graph the equations $y = -1$ and $x = -1$. What is the slope of each line? What is the y-intercept of each line?

$y = -1$

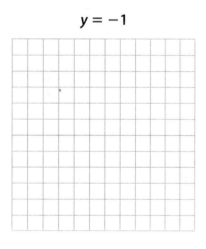

slope: _____

y-intercept: _____

$x = -1$

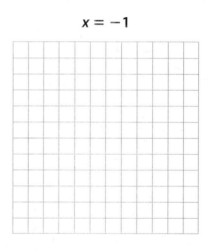

slope: _____

y-intercept: _____

8 Graph the equation $y = -20x + 500$.

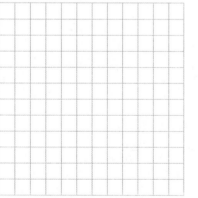

Practice Graphing a Linear Equation of the Form $y = mx + b$

➤ **Study the Example showing how to graph a linear equation of the form $y = mx + b$. Then solve problems 1–4.**

Example

Mr. Díaz uses a hose to fill a kiddie pool with water. When full, the pool holds 300 gallons of water. The equation $y = 25x + 50$ can be used to find the number of gallons of water, y, in the pool x minutes after he turns on the hose. Graph the equation. How long does it take to fill the pool?

The y-intercept is 50, so the line intersects the y-axis at (0, 50). The slope is 25, or $\frac{25}{1}$. There is a **vertical change of 25** for every **horizontal change of 1.**

$(0 + 1, 50 + 25) = (1, 75)$

$(1 + 1, 75 + 25) = (2, 100)$

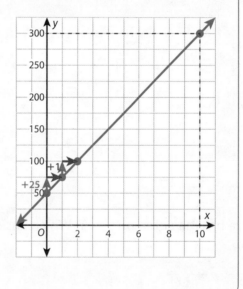

Plot the points and draw a line through them. The pool is filled when the number of gallons, y, is 300. This corresponds to an x-value of 10, so it takes 10 minutes to fill the pool.

---

1 At the end of the day, Mr. Díaz drains the pool. The equation $y = -50x + 300$ can be used to find y, the number of gallons of water left after draining the pool for x minutes. Graph the equation. How long does it take to drain the pool? Explain.

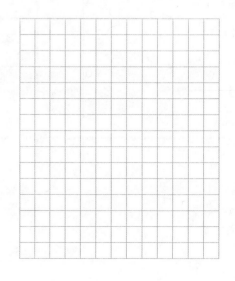

2 Tameka signs up for membership at a rock climbing gym. She pays a
   one-time $100 membership fee. Then she will pay a $25 monthly fee.
   The equation $y = 25x + 100$ can be used to find y, the total cost of
   a gym membership for x months. What is the slope of the line?
   What is the y-intercept?

3 Graph the linear equation $y = -\frac{1}{2}x - 1.5$. Show your work.

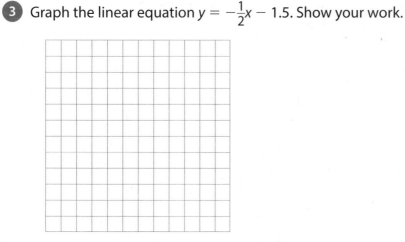

4 Which line has the equation $y = 3$? Which has equation $x = 3$? Explain how
   you know.

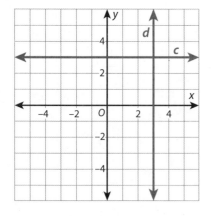

Develop Graphing a Linear Equation Given in Any Form

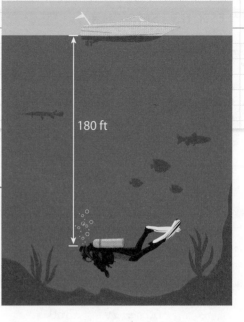

180 ft

➤ **Read and try to solve the problem below.**

A scuba diver dives to 180 feet below sea level. The linear equation $-60x + 2y = -360$ represents his trip back to the surface. The variable y is his elevation in feet relative to sea level after x minutes. Graph the equation.

TRY IT

Math Toolkit graph paper, straightedges

➤ **Explore different ways to graph a linear equation given in any form.**

A scuba diver dives to 180 feet below sea level. The linear equation $-60x + 2y = -360$ represents his trip back to the surface. The variable y is his elevation in feet relative to sea level after x minutes. Graph the equation.

Model It

You can rewrite the linear equation in slope-intercept form, $y = mx + b$.

$$-60x + 2y = -360$$

$$-60x + 60x + 2y = -360 + 60x$$

$$2y = -360 + 60x$$

$$\frac{2y}{2} = \frac{-360}{2} + \frac{60x}{2}$$

$$y = -180 + 30x$$

$$y = 30x - 180$$

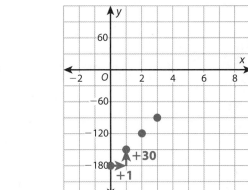

Use the **slope** and **y-intercept** to plot points.

Solve It

You can find two points to graph the linear equation.

Substitute 0 for each variable.

$$-60x + 2y = -360 \qquad\qquad -60x + 2y = -360$$

$$-60(0) + 2y = -360 \qquad\qquad -60x + 2(0) = -360$$

$$2y = -360 \qquad\qquad -60x = -360$$

$$y = -180 \qquad\qquad x = 6$$

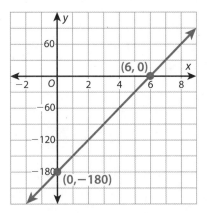

The points $(0, -180)$ and $(6, 0)$ are on the line. Plot these points and draw a line through them.

➤ **Use the problem from the previous page to help you understand how to graph a linear equation in any form.**

1 Look at **Model It**. How does writing the equation in slope-intercept form help you graph it?

2 Look at **Solve It**. To find a point on the line, you can substitute *any* value for one variable and solve for the other. Why might you choose substituting 0 for a variable?

3 What part of the graph represents the situation? How does slope-intercept form help you understand the problem better?

4 Describe two ways you can graph a linear equation if it is not given in slope-intercept form.

5 **Reflect** Think about all the models and strategies you have discussed today. Describe how one of them helped you better understand how to solve the **Try It** problem.

Apply It

➤ **Use what you learned to solve these problems.**

6 Graph the linear equation $-150x + 3y - 300 = 0$. Show your work.

7 Kiara said the line with equation $28x - \frac{1}{2}y = -20$ has a slope of 28. What mistake did Kiara make?

8 A marine biologist is using an underwater drone to study a delicate coral reef. The linear equation $20y - 30x = -900$ gives the drone's elevation, y, in meters from the surface of the water after x seconds. Graph the equation. What are the slope and y-intercept of the line? What part of the graph represents this situation?

Practice Graphing a Linear Equation Given in Any Form

➤ **Study the Example showing how to graph a linear equation given in any form. Then solve problems 1–4.**

Example

Conan has some money to spend on gas for his car. The linear equation $5x + 2y = 100$ represents y, the amount of money he has left after buying x gallons of gas. Graph the equation. What part of the graph represents this situation?

Find two points on the line by substituting 0 for x and y.

$$5(0) + 2y = 100 \qquad\quad 5x + 2(0) = 100$$
$$\qquad\quad 2y = 100 \qquad\qquad\qquad 5x = 100$$
$$\qquad\qquad y = 50 \qquad\qquad\qquad\quad x = 20$$

Plot (0, 50) and (20, 0) and draw a line through them. The situation is represented in Quadrant I of the graph.

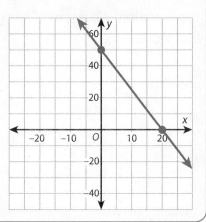

1. **a.** Write the equation from the Example in slope-intercept form.

   b. What is the slope of the line? What is the y-intercept?

2. Madison is reeling in her kite string at a steady rate. The linear equation $3y - 9x = -81$ can be used to find y, the number of feet of kite string she still needs to reel in after x seconds. Are the points $(0, -27)$ and $(-9, 0)$ on the line? Show your work.

Vocabulary

slope

for any two points on a line, the $\frac{\text{rise}}{\text{run}}$ or $\frac{\text{change in } y}{\text{change in } x}$.

slope-intercept form

a linear equation in the form $y = mx + b$, where m is the slope and b is the y-intercept.

y-intercept

the y-coordinate of the point where a line intersects the y-axis.

SOLUTION _____

3 Bruno is a manager at a factory that makes in-line skates. The equation $200x - y + 500 = 0$ relates y, the number of pairs of skates the factory has in the warehouse and x, the number of hours after Bruno starts his shift.

a. Show that the equation is a linear equation by writing it in slope-intercept form. Show your work.

b. Graph the equation. What part of the graph represents this situation? Show your work.

SOLUTION _____

4 Graph the linear equation $16x + 2y = 300$. Show your work.

Refine Deriving and Graphing Linear Equations of the Form $y = mx + b$

➤ **Complete the Example below. Then solve problems 1–8.**

Example

Ichiro lives on an island. He takes a ferry to school. One mile from the dock, the ferry leaves the harbor and travels at a constant speed. A graph relating the ferry's distance from the dock in miles to the time in minutes since it leaves the harbor is a line. The points (3, 2) and (6, 3) are on the line. What is the equation of the line in slope-intercept form? Define your variables.

Look at how you could find the equation of the line using the two points and a graph.

The line goes through (0, 1).

y-intercept: 1

$m = \dfrac{3-2}{6-3} = \dfrac{1}{3}$

y is the distance the ferry traveled in miles after x minutes.

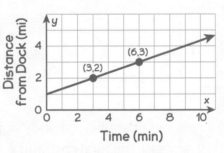

SOLUTION _____

CONSIDER THIS . . .
How can a graph help you find the y-intercept?

PAIR/SHARE
How can you check your equation?

Apply It

1 Graph the equation $y = \dfrac{3}{4}x + \dfrac{1}{2}$. Show your work.

CONSIDER THIS . . .
Understanding what the slope represents could help you set up and label the graph.

PAIR/SHARE
How else could you find points to graph?

2 A botanist is studying the growth of the sequoia tree. He selects one sequoia tree and records its height each year. He makes a graph to show the tree's growth. What is the equation of the line in slope-intercept form? Define your variables.
Show your work.

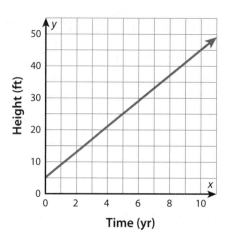

Time (yr)

> **CONSIDER THIS . . .**
> How can you use the graph to help you write the equation?

> **PAIR/SHARE**
> How would the equation change if the y-intercept changed?

SOLUTION _____

3 A movie club is having a new-member sale, so Mindy signs up. The equation $-0.4x + 0.05y - 1.25 = 0$ relates y, the total cost, and x, the number of months. What is the y-intercept of the line represented by the equation?

A -1.25

B 0.05

C 8

D 25

Greg chose C as the correct answer. How might he have gotten that answer?

> **CONSIDER THIS . . .**
> How could rewriting the equation in a different form help you to find the y-intercept?

> **PAIR/SHARE**
> How else could you find the y-intercept?

4 Juanita makes leather lanyards to sell. She charges a base fee and a cost per inch of the finished lanyard. The line shows the cost y for x inches of lanyard. Write an equation for the line in slope-intercept form. Show your work.

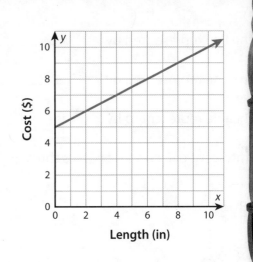

Cost ($)

Length (in)

SOLUTION _____

5 Demarco has some money saved, but wants to save more. He decides to save the same amount every month. The linear equation $10y - 200x = 500$ can be used to find y, the amount of money Demarco has saved after x months. Demarco makes a graph of this equation. Tell whether each statement is *True* or *False*.

	True	False
a. The slope is 20.	○	○
b. The point (0, 500) is on the line.	○	○
c. The line slants downward from left to right.	○	○
d. The slope is −200.	○	○
e. The *y*-intercept is 50.	○	○

6 The slope of the line represented by $y = 5x$ is _____.

The slope of the line represented by $y = 3$ is _____.

The slope of the line represented by $x = 4$ is _____.

7 What is the *y*-intercept of a line that passes through the points (2, 7) and (6, 1)?

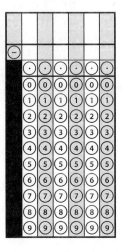

8 **Math Journal** Write a linear equation. Describe two ways you can graph the equation. Then graph the equation.

✓ End of Lesson Checklist

☐ **INTERACTIVE GLOSSARY** Find the entry for *slope-intercept form*. Sketch a graph of an equation in slope-intercept form.

☐ **SELF CHECK** Go back to the Unit 3 Opener and see what you can check off.

Dear Family,

This week your student is learning how to solve linear equations in one variable, also called one-variable linear equations. These are equations that can be written in the form $ax + b = c$, where x is a variable, b and c represent any numbers, and a represents any number except zero.

Previously, your student learned how to solve one-variable linear equations with the variable on one side of the equation. In this lesson, students will extend their knowledge to equations with the variable on both sides. Students will find the solution of an equation by finding the value of x that makes the equation true, like in the example below.

What is the solution of the linear equation?

$$\frac{1}{2}(3x - 1) = \frac{1}{4}(x + 3)$$

➤ **ONE WAY** to find the solution is to first multiply both sides of the equation by the **least common denominator** of the fractions. Then combine like terms.

$$4 \cdot \frac{1}{2}(3x - 1) = 4 \cdot \frac{1}{4}(x + 3)$$

$$2(3x - 1) = 1(x + 3)$$

$$6x - 2 = x + 3$$

$$6x - x - 2 + 2 = x - x + 3 + 2$$

$$5x = 5, \text{ so } x = 1$$

➤ **ANOTHER WAY** is to use the distributive property to multiply by $\frac{1}{2}$ and $\frac{1}{4}$ first. Then combine like terms.

$$\frac{1}{2}(3x - 1) = \frac{1}{4}(x + 3)$$

$$\frac{1}{2}(3x) - \frac{1}{2}(1) = \frac{1}{4}(x) + \frac{1}{4}(3)$$

$$\frac{3}{2}x - \frac{1}{2} = \frac{1}{4}x + \frac{3}{4}$$

$$\frac{5}{4}x = \frac{5}{4}, \text{ so } x = 1$$

Using either method, the solution of the equation is 1.

 Use the next page to start a conversation about linear equations in one variable.

Activity Thinking About Linear Equations in One Variable

➤ **Do this activity together to investigate linear equations in the real world.**

Linear equations can be useful in modeling situations where there is an unknown value, such as in the problem below.

You buy 6 notebooks and a $2 set of pencils. A friend buys 4 notebooks and an $8 set of pencils for the same amount of money. How much does one notebook cost?

The equation $6x + 2 = 4x + 8$ can be used to find x, the cost of one notebook. You can solve the equation to find that a notebook costs $3.

> **?** What different ways could you begin to solve the equations given below? Which store would you rather visit to buy supplies?

PROBLEM 1

In Store A, you can buy 3 notebooks and a $2 set of pencils for the same price as 4 notebooks. How much does a notebook cost at Store A?

The equation $3x + 2 = 4x$ can be used to find x, the cost of 1 notebook.

PROBLEM 2

In Store B, you can buy 2 notebooks and an $11 set of pencils for the same price as 4 notebooks and a $3 set of pencils. How much does a notebook cost at Store B?

The equation $2x + 11 = 4x + 3$ can be used to find x, the cost of 1 notebook.

Explore Linear Equations in One Variable

Previously, you learned how to solve one-variable equations. In this lesson, you will learn about solving one-variable equations that include fractions, decimals, the variable on both sides of the equation, and use of the distributive property.

➤ **Use what you know to try to solve the problem below.**

Teresa is going with her family to watch professional barrel racers. Her family buys 6 tickets. They have a coupon for $1.50 off each ticket. They pay $52.50 altogether for their tickets. Write an equation that you could use to represent the situation. What is the price of a ticket before using the coupon?

TRY IT

 Math Toolkit grid paper, sticky notes

DISCUSS IT

Ask: How did you get started writing the equation?

Share: First, I . . .

Learning Targets SMP 1, SMP 2, SMP 3, SMP 4, SMP 5, SMP 6

Solve linear equations in one variable.
• Solve linear equations with rational number coefficients, including equations whose solutions require expanding expressions using the distributive property and collecting like terms.

1 **Look Back** What is the price of a ticket before using the coupon? What equation did you write? Explain what each part of the equation represents.

2 **Look Ahead** A linear equation in one variable can be written in the form $ax + b = c$, where b and c can be any numbers and a can be any number except zero.

a. Explain why $4(x - 2.1) = 7.2$ is a linear equation in one variable.

b. The solution of a one-variable equation is the value of the variable that makes the equation true. What is the solution of $4(x - 2.1) = 7.2$?

c. Look at the equation $4x - 8.4 = 2x + 5$. The terms $4x$ and $2x$ are *like terms* because they are both written as a coefficient times x. To combine $4x$ and $2x$, you can subtract $2x$ from both sides of the equation. Write the equation in the form $ax + b = c$. What is the solution of this equation?

d. Another way you can combine $4x$ and $2x$ is to subtract $4x$ from both sides of the equation. Write $4x - 4x - 8.4 = 2x - 4x + 5$ in the form $ax + b = c$. What is the solution of this equation?

e. The original equation has the variable on both sides of the equation. What happens to the variable after combining the like terms?

3 **Reflect** Which way of combining like terms in problems 2c and 2d do you prefer? Explain.

Prepare for Solving Linear Equations in One Variable

1 Think about what you know about expressions. Fill in each box.
Use words, numbers, and pictures. Show as many ideas as you can.

Word	In My Own Words	Examples
coefficient		
like terms		
term		
variable		

2 For each expression, circle any like terms and list any variables.

a. $-2.5x + 3.9 + 1.7x$

b. $1\frac{1}{2} + t + \frac{2}{3}s$

c. $15k + \frac{2}{5}k - 3m$

3. Darnell goes to the movies with his friends. The receipt on his phone shows the cost of the tickets after a discount.

a. Write an equation to represent the situation. What is the price of a ticket before the discount? Show your work.

SOLUTION _____

b. Check your answer to problem 3a. Show your work.

Develop Solving Linear Equations in One Variable with the Variable on Both Sides

➤ **Read and try to solve the problem below.**

Emma is $\frac{1}{4}$ as old as her father. In 20 years, Emma will be half as old as her father. The equation $\frac{1}{4}x + 20 = \frac{1}{2}(x + 20)$ represents this situation, where x is Emma's father's age now. How old is Emma's father now? How old is Emma now?

TRY IT   **Math Toolkit** grid paper, sticky notes

DISCUSS IT

Ask: Why did you choose that strategy to find their ages?

Share: I knew . . . so I . . .

➤ **Explore different ways to solve linear equations in one variable with the variable on both sides of the equation.**

Emma is $\frac{1}{4}$ as old as her father. In 20 years, Emma will be half as old as her father. The equation $\frac{1}{4}x + 20 = \frac{1}{2}(x + 20)$ represents this situation, where x is Emma's father's age now. How old is Emma's father now? How old is Emma now?

Model It

You can multiply both sides of the equation by **4** first. Then use the distributive property again and combine like terms.

$$\frac{1}{4}x + 20 = \frac{1}{2}(x + 20)$$

$$4\left(\frac{1}{4}x + 20\right) = 4 \cdot \frac{1}{2}(x + 20)$$

$$x + 80 = 2(x + 20)$$

$$x + 80 = 2x + 40$$

$$x - x + 80 = 2x - x + 40$$

$$80 = x + 40$$

Model It

You can use the distributive property to multiply by $\frac{1}{2}$ first. Then combine like terms.

$$\frac{1}{4}x + 20 = \frac{1}{2}(x + 20)$$

$$\frac{1}{4}x + 20 = \frac{1}{2}x + \frac{1}{2}(20)$$

$$\frac{1}{4}x + 20 = \frac{1}{2}x + 10$$

$$\frac{1}{4}x - \frac{1}{4}x + 20 = \frac{1}{2}x - \frac{1}{4}x + 10$$

$$20 = \frac{1}{4}x + 10$$

$$20 - 10 = \frac{1}{4}x + 10 - 10$$

$$10 = \frac{1}{4}x$$

➤ **Use the problem from the previous page to help you understand how to solve linear equations in one variable with the variable on both sides of the equation.**

1 Explain what each part of the equation $\frac{1}{4}x + 20 = \frac{1}{2}(x + 20)$ represents in the situation.

2 Look at both **Model Its**. Why does it make sense to multiply both sides by 4 first in the first **Model It**? Why does it make sense to use the distributive property first in the second **Model It**?

3 Look at both **Model Its**. Finish the solution for each method. Does it matter which solution method you use? Explain.

4 What is Emma's age now? What is her father's age now? Explain.

5 **Reflect** Think about all the models and strategies you have discussed today. Describe how one of them helped you better understand solving linear equations in one variable with the variable on both sides of the equation.

Apply It

➤ **Use what you learned to solve these problems.**

6 What is the solution of the equation? Show your work.

$$2x + 4 \overset{.}{-} \frac{3}{2}x = \frac{1}{3}(x + 5)$$

SOLUTION _____

7 Mr. Gordon buys packages of clay. Some of the packages are on sale. Five packages that are on sale cost the same as three packages that are not. The equation $5(p - 2.50) = 3p$ describes this situation, where p is the price of a package of clay that is not on sale. What is the price of a package of clay that is not on sale?

A $1.25

B $3.75

C $6.25

D $8.75

8 Solve the equation for m. Show your work.

$$0.4(20 - 10m) = 2.5 - 2m - 12.5$$

SOLUTION _____

Practice Solving Linear Equations in One Variable with the Variable on Both Sides

➤ **Study the Example showing how to solve a linear equation with the variable on both sides. Then solve problems 1–4.**

Example

The weight of Keiko's kitten is $\frac{1}{6}$ the weight of her puppy. If each animal gains 3 pounds, the kitten will weigh $\frac{1}{3}$ as much as the puppy. The equation $\frac{1}{6}w + 3 = \frac{1}{3}(w + 3)$ describes this situation, where w is the weight of the puppy now. How much does the puppy weigh now?

$$6\left(\frac{1}{6}w + 3\right) = 6 \cdot \frac{1}{3}(w + 3)$$

$$6\left(\frac{1}{6}w + 3\right) = 2(w + 3)$$

$$w + 18 = 2w + 6$$

$$w - w + 18 = 2w - w + 6$$

$$18 = w + 6$$

$$12 = w \quad \text{The puppy weighs 12 pounds now.}$$

1. In the Example, how much will the kitten weigh if it gains 3 pounds?
   Show your work.

SOLUTION _____

2. Solve the equation for t. Show your work.

   $$5(2t - 3) - 7.5t = 0.5(12 - t)$$

SOLUTION _____

3 Mrs. Shaw writes this equation on the board. She asks the students to find the solution.

$$-40 - 2\left(3m + \frac{1}{2}\right) = 7m - 2$$

a. Keith's work is shown below. What mistake did Keith make?

$$-40 - 6m + 1 = 7m - 2$$

$$-39 - 6m = 7m - 2$$

$$-39 = 13m - 2$$

$$-37 = 13m$$

$$-2\frac{11}{13} = m$$

b. What is the solution of the equation?

4 Marta practices the long jump. She jumps the same distance on her first four jumps. Her last two jumps are $1\frac{1}{2}$ feet longer than her first four jumps. Her average jump distance is 16 feet. The equation below represents the situation, where j is the distance of each of Marta's first four jumps.

average jump: 16 ft

$$\frac{4j + 2(j + 1.5)}{6} = 16$$

What is the distance of each of Marta's first four jumps? Show your work.

SOLUTION _____

Develop Representing and Solving Problems with One-Variable Equations

➤ **Read and try to solve the problem below.**

Tarik makes two large game mats for a bean bag toss. One mat is square and the other is an equilateral triangle. The square has a side length of $x + 3$ feet. The equilateral triangle has a side length of $3x - 1$ feet. The perimeters of the mats are the same. What are the side lengths of each game mat?

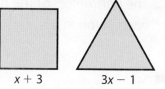

$x + 3$ $3x - 1$

TRY IT   **Math Toolkit** grid paper, sticky notes, algebra tiles

➤ **Explore different ways to represent and solve word problems involving one-variable equations.**

Tarik makes two large game mats for a bean bag toss. One mat is square and the other is an equilateral triangle. The square has a side length of $x + 3$ feet. The equilateral triangle has a side length of $3x - 1$ feet. The perimeters of the mats are the same. What are the side lengths of each game mat?

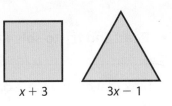

$x + 3$ $3x - 1$

Model It

You can write an equation to model the problem.

	Square Mat	Triangular Mat
Side Length	$x + 3$	$3x - 1$
Perimeter	$4(x + 3)$	$3(3x - 1)$

$4(x + 3) = 3(3x - 1)$

Model It

You can solve the equation for x.

$$4(x + 3) = 3(3x - 1)$$
$$4x + 12 = 9x - 3$$
$$4x - 4x + 12 = 9x - 4x - 3$$
$$12 + 3 = 5x - 3 + 3$$
$$15 = 5x$$
$$3 = x$$

➤ **Use the problem from the previous page to help you understand how to represent and solve word problems involving one-variable equations.**

1 Look at the first **Model It**. Explain how the equation represents the situation.

2 Look at the second **Model It**. Is the solution of the equation also the solution of the problem? Explain.

3 What are the side lengths of each game mat? How do you know?

4 How do you know whether the solution of an equation is also the solution of the original problem?

5 **Reflect** Think about all the models and strategies you have discussed today. Describe how one of them helped you better understand how to represent and solve word problems involving one-variable equations.

Apply It

➤ **Use what you learned to solve these problems.**

6 James and his sister save money for a trip to the water park. James has saved half the amount of money that his sister has saved. If they both save $30 more, James will have saved $\frac{3}{4}$ as much as his sister. Which equation can you use to find how much James has saved?

A $\frac{1}{2}x + 30 = \frac{3}{4}x + 30$

B $\frac{1}{2}(x + 30) = \frac{3}{4}(x + 30)$

C $\frac{1}{2}x + 30 = x + 30$

D $\frac{1}{2}x + 30 = \frac{3}{4}(x + 30)$

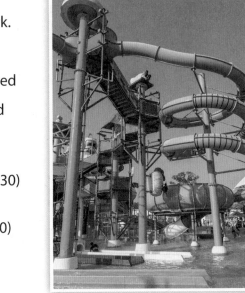

7 **a.** How much money has James saved in problem 6? Show your work.

SOLUTION _____

b. Did solving the equation in problem 7a solve the problem? Explain.

8 The length of Adriana's chicken coop is $3x + 12$ feet. The length of her garden is $6x - 16$ feet. The garden is $\frac{2}{3}$ the length of the chicken coop. What are the lengths of the chicken coop and the garden? Show your work.

3x + 12

Chicken Coop

Garden

6x − 16

SOLUTION _____

Name: _____

Practice Representing and Solving Problems with One-Variable Equations

➤ **Study the Example showing how to write and solve a one-variable equation that represents a word problem. Then solve problems 1–4.**

Example

Jelani has twice as much money on his subway pass as Alexis. If they both add $20 to their passes, Jelani will have 1.5 times as much on his pass as Alexis. Write an equation to represent this situation. How much do Jelani and Alexis have on their subway passes now?

	Jelani	Alexis
Now	$2x$	x
Add $20	$2x + 20$	$x + 20$

$2x + 20 = 1.5(x + 20)$

$2x + 20 = 1.5x + 30$

$0.5x = 10$

$x = 20 \qquad 2x = 40$

Jelani has $40 on his pass and Alexis has $20.

---

1 In the Example, does the value of x answer the question? Explain.

2 An equilateral triangle has a side length of $1.4x + 2$ inches. A regular hexagon has a side length of $0.5x + 2$ inches. The perimeters are equal. What is the side length of the triangle? What is the side length of the hexagon? Show your work.

SOLUTION _____

3 Victoria counts this week's food donations at a pet shelter. There are 16 full cases of canned food. There are 4 cases of canned food that are each missing 5 cans. Victoria records a total of 220 cans of food.

16 full cases of canned food
220 cans of food

a. Use c to represent the number of cans in a full case. What expression could represent the number of cans in each case that is missing cans?

b. Write an equation you could use to find c.

c. How many cans are in a full case? How many cans are in each of the 4 other cases? Show your work.

SOLUTION _____

4 Five less than twice the value of a number is equal to three times the quantity of four more than one-half the number. What is the number?

a. Let x be the number. Write and solve an equation to find x. Show your work.

SOLUTION _____

b. Does the solution of your equation solve the original problem? Explain.

Refine Solving Linear Equations in One Variable

➤ **Complete the Example below. Then solve problems 1–8.**

Example

Patrick divides a triangle into two smaller triangles. He labels some of the angle measures. What are the measures of $\angle 1$, $\angle 2$, and $\angle 3$?

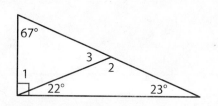

Look at how you could use equations to find the angle measures.

$$m\angle 2 + 22° + 23° = 180°$$
$$m\angle 2 + 45° = 180°$$
$$m\angle 2 = 135°$$

$$m\angle 3 + 135° = 180°$$
$$m\angle 3 = 45°$$

$$m\angle 1 + 67° + 45° = 180°$$
$$m\angle 1 + 112° = 180°$$
$$m\angle 1 = 68°$$

SOLUTION _____

Apply It

1. What is the solution of the equation? Show your work.

$$\frac{1}{4}(2x + 1.2) = 3(0.7x + 3) - 5\frac{1}{2}$$

SOLUTION _____

2 Laqueta has three times as many quarters as Pablo. If they each spend $0.50, Laqueta will have five times as many quarters as Pablo. How many quarters do Laqueta and Pablo each have now? Show your work.

CONSIDER THIS . . .
How many quarters are there in $0.50?

SOLUTION _____

PAIR/SHARE
What is another way you could write the equation?

3 Mr. McClary writes the equation $3(3x - 10) = 5(x + 10)$. The equation shows the relationship between the perimeter of an equilateral triangle and the perimeter of a regular pentagon. What is the perimeter of the pentagon?

A 20

B 50

C 100

D 150

Nikia chose A as the correct answer. How might she have gotten that answer?

CONSIDER THIS . . .
How can you use like terms to help find the solution of the equation?

PAIR/SHARE
Does it matter which perimeter you find?

4 What is the value of k? Show your work.

$$\frac{5}{4}(2 - k) = 2(3k - 1) - \frac{2}{3}k$$

SOLUTION _____

5 Alita is 2 times as old as Jiro. Jiro is 4 years younger than Erik. Erik is $\frac{1}{3}$ as old as Dawn. The sum of all their ages is 72.

a. What equation could you write to represent this situation? Show your work.

SOLUTION _____

b. What is the solution of your equation? Show your work.

SOLUTION _____

c. Fill in the blanks to complete each statement.

Alita is _____ years old.   Jiro is _____ years old.

Erik is _____ years old.   Dawn is _____ years old.

6 Moses makes a school spirit flag. He has $\frac{1}{3}$ as many yards of red fabric as blue fabric. He buys $2\frac{2}{3}$ yards more red fabric. Now he has equal amounts of red and blue fabric. Use x to represent the amount of blue fabric. Which equations could you use to find the amount of red fabric Moses has? Select all that apply.

A $x = \frac{1}{3}x + 2\frac{2}{3}$

B $\frac{1}{3}x = x + 2\frac{2}{3}$

C $x = \frac{1}{3}x - 2\frac{2}{3}$

D $x - 2\frac{2}{3} = \frac{1}{3}x$

E $x + 2\frac{2}{3} = \frac{1}{3}x + 2\frac{2}{3}$

F $x = \frac{1}{3}\left(x + 2\frac{2}{3}\right)$

7 Lian draws three lines on the board. Lines m and n are parallel. Lian says that the measure of $\angle 2$ is $\frac{2}{3}$ the measure of $\angle 1$. What is the measure of $\angle 2$?

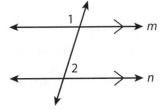

8 **Math Journal** Ava's turtle is half as old as her parrot. In 10 years, her turtle will be $\frac{3}{4}$ as old as her parrot. Write an equation to represent this situation. How old is Ava's turtle?

✔ End of Lesson Checklist

☐ **INTERACTIVE GLOSSARY** Find the entry for *variable*. Write a definition for a younger student. Show an example.

☐ **SELF CHECK** Go back to the Unit 3 Opener and see what you can check off.

Dear Family,

This week your student is learning that one-variable linear equations can have one solution, infinitely many solutions, or no solution. Students will learn that an equation has:

- one solution if the equation can be written as a statement that shows a value for a variable, like $x = 2$.

- infinitely many solutions if the equation can be written as a statement that shows a true statement, like $3 = 3$ or $2x + 3 = 2x + 3$.

- no solution if the equation can be written as a statement that shows a false statement, like $2 = 3$.

Students will learn how to find the number of solutions to a linear equation, as in the problem below.

Consider the linear equation $\frac{1}{4}(4x + 4) = x + 6$. How many solutions does the equation have?

▶ **ONE WAY** to find the number of solutions is to solve the equation by first applying the distributive property.

$$\frac{1}{4}(4x + 4) = x + 6$$

$$x + 1 = x + 6 \longleftarrow \text{Distribute the } \frac{1}{4}.$$

$$1 = 6$$

▶ **ANOTHER WAY** is to solve the equation by first eliminating the fraction.

$$4 \cdot \frac{1}{4}(4x + 4) = 4(x + 6) \longleftarrow \text{Multiply both sides by } 4.$$

$$4x + 4 = 4x + 24$$

$$4x - 4x + 4 - 4 = 4x - 4x + 24 - 4$$

$$0 = 20$$

Using either method, you get a false statement. The equation has no solution.

 Use the next page to start a conversation about solutions to one-variable linear equations.

Activity Thinking About Solutions of One-Variable Linear Equations

➤ **Do this activity together to investigate solutions of one-variable linear equations.**

Solutions of a one-variable linear equation are values of x that make the equation true. There can be one value of x that makes an equation true. There can be no values of x that make an equation true. There can be infinitely many values of x that make an equation true.

? What are some patterns you notice about the number of solutions to the equations below?

EQUATION SET 1

These equations have one solution.

$4x = 8$
$x = 9$
$5x = 20$

EQUATION SET 2

These equations have no solution.

$y + 1 = y + 4$
$2y + 3 = 2y + 5$
$3y + 4 = 3y - 2$

EQUATION SET 3

These equations have infinitely many solutions.

$2z + 3 = 2z + 3$
$z - 7 = z - 7$
$3z + 12 = 3z + 12$

Explore The Number of Solutions to One-Variable Linear Equations

Previously, you learned to use the distributive property and combine like terms to solve one-variable linear equations. In this lesson, you will learn that not all one-variable linear equations have exactly one solution.

➤ **Use what you know to try to solve the problem below.**

Solve the equation.

$$4(x + 6) = 2(2x + 12)$$

TRY IT

Math Toolkit algebra tiles, grid paper

DISCUSS IT

Ask: How did you decide to solve the equation?

Share: I knew . . . so I . . .

◎ **Learning Targets** SMP 1, SMP 2, SMP 3, SMP 4, SMP 5, SMP 6, SMP 7, SMP 8

Solve linear equations in one variable.
• Give examples of linear equations in one variable with one solution, infinitely many solutions, or no solutions. Show which of these possibilities is the case by successively transforming the given equation into simpler forms, until an equivalent equation of the form $x = a$, $a = a$, or $a = b$ results.

CONNECT IT

1 **Look Back** What happened when you solved the equation? What happens when you substitute any number for x in the equation?

2 **Look Ahead** You know how to solve equations where you get a statement like $x = 5$ or $t = 17.8$. This means the equation is true for this one value of the variable. The equation has one solution. However, sometimes you solve an equation and get a statement like $32 = 32$ or $0 = 0$. This means the equation is true for any value of the variable. The equation has infinitely many solutions.

a. Solve $5x = 2$. How many solutions does the equation have? Show your work.

b. Solve $9x - 5 = 9x - 5$. How many solutions does the equation have? Show your work.

3 **Reflect** Look at the equation in problem 2b. How could you know that $9x - 5 = 9x - 5$ has infinitely many solutions without solving the equation?

Name:

Prepare for Determining the Number of Solutions to an Equation

1 Think about what you know about expressions in mathematical statements. Fill in each box. Use words, numbers, and pictures. Show as many ideas as you can.

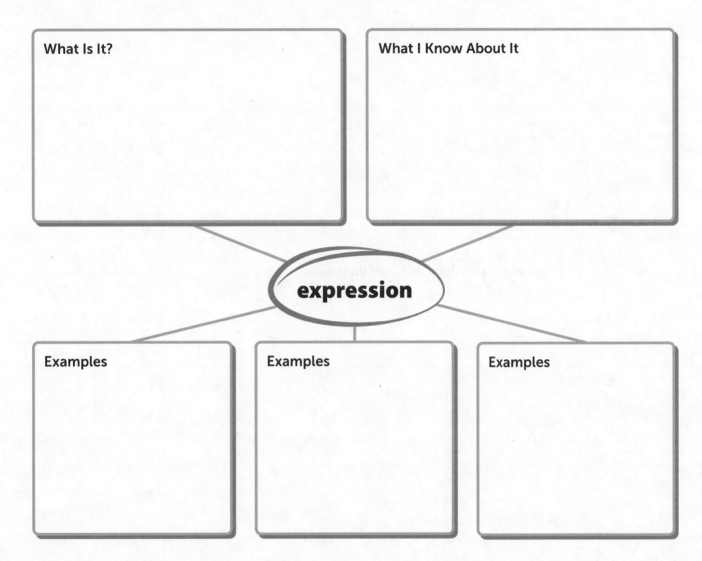

What Is It?

What I Know About It

expression

Examples

Examples

Examples

2 Which of the following are expressions? Circle your answers.

$4x + 7$ $6b + 1 = 13$

$192 \div 8 = 24$ $y - 17$

a. Solve the equation $6(x + 2) = 3(2x + 4)$. How many solutions are there? Show your work.

SOLUTION _____

b. Check your answer to problem 3a. Show your work.

Develop Determining the Number of Solutions to One-Variable Equations

➤ **Read and try to solve the problem below.**

A zoologist observes two sloths sitting in a tree at different heights. Both sloths start climbing at the same time. They stop after x minutes and she notes one sloth's height in the tree is $\frac{1}{2}(2x + 4)$ meters and the other's height is $x + 3$ meters. How many values of x make the equation $\frac{1}{2}(2x + 4) = x + 3$ true?

Math Toolkit algebra tiles

DISCUSS IT

Ask: What did you do first to decide how many solutions the equation has?

Share: I started by …

➤ **Explore different ways to determine the number of solutions to a one-variable linear equation.**

A zoologist observes two sloths sitting in a tree at different heights. Both sloths start climbing at the same time. They stop after x minutes and she notes one sloth's height in the tree is $\frac{1}{2}(2x + 4)$ meters and the other's height is $x + 3$ meters. How many values of x make the equation $\frac{1}{2}(2x + 4) = x + 3$ true?

Model It

You can solve the equation by first using the distributive property.

$$\frac{1}{2}(2x + 4) = x + 3$$
$$x + 2 = x + 3$$
$$2 = 3$$

Model It

You can solve the equation by first eliminating the fraction.

$$\frac{1}{2}(2x + 4) = x + 3$$
$$2\left[\frac{1}{2}(2x + 4)\right] = 2(x + 3)$$
$$2x + 4 = 2x + 6$$
$$4 = 6$$

> **Use the problem from the previous page to help you understand how to determine the number of solutions to a one-variable linear equation.**

1 The final statements for the **Model Its** are $2 = 3$ and $4 = 6$. Is either a true statement? Is 2, 3, 4, or 6 a solution of the equation? Explain.

2 Does the equation $\frac{1}{2}(2x + 4) = x + 3$ have infinitely many solutions? Does it have exactly one solution? Explain.

3 The statements $2 = 3$ and $4 = 6$ are simplified versions of the original equation. Because they are false statements, the original equation is also a false statement. Why does it make sense to conclude that the equation has no solution? What does this mean in terms of the situation?

4 Look at the equation $x + 2 = x + 3$ in the first **Model It**. How can you tell that this equation has no solution without solving further?

5 **Reflect** Think about all the models and strategies you discussed today. Describe how one of them helped you better understand how to solve the **Try It** problem.

Apply It

➤ **Use what you learned to solve these problems.**

6 Gabriel solves the equation $6g + 5 = 7g + 5$. He gets $g = 0$. He concludes the equation has no solution. Is Gabriel correct? Explain your reasoning.

7 Which equations have no solution? Select all that apply.

A $x + 5 = x - 5$

B $0.5y = 0$

C $x - 7 = x - 7$

D $9(-1 + x) + 1 = 12x + 1$

E $8 + 4 \cdot f = 4(3 + f)$

8 Erin and Santo are stopped at different points along a bike trail. They happen to start riding again at the same time. After x hours, the distance each is from the start of the trail is shown.

a. Solve the equation $4x + 3.5 = 2(2x + 2)$ for x. Show your work.

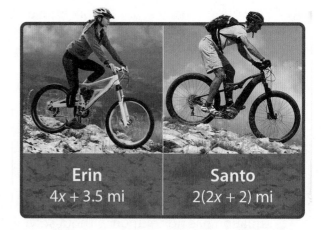

Erin
$4x + 3.5$ mi

Santo
$2(2x + 2)$ mi

SOLUTION _____

b. What does your answer to problem 8a mean in terms of the situation?

Practice Determining the Number of Solutions to One-Variable Equations

➤ **Study the Example showing how to determine the number of solutions to a one-variable equation. Then solve problems 1–6.**

Example

How many solutions does $\frac{1}{3}(6w - 12) = 2w + 2$ have?

You can rewrite the equation until you identify a true statement like $3 = 3$, identify a false statement like $1 = 4$, or solve for w.

$$\frac{1}{3}(6w - 12) = 2w + 2$$
$$2w - 4 = 2w + 2$$
$$-4 = 2$$

$-4 = 2$ is a false statement. No value of w makes the equation true. So the equation has no solution.

---

1 Could you have stopped solving the equation in the Example sooner, before you reached the false statement $-4 = 2$? Explain.

2 Tell whether each equation has *no solution, one solution,* or *infinitely many solutions.*

a. $1 + 3x = 3x + 1$

b. $4x + 1 = 3x + 2$

c. $5x + 1 = 5x - 2$

d. $-3(x + 1) = -3x + 3$

③ How many solutions does $3(x + 5) - 3 = 2(3x + 1) - 3x$ have? Show your work.

SOLUTION _____

④ Complete the following sentences about one-variable equations.

a. You solve an equation and get $8x + 7 = 8x + 7$. The equation has

_____ solution(s).

b. You solve an equation and get $10t - 6 = 10t + 6$. The equation has

_____ solution(s).

⑤ How many solutions does $4x + 5 = 6(x + 3) - 20 - 2x$ have? Show your work.

SOLUTION _____

⑥ Ria solves the equation $5 + 3r = 4 + 4r$ and gets $r = r$. She concludes that the equation has infinitely many solutions. What is the correct solution? What mistake did Ria make?

Develop Writing an Equation with No, One, or Infinitely Many Solutions

➤ **Read and try to solve the problem below.**

Mrs. Quinn writes this problem on the board. What number can you write on the line so the equation has no solution? What number can you write on the line so the equation has infinitely many solutions?

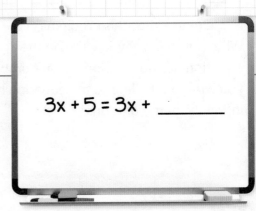

$$3x + 5 = 3x + \underline{\hspace{2cm}}$$

TRY IT

Math Toolkit algebra tiles

LESSON 11 Determine the Number of Solutions to One-Variable Equations **259**

➤ **Explore different ways to write one-variable linear equations with no, one, or infinitely many solutions.**

Mrs. Quinn writes this problem on the board. What number can you write on the line so the equation has no solution? What number can you write on the line so the equation has infinitely many solutions?

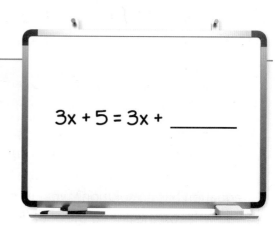

$$3x + 5 = 3x + \underline{\hspace{1.5cm}}$$

Model It

You can solve the equation.

$$3x + 5 = 3x + \underline{\hspace{2.5cm}}$$

$$3x - 3x + 5 = 3x - 3x + \underline{\hspace{2.5cm}}$$

$$5 = \underline{\hspace{2cm}}$$

Think about what number gives you a false statement.

Think about what number gives you a true statement.

Analyze It

You can analyze the structure of the equation.

$$3x + 5 = 3x + \underline{\hspace{2.5cm}}$$

Compare the **variable terms** on each side of the equation.

Think about how the **constant terms** on each side of the equation should compare for the equation to have no solution.

Think about how the **constant terms** on each side of the equation should compare for the equation to have infinitely many solutions.

©Curriculum Associates, LLC   Copying is not permitted.

> ➤ **Use the problem from the previous page to help you understand how to write one-variable linear equations with different numbers of solutions.**

1 Look at **Analyze It**. What must be true about the constant terms on each side of the equation if the equation has no solution? What must be true about the constant terms on each side of the equation if the equation has infinitely many solutions? How do you know?

2 **a.** Is there more than one number you could write on the line so the equation has no solution? Explain.

b. Is there more than one number you could write on the line so the equation has infinitely many solutions? Explain.

3 What constant term or *x*-term could you write on the line so the equation has exactly one solution? Is there more than one possibility? How do you know?

4 **Reflect** Think about all the models and strategies you have discussed today. Describe how one of them helped you better understand how to write one-variable linear equations with no solution, one solution, or infinitely many solutions.

Apply It

➤ **Use what you learned to solve these problems.**

5 Hai's teacher writes the equation $3x - 4 = 2(x + 3) + x$. Hai concludes that the equation has infinitely many solutions. Is Hai correct? Explain.

6 Which numbers could you substitute for c so the equation $4(4x + c) = 2(8x + 1)$ has no solution? Select all that apply.

A 0

B $\frac{1}{4}$

C $\frac{1}{2}$

D 1

E 2

7 Write a constant term or variable term on the line so that each equation has the number of solutions shown.

a. No solution:

$\frac{2}{7}m + 1 = \frac{2}{7}m +$ _____

b. One solution:

$m + 1 = m +$ _____

c. Infinitely many solutions:

$3p + 3 = 3p +$ _____

d. Infinitely many solutions:

$2x + 4 = 2x -$ _____

Practice Writing an Equation with No, One, or Infinitely Many Solutions

➤ **Study the Example showing how to write a one-variable linear equation with no, one, or infinitely many solutions. Then solve problems 1–4.**

Example

Write a constant term or variable term on the line to form an equation that has no solution, one solution, or infinitely many solutions.

$4x + 7 = 4x + $ _____

No solution: The x-terms on both sides of the equation are the same. Write a **constant term** so the constant terms on each side are different.

$4x + 7 = 4x + \textbf{8}$

One solution: Write an x-**term** so the x-terms on each side of the equation will have different coefficients.

$4x + 7 = 4x + \textbf{14}x$

Infinitely many solutions: **7** results in identical expressions on both sides of the equation.

$4x + 7 = 4x + \textbf{7}$

1 Look at the Example. Decide whether there is more than one possible answer that will result in no solution, one solution, or infinitely many solutions. Where possible, write a different constant term or variable term.

   a. No solution: $4x + 7 = 4x + $ _____

   b. One solution: $4x + 7 = 4x + $ _____

   c. Infinitely many solutions: $4x + 7 = 4x + $ _____

2 Complete the following sentences.

   a. The one-variable linear equation $13x + 6 = 13x + $ _____ has infinitely many solutions.

   b. The one-variable linear equation $x + 6 = x + $ _____ has no solution.

   c. The one-variable linear equation $4x + 5 = $ _____ $ + 10$ has one solution.

3 Two garden beds are shown. The perimeters of the two gardens are equal.

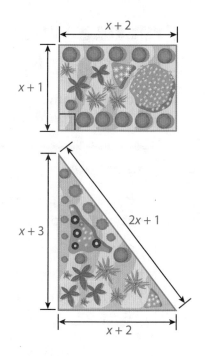

a. Write an equation that sets the perimeters equal. Then solve the equation.

b. The side length of a garden cannot be a negative number or zero. What value(s) of x make the equation you wrote in problem 3a true in the context of this problem?

4 Write an expression on the line to form an equation that has no solution, one solution, or infinitely many solutions.

a. No solution

$2(h + 3) = $ _____

b. One solution

$2h + 5 = $ _____

c. Infinitely many solutions

$2h - 12 = $ _____

Refine Determining the Number of Solutions to One-Variable Equations

➤ **Complete the Example below. Then solve problems 1–9.**

Example

The equation $10x - 12 = 8x - 6$ has one solution. Solve for x.
Then change *one term* in the equation so that your new equation
has no solution.

Look how you could solve the equation.

$$10x - 12 = 8x - 6$$
$$2x - 12 = -6$$
$$2x = 6$$
$$x = 3$$

The equation will have no solution if you change $8x$ to $10x$
or if you change $10x$ to $8x$.

SOLUTION _____

CONSIDER THIS . . .
What is true about the
variable terms on both
sides in an equation
with no solution?

PAIR/SHARE
How could you change
the equation in your
answer to get an
equation with infinitely
many solutions?

Apply It

1 How many solutions does each equation have? Explain how you know.

a. $2x + 6 = 7x + 5$

b. $6v + 8 = 8 + 6v$

c. $10 - e = e - 10$

CONSIDER THIS . . .
You can analyze the
structure of an equation
to determine how many
solutions it has.

PAIR/SHARE
How would your
answer to part b change
if the equation was
$6v + 8 = -8 + 6v$?

2 What constant term or variable term could you write on the line to create an equation with the number of solutions shown? Explain how you know your answer is correct.

$$12x - 3 = 12x + \underline{\hspace{3cm}}$$

CONSIDER THIS ...
What is true about the constant terms on both sides in an equation with no solution?

a. One solution

b. No solution

c. Infinitely many solutions

PAIR/SHARE
Which parts have more than one possible answer?

3 How many solutions does $\frac{2}{3}(3x - 15) = x - 10$ have?

A Infinitely many solutions

B No solution

C One solution

D Two solutions

CONSIDER THIS ...
Why might it be helpful to multiply both sides of the equation by 3?

Mia chose B as the correct answer. How might she have gotten that answer?

PAIR/SHARE
How could you check that you solved the equation correctly?

4 **a.** What are all the possible values of a and b that make $3x + 6 = ax + b$ have one solution?

b. What are all the possible values of c and d that make $3x + 6 = cx + d$ have infinitely many solutions?

c. What are all the possible values of e and f that make $3x + 6 = ex + f$ have no solution?

5 Which of the following expressions can be set equal to $2.74x - 7.9$ to form an equation that has no solution?

A $2.74x - 7.9$

B $7.9x - 7.9$

C $2.74x + 7.9$

D $7.9x + 2.74$

6 Which of the following statements are true? Select all that apply.

A If you rewrite a one-variable linear equation and see a statement like $4 = 4$ or $4a + 6 = 4a + 6$, then the equation has infinitely many solutions.

B If you rewrite a one-variable linear equation and the variable terms are the same on each side of the equation, then you can solve the equation and find the value of the variable.

C If a one-variable linear equation has one solution, then every value of the variable makes the equation true.

D If both sides of a one-variable linear equation have the same variable term and different constant terms, then the equation has infinitely many solutions.

E If a one-variable linear equation has no solution, then no value of the variable will make the equation true.

7 The cost of p inches of plain ribbon is represented by $6p$. The cost of p inches of striped ribbon is represented by $6p + 9$. Vivian says that $6p = 6p + 9$ for any value of p because the coefficients of p are the same on both sides of the equation. Is Vivian correct? Explain.

8 Write an equation that has the given number of solutions.

a. No solution

b. Infinitely many solutions

9 **Math Journal** Write a one-variable linear equation that has infinitely many solutions. Then change *one term* in your equation so that it has no solution. How do you know that each of your equations has the correct number of solutions?

✓ **End of Lesson Checklist**

☐ **INTERACTIVE GLOSSARY** Find the entry for *linear equation*. Give 3 examples of linear equations.

☐ **SELF CHECK** Go back to the Unit 3 Opener and see what you can check off.

Dear Family,

This week your student is exploring **systems of linear equations**. A system of linear equations is two or more related equations that are solved together in order to find a solution common to all the equations. This solution is the (x, y) pair(s) that make all equations in the system true. On a graph, the solution is represented by the points(s) that the graphs of all the equations have in common. A system of linear equations can have one, zero, or infinitely many solutions.

Your student will first explore systems of linear equations by looking at their graphs. The following examples show the ways the graph of a system can tell you how many solutions the system has.

➤ **ONE WAY:** One solution

The lines in this graph intersect at one point. The (x, y) pair for this point makes both equations in the system true.

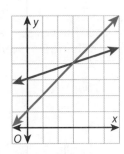

➤ **ANOTHER WAY:** No solution

The lines in this graph do not intersect at all. There are no (x, y) pairs that make both equations in the system true.

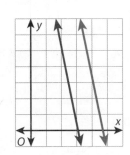

➤ **ANOTHER WAY:** Infinitely many solutions

The lines in this graph intersect at every point and represent the same line. The (x, y) pairs for all the points on the line make both equations in the system true.

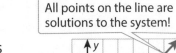

All points on the line are solutions to the system!

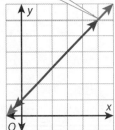

▶ Use the next page to start a conversation about systems of linear equations.

Activity Thinking About Systems of Linear Equations

➤ **Do this activity together to investigate systems of linear equations in the real world.**

Systems of equations help answer questions about when, or if, two relationships share the same pair of related values. For example, suppose two runners in a race are at different distances from the finish line. A system of linear equations based on their two rates of running can be used to determine if and when the runner who is behind will be able to catch up.

? Can you think of some other real-world examples where solving a system of linear equations is helpful?

UNDERSTAND: What does it mean to solve a system of linear equations?

Explore Systems of Linear Equations in Two Variables

Model It

➤ **Complete the problems about graphing related linear equations.**

1 Elias reads 15 pages of his book each day. The graph of $p = 15d$ shows how many pages Elias reads in d days.

Before Elias starts reading, Jaime has already read 20 pages of the same book. Jaime then reads 10 pages each day. The equation $p = 10d + 20$ tells how many pages Jaime has read since Elias started reading.

a. Graph Jaime's equation in the same coordinate plane as Elias's graph. What point is on both lines?

b. On what day have both Elias and Jaime read the same number of pages? How many pages have they read on that day? Use your answer to problem 1a to explain.

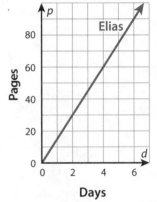

2 The related equations in problem 1 for which you found a common solution form a **system of linear equations**. You can graph the equations in a system to see if the lines intersect. Any point that is common to both lines represents a solution to the system of equations. This means that the ordered pair for this point makes both equations in the system true.

a. Graph the equations $y = x + 2$ and $y = -x$. Where do the lines intersect?

b. You cannot always know the exact coordinates of a point of intersection from a graph. How can you be sure that the point you identified in problem 2a is a solution to the system?

DISCUSS IT

Ask: What can the graph of a system of equations tell you?

Share: Seeing the graphs of the equations is helpful because . . .

 Learning Targets SMP 2, SMP 3, SMP 4, SMP 7
Analyze and solve pairs of simultaneous linear equations.
• Understand that solutions to a system of two linear equations in two variables correspond to points of intersection of their graphs, because points of intersection satisfy both equations simultaneously.

Model It

➤ **Complete the problems about solving systems of linear equations.**

3 Another way to find a solution to a system of equations is to list ordered pairs that make each equation in the system true. An ordered pair that makes *both* equations true is a solution to the system.

Look at the system of equations below.

$y = 2x$

$y = x - 1$

a. Complete the table. For each equation, find the *y*-value for each *x*-value. What is the solution to the system of equations? How do you know?

x	−4	−3	−2	−1	0	1	2	3	4
y = 2x	−8								
y = x − 1	−5								

Ask: How does using a table help you find the solution to a system of equations?

Share: Using a table is different from using a graph because . . .

b. Graph the system of equations to check that your answer to problem 3a is reasonable.

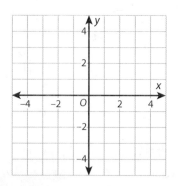

4 **Reflect** How is the solution to the system of equations in problem 3 related to the solutions of the individual equations $y = 2x$ and $y = x - 1$?

Name:

Prepare for Systems of Linear Equations in Two Variables

1 Think about what you know about linear equations. Fill in each box. Use words, numbers, and pictures. Show as many ideas as you can.

What Is It?

What I Know About It

linear equation

Examples

Examples

2 Graph the linear equation $y = x - 2$.

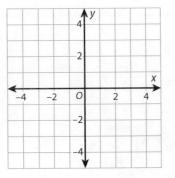

➤ **Complete problems 3–5.**

3 The graph of the system of linear equations below is shown in the coordinate plane.

$$4y = -3x - 1$$

$$2y = x - 13$$

Why is the point (5, −4) a solution to the system?

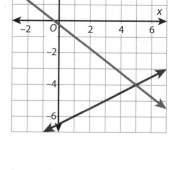

4 **a.** Graph the following system of equations.

$$y = -3x$$

$$y = x + 4$$

b. What does the graph show to be the solution of the system?

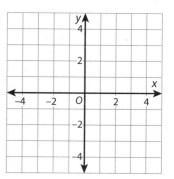

5 DeAndre and Leah are making origami cranes. Their goal is to complete 1,000 cranes by the end of the summer.

• DeAndre already has 30 cranes and makes 5 more each day.

• Leah already has 10 cranes and makes 15 more each day.

The graph shows how many cranes, c, each person has made after d days.

a. What does the graph show to be the solution of the system?

b. What does the solution mean in this context?

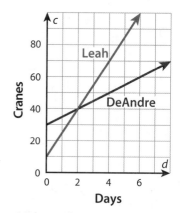

origami cranes

Develop Understanding of the Number of Solutions to a System of Linear Equations

Model It: No Solution

➤ **Try these two problems involving systems of linear equations with no solution.**

1 You have seen that a solution to a system of equations is represented on its graph as a point of intersection. The ordered pair for this point makes both equations true.

    a. Graph the system $y = x + 2$ and $y = x - 1$.

    b. Does this system have a solution? How do you know?

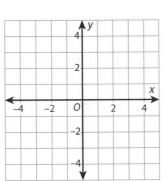

2 Charlotte and Paloma both walk the same trail at the same rate. Charlotte starts to walk first. The graph shows each girl's distance along the trail for the first 40 minutes of Paloma's hike.

    a. Does Paloma catch up to Charlotte? How do you know?

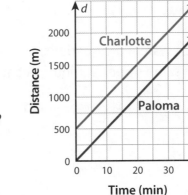

Time (min)

    b. Look at the system of equations. How can you tell by looking at the equations that the system has no solution?

        Paloma: $d = 50t$

        Charlotte: $d = 50t + 500$

hiking trail

DISCUSS IT

Ask: How are the equations of the system in problem 1 like the equations of the system in problem 2?

Share: I can tell there is no solution if...

Model It: Infinitely Many Solutions

➤ **Try this problem about a system of linear equations with infinitely many solutions.**

3 The graph of the equation $y - 1 = 2x$ is shown.

a. Graph the equation $y = 2x + 1$ in the same coordinate plane to represent a system.

b. At which point(s) do the two lines intersect?

c. How many ordered pairs are solutions of the system? Explain.

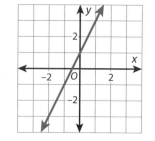

DISCUSS IT

Ask: Suppose Charlotte and Paloma start at the same time in problem 2. Why would the system representing this context have infinitely many solutions?

Share: I can tell there are infinitely many solutions if . . .

CONNECT IT

➤ **Complete the problems below.**

4 Look at problems 1–3. In each system of equations, both lines have the same slope. Can two lines with the same slope ever intersect at exactly one point? Explain.

5 What values of m and b will result in a system with no solution?

$y = 4x + 5$

$y = mx + b$

Practice Determining the Number of Solutions to a System of Linear Equations

▶ **Study the Example showing how to determine the number of solutions to a system of linear equations. Then solve problems 1–7.**

Example

How many solutions does each system of equations have?

a.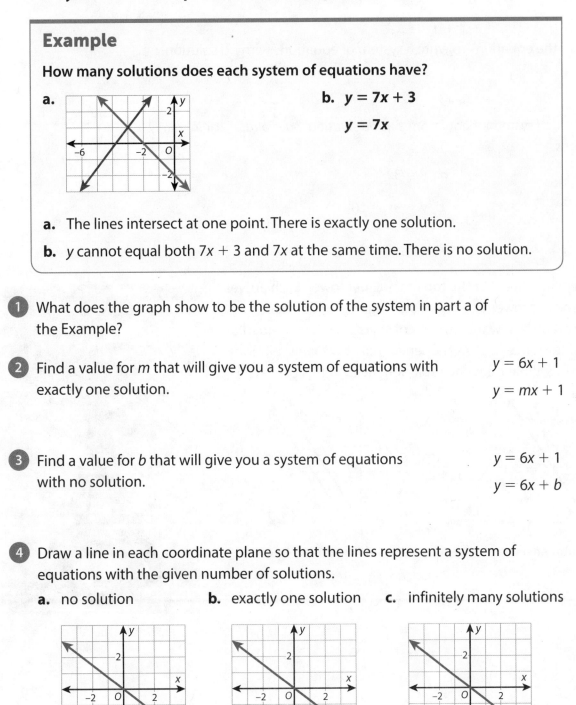

b. $y = 7x + 3$

$y = 7x$

a. The lines intersect at one point. There is exactly one solution.

b. y cannot equal both $7x + 3$ and $7x$ at the same time. There is no solution.

① What does the graph show to be the solution of the system in part a of the Example?

② Find a value for m that will give you a system of equations with exactly one solution.

$y = 6x + 1$

$y = mx + 1$

③ Find a value for b that will give you a system of equations with no solution.

$y = 6x + 1$

$y = 6x + b$

④ Draw a line in each coordinate plane so that the lines represent a system of equations with the given number of solutions.

a. no solution

b. exactly one solution

c. infinitely many solutions

5 Use the equations below.

$$y = 4x + 2 \qquad y = 9x + 2 \qquad y = 9x + 5$$

a. Use two of the equations to write a system of equations with exactly one solution.

b. Use two of the equations to write a system of equations with no solution.

6 Tell whether each system of equations has *no solution, one solution,* or *infinitely many solutions.*

a. $y = x$

$-y = -x$

b. $y = 3x$

$y = 3x - 10$

c. $y = x$

$y = 2x$

7 Four friends plan to meet at the top of the Eiffel Tower. Each arrives about the time the tower opens and starts climbing the stairs to the top. The graphs show the number of stairs each has climbed, *s*, in the *m* minutes since the tower opened. Tell how many solutions each system has. What does each solution mean in this context?

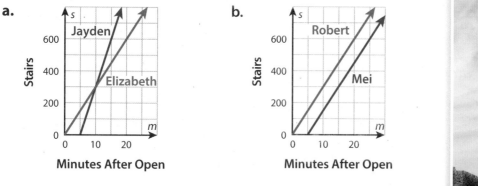

Eiffel Tower, Paris, France

UNDERSTAND: What does it mean to solve a system of linear equations?

Refine Ideas About Systems of Linear Equations in Two Variables

Apply It

➤ **Complete problems 1–5.**

1 **Generalize** A system of linear equations has exactly one solution. What can you say about the slopes of the lines when the equations are graphed? How do you know?

2 **Analyze** Can you identify the solution of this system without graphing the equations? Explain.

$x = 4$

$y = 6$

3 **Examine** Rachel graphs this system of equations. She says there is no solution to the system because the lines do not intersect. Do you agree or disagree with Rachel? Explain.

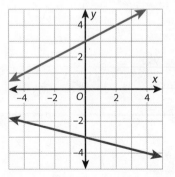

4 Kenji and Ramón are running cross country. Kenji runs at a rate of 150 meters per minute. Kenji has already run 750 meters before Ramón starts running. Ramón runs at a rate of 300 meters per minute.

PART A The system of equations represents the distance, d, from the starting point of each runner t minutes after Ramón starts running. Graph the system and label each line with the runner it represents.

$$d = 150t + 750$$

$$d = 300t$$

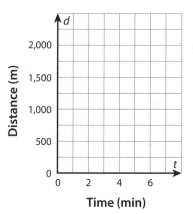

PART B What does the graph show to be the solution of the system in Part A? What does the solution mean in the context of the problem?

PART C Describe a situation in which Kenji and Ramón are running cross country but are never the same distance from the starting point at the same time. Write a system of equations or draw a graph to model the situation. How many solutions does the system have?

5 **Math Journal** What does it mean to solve a system of linear equations? Use models to show the possible numbers of solutions a system can have.

✓ **End of Lesson Checklist**

☐ **INTERACTIVE GLOSSARY** Write a new entry for *common*. What does it mean when a point is *common* to two lines?

Dear Family,

This week your student is learning about solving systems of linear equations. Previously, students learned to estimate solutions to systems by graphing. Now they will see that they can solve systems algebraically. Look at this example.

Gym A membership costs $15 per month plus a one-time fee of $45. **Gym B membership** costs $20 per month plus a one-time fee of $30. This situation can be represented by the system of equations below, where c is the total cost and t is the time in months.

$$c = 15t + 45$$

$$c = 20t + 30$$

When is the total cost for both gyms the same?

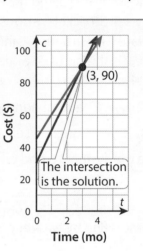

The intersection is the solution.

➤ **ONE WAY** to solve a system of linear equations is by substitution.

$$c = 15t + 45 \qquad 20t + 30 = 15t + 45 \qquad c = 20t + 30$$
$$c = 20t + 30 \qquad 20t - 15t = 45 - 30 \qquad c = 20(3) + 30$$
$$5t = 15 \qquad c = 60 + 30$$
$$t = 3 \qquad c = 90$$

➤ **ANOTHER WAY** is by elimination.

$$c = 15t + 45 \qquad\qquad c = 15t + 45 \qquad c = 15t + 45$$
$$\underline{-\,(c = 20t + 30)} \longrightarrow \underline{+\,-c = -20t - 30} \qquad c = 15(3) + 45$$
$$0 = -5t + 15 \qquad c = 45 + 45$$
$$5t = 15 \qquad\qquad c = 90$$
$$t = 3$$

Using either method, the total cost is the same ($90) at 3 months. This is the same solution as shown by the graph of the system.

▶ Use the next page to start a conversation about systems of linear equations.

Activity Thinking About Solving Systems of Linear Equations

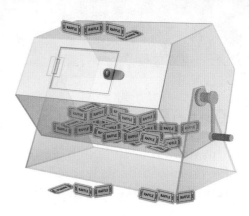

➤ **Do this activity together to investigate solving systems of linear equations in the real world.**

Systems of linear equations can be used in situations that can be modeled by two related equations, as in the example below.

Augustine and Raúl are selling tickets for a raffle. Together they sell 36 tickets. Augustine sells 10 more tickets than Raúl. The situation can be represented by the system of equations shown, where x is the number of tickets Augustine sells and y is the number of tickets Raúl sells.

$x + y = 36$ ← The total number of tickets they sell is 36.

$x = y + 10$ ← Augustine sells 10 more tickets than Raúl.

You can solve the system to find out how many raffle tickets each sold.

? What other situations can you think of that can be modeled by two related equations?

Explore Solving Systems of Linear Equations Algebraically

7 books
bought

3 puzzles
bought

Previously, you learned how to estimate or check solutions to systems of linear equations by graphing. In this lesson, you will learn how to solve systems of linear equations algebraically.

➤ **Use what you know to try to solve the problem below.**

Neena buys books and puzzles at a yard sale. The price of a book is the same as the price of a puzzle. She spends $15. The situation can be represented by the graph and system of equations shown, where b is the price of each book and p is the price of each puzzle.

$7b + 3p = 15$ ⬅ Neena spends $15 buying 7 books and 3 puzzles.

$b = p$ ⬅ A book is the same price as a puzzle.

What is the price of each book? What is the price of each puzzle?

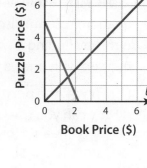

TRY IT

DISCUSS IT

Ask: What strategy did you use to find the exact prices of the books and puzzles?

Share: To find the exact prices, I …

◎ **Learning Targets** SMP 1, SMP 2, SMP 3, SMP 4, SMP 5, SMP 6, SMP 7
Analyze and solve pairs of simultaneous linear equations.
• Solve systems of two linear equations in two variables algebraically, and estimate solutions by graphing the equations. Solve simple cases by inspection.

CONNECT IT

1 **Look Back** What is the price of each book? What is the price of each puzzle? How did you find your answers?

2 **Look Ahead** In earlier lessons, you learned strategies for solving a one-variable equation. You can also use those strategies to solve a system of equations. You can do this by finding a way to combine the two equations with two variables into one equation with one variable.

   a. In **Try It**, the price of each book is the same as the price of each puzzle. How can you use this fact to write a one-variable equation for the money Neena spends? What is the equation?

   b. Solve the equation you wrote in problem 2a. Do you get the same prices for the books and puzzles as in problem 1?

   c. Why might someone prefer using the strategy in problems 2a and 2b over solving a system by graphing? How can a graph be helpful when solving a system?

3 **Reflect** Explain how you used both equations in the system to write the one-variable equation in problem 2a.

Prepare for Solving Systems of Linear Equations Algebraically

1　Think about what you know about systems of linear equations. Fill in each box. Use words, numbers, and pictures. Show as many ideas as you can.

Definition	What I Know About It

system of linear equations

Examples	Examples	Examples

2　Start with the linear equation $y = -2x + 0.5$. Write an equation that results in a system of equations with the given number of solutions.

a. No solution

b. One solution

c. Infinitely many solutions

3 Riley and her friends buy snacks at the movies. They buy 3 pretzels and 4 drinks for $17.50. The cost of a pretzel is the same as the cost of a drink. The situation can be represented by the graph and the system of equations shown, where p is the cost of a pretzel and d is the cost of a drink.

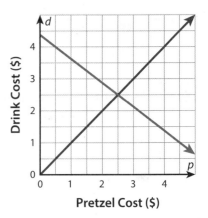

$3p + 4d = 17.50$ ⟵ They spend $17.50 on 3 pretzels and 4 drinks.

$p = d$ ⟵ A pretzel costs the same as a drink.

a. What is the cost of each pretzel? What is the cost of each drink? Show your work.

SOLUTION _____

b. Check your answer to problem 3a. Show your work.

Develop Solving Systems of Linear Equations by Substitution

4 beds of vegetables   **1 bed of flowers**

➤ **Read and try to solve the problem below.**

The residents of a downtown apartment building are starting a rooftop garden. They will plant 4 beds of vegetables for every 1 bed of flowers, plus have 5 extra beds of vegetables. They plan to plant a total of 30 garden beds. In the system of equations shown, v is the number of vegetable beds and f is the number of flower beds.

$v = 4f + 5$

$v + f = 30$

How many vegetable beds and how many flower beds will be in the rooftop garden?

Math Toolkit graph paper, straightedges

DISCUSS IT

Ask: How did you use the equations given in the problem?

Share: I began by . . .

➤ **Explore different ways to solve a system of equations by substitution.**

The residents of a downtown apartment building are starting a rooftop garden. They will plant 4 beds of vegetables for every 1 bed of flowers, plus have 5 extra beds of vegetables. They plan to plant a total of 30 garden beds. In the system of equations shown, v is the number of vegetable beds and f is the number of flower beds.

$$v = 4f + 5$$
$$v + f = 30$$

How many vegetable beds and how many flower beds will be in the rooftop garden?

Model It

You can substitute an expression from one equation into the other equation.

Since $v = 4f + 5$, you can substitute $4f + 5$ for v in the other equation. You can also show this using bar models.

$v = 4f + 5$

$v + f = 30$

$v + f = 30 \longrightarrow 4f + 5 + f = 30$

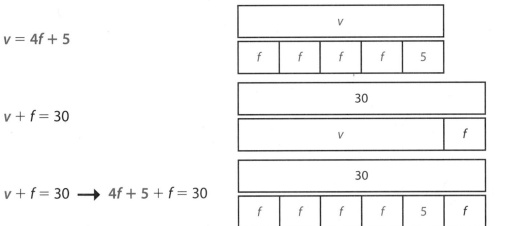

Model It

You can rewrite the second equation so both equations are solved for v.

$$v + f = 30 \longrightarrow v = -f + 30$$

The system is now: $v = 4f + 5$

$$v = -f + 30$$

Set the two expressions for v equal to each other.

$$4f + 5 = -f + 30$$

> **Use the problem from the previous page to help you understand how to use substitution to solve a system of equations.**

1 Explain what $v = 4f + 5$ and $v + f = 30$ tell you about the situation.

2 **a.** Look at both **Model Its**. You started with a system of two equations in two variables. In each case you end up with a single one-variable equation, $4f + 5 + f = 30$ and $4f + 5 = -f + 30$. How did this happen?

   b. How many flower beds will there be in the garden? How many vegetable beds? Explain how you know.

3 Solve $v + f = 30$ for f. Use this result to solve the system by substituting for f. Does it matter into which equation or for which variable you substitute when solving a system of equations? Explain.

4 Do you think using substitution will always work when solving a system of equations? Explain.

5 **Reflect** Think about all the models and strategies you have discussed today. Describe how one of them helped you better understand how to solve the **Try It** problem.

Apply It

➤ **Use what you learned to solve these problems.**

6 Tara begins solving the system below. What do you think her next step will be?

$$6x + 8y = 7$$
$$-2x + 4y = -8 \longrightarrow \quad -2x = -4y - 8$$
$$x = 2y + 4$$

7 A football team scores 7 times and earns 27 points. All their points come from 6-point touchdowns and 3-point field goals.

Let t be the number of touchdowns and f be the number of field goals. The equation $t + f = 7$ represents the number of times the team scores. The equation $6t + 3f = 27$ represents the total number of points scored. How many touchdowns and how many field goals does the team make? Show your work.

SOLUTION _____

8 Solve this system of equations. Show your work.

$$3x = 6y - 21$$
$$6x - 9y = -30$$

SOLUTION _____

Practice Solving Systems of Linear Equations by Substitution

➤ **Study the Example showing how to solve a system of equations by substitution. Then solve problems 1–3.**

Example

What is the solution to the system of equations?

$x + y = 1$

$2y = -2 - 5x$

Solve the first equation for x. Then substitute the expression into the second equation.

$x + y = 1$	$2y = -2 - 5(-y + 1)$	$x + y = 1$
$x = -y + 1$	$2y = -2 + 5y - 5$	$x + \frac{7}{3} = 1$
	$7 = 3y$	$x = -\frac{4}{3}$
	$\frac{7}{3} = y$	

1 Describe a different way to use substitution to solve the problem in the Example.

2 Antonio is a set designer. He is gluing ribbon on 4 square and 2 triangular posters to be used as stage props in an upcoming play. Use the system of equations to find s, the amount of ribbon needed for a square poster, and t, the amount of ribbon needed for a triangular poster. Show your work.

$s = t + 5$

$4s + 2t = 110$

SOLUTION _____

3 What is the solution of each system of equations? Show your work.

a. $-6x - 5y = 6$

$4x + y = 3$

SOLUTION _____

b. $3x - 4y = 11$

$3x + 2y = 2$

SOLUTION _____

c. $8x + 9y = 20$

$x = -3y$

SOLUTION _____

Develop Solving Systems of Linear Equations by Elimination

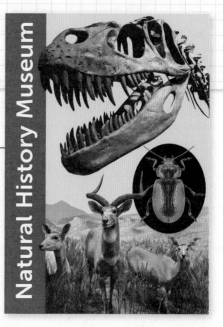

Natural History Museum

➤ **Read and try to solve the problem below.**

Amare is buying museum souvenirs. He buys 3 animal figures and 6 bookmarks for $33. Later he goes back to buy 3 more figures and return 3 of the bookmarks, spending another $6. In the system, f is the price of a figure and b is the price of a bookmark.

$$3f + 6b = 33$$

$$3f - 3b = 6$$

How much does each figure cost? How much does each bookmark cost?

TRY IT

Math Toolkit graph paper, straightedges

DISCUSS IT

Ask: What strategy did you use?

Share: I began by …

➤ **Explore different ways to solve systems of equations by elimination.**

Amare is buying museum souvenirs. He buys 3 animal figures and 6 bookmarks for \$33. Later he goes back to buy 3 more figures and return 3 of the bookmarks, spending another \$6. In the system, f is the price of a figure and b is the price of a bookmark.

$$3f + 6b = 33$$
$$3f - 3b = 6$$

How much does each figure cost? How much does each bookmark cost?

Model It

You can first eliminate the variable b.

Multiply the second equation by 2 so the b terms are opposites. Then add the like terms in the two equations. This gives you a one-variable equation for f.

$$3f + 6b = 33$$
$$2(3f - 3b = 6)$$
➡
$$\begin{array}{r} 3f + 6b = 33 \\ + \ 6f - 6b = 12 \\ \hline 9f + 0b = 45 \end{array}$$

Model It

You can first eliminate the variable f.

Multiply the second equation by -1 so the f terms are opposites. Then add the like terms in the two equations. This gives you a one-variable equation for b.

$$3f + 6b = 33$$
$$-(3f - 3b = 6)$$
➡
$$\begin{array}{r} 3f + 6b = 33 \\ + \ -3f + 3b = -6 \\ \hline 0f + 9b = 27 \end{array}$$

➤ **Use the problem from the previous page to help you understand how to use elimination to solve a system of equations.**

 1 Explain what $3f + 6b = 33$ and $3f - 3b = 6$ tell you about the situation.

2 **a.** Look at the first **Model It**. Why does the equation $6f - 6b = 12$ have the same solutions as $3f - 3b = 6$?

    b. How does knowing that $6f - 6b = 12$ allow you to add $6f - 6b$ to one side and 12 to the other side of the equation $3f + 6b = 33$?

    c. How much does each figure cost? How much does each bookmark cost?

3 Solve the equation $0f + 9b = 27$ in the second **Model It** for b. Do you get the same answer as you did in problem 1c?

4 How could you use substitution to find how much each figure and bookmark cost? When do you think you might choose to use substitution to solve a system instead of elimination?

5 **Reflect** Think about all the models and strategies you have discussed today. Describe how one of them helped you better understand how to solve the **Try It** problem.

Apply It

➤ **Use what you learned to solve these problems.**

6 Adela has 24 bracelets. She makes 3 more each day. Isaiah has 10 bracelets. He makes 5 more each day. The equations represent the number of bracelets y each person has after x days.

Adela: $y = 3x + 24$

Isaiah: $y = 5x + 10$

Use elimination to solve the system of equations. What does the solution mean in the situation?

7 Which of these strategies will eliminate a variable to help you solve the system of equations to the right? Select all that apply.

$$12x + 5y = 7$$
$$-4x + 10y = -7$$

A Multiply the first equation by 2 and add it to the second equation.

B Multiply the first equation by -2 and add it to the second equation.

C Multiply the first equation by $\frac{1}{3}$ and add it to the second equation.

D Multiply the second equation by 3 and add it to the first equation.

E Multiply the second equation by $\frac{1}{2}$ and add it to the first equation.

8 Solve the system of equations. Show your work.

$$-6x + 4y = -28$$
$$-9x + 5y = -33$$

SOLUTION _____

Practice Solving Systems of Linear Equations by Elimination

➤ **Study the Example showing how to use elimination to solve systems of equations. Then solve problems 1–4.**

Example

What is the solution of the system of equations? $-5x + 2y = 22$

$10x + 2y = -8$

$$2(-5x + 2y = 22) \longrightarrow$$

$$\begin{array}{c} -10x + 4y = 44 \\ +\quad 10x + 2y = -8 \\ \hline 6y = 36 \\ y = 6 \end{array}$$

$$\begin{array}{c} 10x + 2y = -8 \\ 10x + 2(6) = -8 \\ 10x + 12 = -8 \\ 10x = -20 \\ x = -2 \end{array}$$

The solution is $(-2, 6)$.

---

1 Show a different way to use elimination to solve the system in the Example.

2 Cheryl says that the system of equations at the right MUST be solved by elimination rather than by substitution. $-7x + 12y = 13$

$7x - 11y = -9$

a. Explain why Cheryl is not correct.

b. Why might Cheryl think this is true?

> **Vocabulary**
>
> **system of linear equations**
> a group of related linear equations in which a solution makes all the equations true at the same time.

LESSON 13 Solve Systems of Linear Equations Algebraically   **297**

3 Use the system of equations shown.

$$-2x - 4y = 24$$
$$6x - 8y = 28$$

a. How could you change one of the equations so that you could add it to the other equation and eliminate the *x* terms?

b. How could you change one of the equations so that you could add it to the other equation and eliminate the *y* terms?

c. What is the solution of the system? Show your work.

SOLUTION _____

4 Use the system of equations shown.

$$3x + 4y = -9$$
$$9x + 2y = 3$$

a. Would you choose substitution or elimination to solve this system? Explain.

b. Solve the system using the method you chose in problem 4a. Show your work.

SOLUTION _____

Develop Determining When a System Has Zero or Infinitely Many Solutions

➤ **Read and try to solve the problem below.**

How many solutions does the system of equations have?

$$-\frac{1}{2}x + y = 3$$
$$x - 2y = 4$$

TRY IT

Math Toolkit graph paper, straightedges

DISCUSS IT

Ask: How did you find how many solutions the system has?

Share: I noticed that . . .

➤ **Explore different ways to determine the number of solutions a system of equations has.**

How many solutions does the system of equations have?

$$-\frac{1}{2}x + y = 3$$
$$x - 2y = 4$$

Model It

You can solve the system.

Solve by substitution.

$x - 2y = 4$

$x = 2y + 4$ ⟶ $-\frac{1}{2}(2y + 4) + y = 3$

$-y - 2 + y = 3$

$-2 = 3$

Solve by elimination.

Multiply the first equation by 2.

$2(-\frac{1}{2}x + y = 3)$ ⟶ $-x + 2y = 6$

$x - 2y = 4$ $+ \quad x - 2y = 4$

                                  $0 = 10$

Model It

You can write the equations in slope-intercept form and compare.

$-\frac{1}{2}x + y = 3$ $x - 2y = 4$

$y = \frac{1}{2}x + 3$ $-2y = -x + 4$

                                       $y = \frac{1}{2}x - 2$

The slopes are the same and the *y*-intercepts are different.

➤ **Use the problem from the previous page to help you understand how to determine the number of solutions a system of equations has.**

1 Look at the first **Model It**. What happens to the variables when you solve by either method? What kind of statements are $-2 = 3$ and $0 = 10$?

2 Look at the second **Model It**. What will the graph of this system look like? How many solutions does this system have?

3 **a.** Solve this system of equations by either substitution or elimination. What happens to the variables? What result do you get?

$$5x - y = 8$$
$$10x - 2y = 16$$

b. Write both equations in slope-intercept form. Compare slopes and y-intercepts. What will the graph of this system look like? How many solutions does this system have?

c. Suppose the equations had different slopes. How many solutions would the system have?

4 Suppose you solve a system of equations and both variables are eliminated. What do you know about the number of solutions the system has? Do you need to solve the system to find the number of solutions? Explain.

5 **Reflect** Think about all the models and strategies you have discussed today. Describe how one of them helped you better understand how to determine whether a system has no solution or infinitely many solutions.

Apply It

➤ **Use what you learned to solve these problems.**

6 How many solutions does the system of equations have? How do you know?

$$-2x = 1$$

$$x = -2$$

7 Which system of equations has exactly one solution?

A $3x + 6y = 5$
$-3x - 6y = 5$

B $3x - 6y = 0$
$-2x + 4y = 0$

C $3x + 6y = 12$
$2x - 4y = -8$

D $-3x + 2y = 7$
$-6x + 4y = 14$

8 Alec is building a rectangular picture frame. He wants the sum of the length and width to be 12 in. and the perimeter to be 30 in. Use the system of equations to determine how many possibilities there are for the length and width of the frame.

$$\ell + w = 12$$

$$2\ell + 2w = 30$$

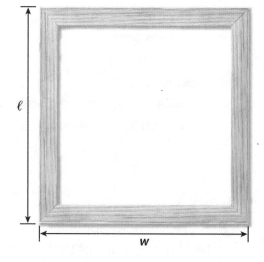

Practice Determining When a System Has Zero or Infinitely Many Solutions

➤ **Study the Example showing how to determine the number of solutions a system of equations has. Then solve problems 1–4.**

Example

How many solutions does each system of equations have?
Explain how you can tell.

a. $4x - 12y = 13$

   $2x - 6y = 9$

b. $-5x + 9y = 17$

   $5x - 9y = -17$

a. No solution; Multiply the second equation by -2 and add it to the first equation. Both variables are eliminated, resulting in $0 = -5$, a false statement.

b. Infinitely many solutions; Add the equations together. Both variables are eliminated, resulting in $0 = 0$, a true statement.

1 How many solutions does each system of equations have? Explain how you can tell.

a. $x + 6y = 19$

   $x - 6y = 13$

b. $8x + y = 3$

   $-8x - y = 3$

Vocabulary

system of linear equations

a group of related linear equations in which a solution makes all the equations true at the same time. A system of equations can have zero, one, or infinitely many solutions.

2 Mariko is fencing her garden. She wants to use 50 feet of fencing. Mariko also wants the sum of the length and the width of the garden to be 25 feet. Use the system of equations to confirm that there are infinitely many possibilities for the length and width. Are there any limits to what values the length and width can be? Explain your reasoning.

$$2\ell + 2w = 50$$

$$\ell + w = 25$$

3 Use the system of equations shown.

$$gx - 6y = h$$
$$5x - 2y = 9$$

a. What values could you substitute for g and h to create a system of equations with infinitely many solutions?

b. What values could you substitute for g and h to create a system of equations with no solution?

c. What values could you substitute for g and h to create a system of equations with exactly one solution?

4 Tell how many solutions each system of equations has.

a. $3x - 2y = -1$

$-6x + 4y = 2$

b. $12x - 15y = 24$

$-8x + 10y = -36$

c. $\frac{1}{5}y = 1$

$y = 5$

d. $-4y = 8x + 20$

$y = 2x + 5$

Refine Solving Systems of Linear Equations Algebraically

➤ **Complete the Example below. Then solve problems 1–9.**

Example

What is the solution of the system of equations?

$$3x = 4y - 20$$

$$3x = -y + 10$$

Look at how you could solve the system by substitution.

$4y - 20$ and $-y + 10$ are both equal to $3x$.

$$4y - 20 = -y + 10 \qquad 3x = -y + 10$$

$$5y = 30 \qquad\qquad 3x = -6 + 10$$

$$y = 6 \qquad\qquad 3x = 4p$$

$$\qquad\qquad\qquad x = \frac{4}{3}$$

SOLUTION _____

CONSIDER THIS...
The equations show two different expressions that are equal to $3x$.

PAIR/SHARE
How could you use elimination to solve this problem?

Apply It

1 What is the solution of the system of equations? Show your work.

$$y = x + 3$$

$$3x - 4y = -7$$

CONSIDER THIS...
Look at how the equations are written. Does this make you want to use a particular strategy?

SOLUTION _____

PAIR/SHARE
How can you check your answer?

2　What is the solution of the system of equations? Show your work.

$$10x + 16y = 6$$

$$5x - 8y = 5$$

CONSIDER THIS...
How can you combine the two equations to make a one-variable equation?

PAIR/SHARE
Does it matter which variable you solve for first?

SOLUTION _____

3　Which of these systems of equations has no solution?

A　$3x + 2y = -12$
　　$2x + 3y = -12$

B　$2x + 3y = 12$
　　$2x - 3y = 12$

C　$-3x + 3y = 12$
　　$2x - 2y = -12$

D　$-3x - 2y = 12$
　　$3x + 2y = -12$

Mateo chose C as the correct answer. How might he have gotten that answer?

CONSIDER THIS...
How can the coefficients of the variables help you determine the number of solutions the system has?

PAIR/SHARE
Do any of the systems have infinitely many solutions?

4 The first part of a solution to a problem is shown. Which of these equations could you substitute the value of y into in order to find x?

$$-2x + 5y = 10 \quad \longrightarrow \quad -6x + 15y = 30$$
$$3x - 2y = -4 \quad \longrightarrow \quad + \quad 6x - 4y = -8$$
$$\overline{11y = 22}$$
$$y = 2$$

A $-2x + 5y = 10$

B $3x - 2y = -4$

C $-6x + 15y = 30$

D $6x - 4y = -8$

E $11y = 22$

F $2y = 3x + 4$

5 Sebastián tried to solve the system of equations below. He says there are infinitely many solutions. Do you agree? Explain.

$$x - 2y = 1 \quad \longrightarrow \quad x = 2y + 1 \qquad\qquad x - 2y = 1$$
$$4x - 4y = 11 \qquad\qquad\qquad\qquad\qquad (2y + 1) - 2y = 1$$
$$2y + 1 - 2y = 1$$
$$1 = 1$$

6 **a.** Use a graph to estimate the solution of the system.

$$-8x + 4y = 11$$

$$4x - y = 2$$

b. Find the exact solution of the system in problem 6a. Show your work.

SOLUTION _____

7 Hasina and her sister Jada ride their bikes to school. Hasina starts first. The equations show the distance d each girl is from home m minutes after Jada starts. What is the solution of the system of equations? What does this mean in this situation?

Hasina: $d = 300m + 1{,}500$

Jada: $d = 300m$

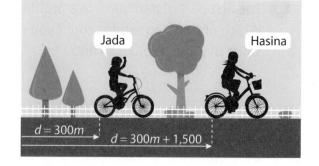

8 To eliminate the y-terms in the system of equations below, multiply the first

equation by _____ and add it to the second equation.

$9x + 5y = -3$

$11x + 15y = -1$

9 **Math Journal** For each system of equations, tell whether it would take fewer steps to solve by substitution or by elimination. Then use that strategy to solve the system.

a. $3x - 8y = 31$

$7x + 8y = 19$

b. $y = 2x$

$-5x + 3y = -4$

✓ End of Lesson Checklist

☐ **INTERACTIVE GLOSSARY** Write a new entry for *eliminate*. Tell what you do when you *eliminate* a variable to solve a system of equations.

☐ **SELF CHECK** Go back to the Unit 3 Opener and see what you can check off.

Dear Family,

This week your student is learning how to use systems of equations to solve real-world and mathematical problems. By assigning variables to real-world quantities, students will solve problems like the one below.

> Lilia volunteers at an animal shelter and a retirement community on the weekends. She spends twice as much time volunteering at the animal shelter as she does at the retirement community. She volunteers a total of 6 hours each weekend. How many hours does she spend volunteering at each location?

➤ **ONE WAY** to solve the problem is to use a table.

Let a be the time spent at the animal shelter. Let r be the time spent at the retirement community. List possible combinations of time spent at each place that give a total of 6 hours.

a	r	$2r$
1	5	10
2	4	8
3	3	6
4	2	4

If $a = 4$ and $r = 2$, then $2r = a$ and $a + r = 6$.

➤ **ANOTHER WAY** is to write and solve a system of equations.

Solve algebraically using substitution.

$$2r = a$$

$$r + a = 6 \longrightarrow r + (2r) = 6 \longrightarrow 3r = 6 \longrightarrow r = 2$$

$$2r = a \longrightarrow 2(2) = a \longrightarrow 4 = a$$

Using either method, you find that $r = 2$ and $a = 4$. So, Lilia spends 2 hours volunteering at the retirement community and 4 hours volunteering at the animal shelter.

Use the next page to start a conversation about solving problems with systems of linear equations.

Activity Thinking About Systems of Linear Equations

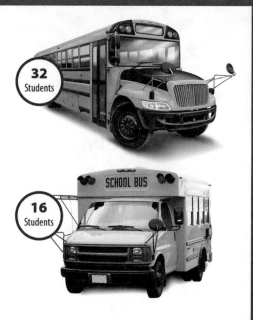

32 Students

16 Students

➤ **Do this activity together to investigate systems of linear equations in the real world.**

Students will learn to use systems of linear equations to represent and solve problems. Below are three real-world problems and three systems of equations. Decide which system of equations represents each problem. Draw lines to show your answers.

PROBLEM 1

Hailey is organizing a field trip. The school has small buses that can seat 16 students and large buses that can seat 32 students. There are 112 students and 4 bus drivers. How many buses of each size are required?

$$x = 2y$$
$$x + y = 6$$

PROBLEM 2

Nicanor spends $6 on gum. Brand A costs $1 per pack. Brand B costs $2 per pack. Nicanor buys two more packs of brand A gum than brand B gum. How many packs of each gum does he buy?

$$x + y = 4$$
$$16x + 32y = 112$$

PROBLEM 3

It takes Francisco 6 hours to read both a book and a magazine. It takes him twice as long to read the book as the magazine. How long does it take Francisco to read each?

$$x + 2y = 6$$
$$y + 2 = x$$

? How did you match the real-world situation with the system of linear equations that represents it?

Explore Representing and Solving Problems with Systems of Linear Equations

Previously, you learned how to solve systems of linear equations. In this lesson, you will learn how to solve real-world and mathematical problems involving systems of linear equations.

➤ **Use what you know to try to solve the problem below.**

Jade and Enrique are saving money. Jade has $0 saved. She plans to save $5 each week. Enrique has $12 saved. He plans to save $3 each week. In how many weeks will they have the same amount of money saved? How much will they each have?

TRY IT

 Math Toolkit counters, graph paper, straightedges

DISCUSS IT

Ask: How did you use the dollar amounts given in the problem?

Share: I used the amounts saved each week when I . . .

⊚ **Learning Targets** SMP 1, SMP 2, SMP 3, SMP 4, SMP 5, SMP 6
Analyze and solve pairs of simultaneous linear equations.
• Solve real-world and mathematical problems leading to two linear equations in two variables.

CONNECT IT

1 **Look Back** In how many weeks will Jade and Enrique have the same amount of money saved? How much will they each have? How did you find your answer?

2 **Look Ahead** You can use a different variable for each quantity when a problem has two unknown quantities. You can write a system of equations to solve for both variables.

   a. What two quantities were you were asked to find in the **Try It** problem?

   b. Explain why you cannot find both values by writing and solving a one-variable equation.

   c. Write an expression for the number of dollars that Jade will save in x weeks.

   d. Write an expression for the number of dollars Enrique will have in x weeks.

   e. Use the expressions you wrote in problems 2c and 2d to write two equations for y, the number of dollars saved after x weeks. Write one equation for each person.

3 **Reflect** How would you use the equations you wrote in problem 2e to find the answer to the **Try It**? What values would you get for x and y?

Prepare for Representing and Solving Problems with Systems of Linear Equations

1 Think about what you know about graphing lines. Fill in each box. Use words, numbers, and pictures. Show as many ideas as you can.

What Is It?	What I Know About It

y-intercept

Examples	Examples	Examples

2 What is the *y*-intercept of the graph of the equation $6x + 3y = -18$?

3) Adrian and Cyrus volunteer for a community service organization the number of hours shown. Cyrus has already volunteered 8 hours when Adrian begins to volunteer.

a. After how many weeks will they both have volunteered the same number of hours? How many hours will each of them have volunteered at that time? Show your work.

Community Service Hours

Adrian	Cyrus
4 h per week	2 h per week

SOLUTION _____

b. Check your answer to problem 3a. Show your work.

Develop Solving Real-World Problems with Systems of Linear Equations

MAIN STREET CAFE

Seating Capacity: 32

small table   large table

➤ **Read and try to solve the problem below.**

The Drama Club holds a cast party at a local café. All 12 of the café's tables are used to full capacity. Small tables seat 2 people and large tables seat 4 people. How many tables of each size are there?

TRY IT   **Math Toolkit** counters, graph paper, straightedges

DISCUSS IT

Ask: How did you represent the number of tables and the number of people?

Share: I modeled the situation by . . .

➤ **Explore different ways to solve a real-world problem with two unknowns.**

The Drama Club holds a cast party at a local café. All 12 of the café's tables are used to full capacity. Small tables seat 2 people and large tables seat 4 people. How many tables of each size are there?

Model It

You can use a table.

Let s be the number of small tables and ℓ be the number of large tables.

List possible combinations of each size that give you a total of 12 tables.

s	ℓ	$2s + 4\ell$
12	0	24
11	1	26
10	2	
9	3	
8	4	
7	5	
6	6	

Model It

You can write a system of equations.

Let s be the number of small tables and ℓ be the number of large tables.

$$s + \ell = 12$$
$$2s + 4\ell = 32$$

©Curriculum Associates, LLC   Copying is not permitted.

➤ **Use the problem from the previous page to help you understand how to solve problems with two unknowns.**

1 **a.** Look at the first **Model It**. What does the expression $2s + 4\ell$ represent?

b. Complete the table. What combination of tables will seat 32 people? How do you know?

2 **a.** Look at the second **Model It**. What does each equation in the system represent?

b. Solve the system. Do you get the same answer as you did in problem 1b?

3 Look at this problem: A banquet hall has seating for 200 people. Some tables seat 6 people and some tables seat 10 people. There are 26 tables in all. How many tables are there of each size?

a. Write a system of equations to represent the problem.

b. Why might someone choose to use a system of equations to solve this problem instead of making a table?

4 **Reflect** Think about all the models and strategies you have discussed today. Describe how one of them helped you better understand how to solve the **Try It** problem.

Apply It

➤ **Use what you learned to solve these problems.**

5 Crew teams are racing in a regatta. Every 15 seconds a new crew starts the race. Today, the first crew rows at a speed of 240 meters per minute. They are 60 m ahead when the next crew starts, rowing 260 m per minute. Let x be the number of minutes after the second crew starts and y be the distance rowed. Write a system of equations that can be solved to find out when the two crews are the same distance from the start.

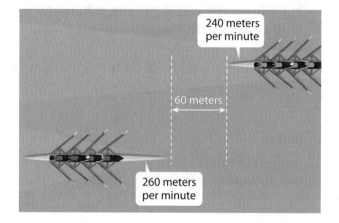

240 meters per minute

60 meters

260 meters per minute

6 Lian buys 10 packs of batteries. C batteries are sold in packs of 6. AAA batteries are sold in packs of 8. Lian buys 72 batteries in all. Let x be the number of packs of C batteries. Let y be the number of packs of AAA batteries. Write and solve a system of equations to find how many packs of each type of battery Lian buys. Show your work.

SOLUTION _____

7 You have $3.10 in dimes and quarters. You have 3 more dimes than quarters. Write an equation that relates the number of coins and an equation for the value of the coins. How many of each kind of coin do you have? Show your work.

SOLUTION _____

Practice Solving Real-World Problems with Systems of Linear Equations

➤ **Study the Example showing how to use systems of equations to solve real-world problems. Then solve problems 1–4.**

Example

Sophia babysits for $15 per hour. She mows lawns for $12 per hour. This weekend, Sophia babysits 4 more hours than she mows lawns. She earns a total of $195. Write a system of equations that can be used to find how many hours she worked at each job.

Let b be hours babysitting. Let m be hours mowing.

$$b = m + 4 \qquad \longleftarrow \quad \text{hours worked}$$
$$15b + 12m = 195 \quad \longleftarrow \quad \text{total money earned}$$

1 **a.** What do the expressions $15b$ and $12m$ represent in the Example?

b. Solve the problem in the Example. Show your work.

SOLUTION _____

2 You have 15 nickels and dimes. The coins are worth $1.20. How many of each coin do you have? Show your work.

SOLUTION _____

3 Mr. Lincoln buys juice and water for the school picnic. A pack of 8 juice boxes costs $5. A pack of 6 water bottles costs $3. Mr. Lincoln spends $95 for 170 juice boxes and bottles of water.

    a. Choose variables for the two unknown quantities in the problem and tell what each variable represents.

    b. Use the variables you chose in problem 3a to write an equation for the amount of money Mr. Lincoln spends.

    c. Use the variables you chose in problem 3a to write an equation for the number of drinks Mr. Lincoln buys.

    d. Solve the system of equations. How many packs of juice boxes and how many packs of water does Mr. Lincoln buy? Show your work.

SOLUTION _____

4 A taxicab fare starts with a base charge. Then an additional amount is added for each mile. The system of equations shows the fares for two different cab companies.

    Cab company A: $y = 3 + 2.25x$

    Cab company B: $y = 2 + 3.50x$

    a. What do x and y represent in each equation?

    b. Solve the system to find x and y. What does the solution tell you about the two cab companies?

Develop Solving Mathematical Problems Involving Systems of Linear Equations

➤ **Read and try to solve the problem below.**

Lines *a* and *b* are a graph of a system of equations. Line *a* passes through the points (0, 4) and (8, 6). Line *b* passes through the points (0, −2) and (8, 1). Do the lines intersect?

 TRY IT

Math Toolkit graph paper, straightedges

DISCUSS IT

Ask: How did you use the points given in the problem?

Share: I began solving the problem by . . .

➤ **Explore different ways to solve mathematical problems involving systems of equations.**

Lines a and b are the graph of a system of equations. Line a passes through the points (0, 4) and (8, 6). Line b passes through the points (0, −2) and (8, 1). Do the lines intersect?

Picture It

You can use the points to graph the lines and see if they intersect.

Plot the points (0, 4) and (8, 6) to graph **line** a.

Plot the points (0, −2) and (8, 1) to graph **line** b.

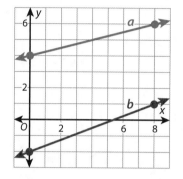

Model It

You can use the points to find and compare the slopes of the lines.

slope of **line** a: $\dfrac{6-4}{8-0} = \dfrac{2}{8} = \dfrac{1}{4}$

slope of **line** b: $\dfrac{1-(-2)}{8-0} = \dfrac{3}{8}$

➤ **Use the problem from the previous page to help you understand how to solve mathematical problems involving systems of equations.**

1 Look at the graph in **Picture It**. How far apart are the lines at $x = 0$? At $x = 8$? How does this help you determine whether the lines intersect?

2 Look at **Model It**. How can the slopes of the lines help you determine whether the lines intersect?

3 **a.** Write the system of equations represented by lines a and b. At what point do the lines intersect?

b. Was it necessary to solve a system of equations to determine whether the lines intersect? Was it necessary to solve a system of equations to answer problem 3a? Explain.

4 Suppose line c passes through the points (20, 8) and (24, 9). Explain why knowing the slope of line c is not enough information to conclude that lines a and c intersect.

5 **Reflect** Think about all the models and strategies you have discussed today. Describe how one of them helped you better understand how to solve the **Try It** problem.

Apply It

➤ **Use what you learned to solve these problems.**

6 Three times the sum of two numbers is 15. One of the numbers is 9 more than one-third of the other number.

   a. How can you use a system of equations to find the two numbers?

   b. What are the two numbers? Show your work.

     SOLUTION _____

7 In the system of equations below, c and d are constants. In the coordinate plane, the graphs of the equations intersect at point P.

$$y = -2x + c$$

$$y = 5x + d$$

The x-coordinate of point P is 1. Which of the following statements is true? Select all that apply.

A $c < d$ **B** $d < 0$

C $c > d$ **D** $c - d = 7$

E $c > 0$ **F** $c + d = 7$

8 The solution of a system of equations is $(-4, -6)$. The graph of one of the equations is a vertical line. The graph of the other equation passes through the origin. What are the equations of the lines?

Practice Solving Mathematical Problems Involving Systems of Linear Equations

➤ **Study the Example showing how to solve a mathematical problem involving systems of linear equations. Then solve problems 1–6.**

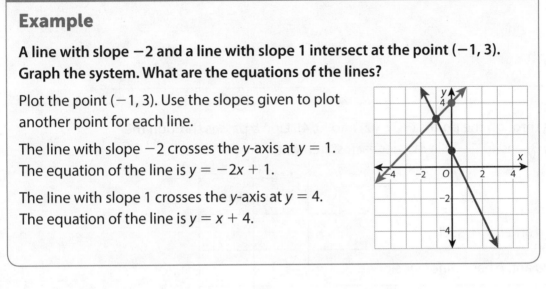

Example

A line with slope -2 and a line with slope 1 intersect at the point $(-1, 3)$. Graph the system. What are the equations of the lines?

Plot the point $(-1, 3)$. Use the slopes given to plot another point for each line.

The line with slope -2 crosses the y-axis at $y = 1$. The equation of the line is $y = -2x + 1$.

The line with slope 1 crosses the y-axis at $y = 4$. The equation of the line is $y = x + 4$.

---

1 Two lines intersect at the point $(2, -5)$. The lines cross the y-axis at $(0, 1)$ and $(0, -6)$.

   a. Graph the system.

   b. What are the equations of the lines?

   c. Check that $(2, -5)$ is the solution of the system of equations you wrote in problem 2b.

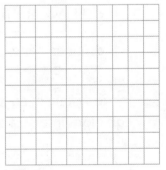

2 The sum of two numbers is 147. The difference of the two numbers is 25. What are the two numbers? Show your work.

Vocabulary

system of linear equations
a group of related linear equations in which a solution makes all the equations true at the same time.

SOLUTION _____

3 One number is 3 less than 4 times a second number. The difference of the first number and twice the second number is 7. What are the two numbers? Show your work.

SOLUTION _____

4 Line *a* passes through the points $(-3, -2)$ and $(0, 4)$. Line *b* passes through the points $(-2, -3)$ and $(0, 1)$. Tell whether each statement is *True* or *False*.

	True	False
a. Lines *a* and *b* intersect.	○	○
b. Lines *a* and *b* have different slopes.	○	○
c. Lines *a* and *b* have different *y*-intercepts.	○	○
d. Lines *a* and *b* are parallel.	○	○

5 In the system of equations shown, *j* and *k* are constants. The graphs of the equations intersect at point *P*.

$$y = 8x + j$$

$$y = -12x + k$$

The *x*-coordinate of point *P* is 2. Which of the following expressions are equal to the *y*-coordinate of point *P*?

A $-24 + k$ **B** $4 + j$ **C** $k - 40$

D $40 - j$ **E** $-6 + k$ **F** $16 + j$

6 Look at the equations in this system. Where do the lines intersect? Explain how you can tell without graphing or solving the system. $y = 7x + 4$
    $y = -5x + 4$

Refine Representing and Solving Problems with Systems of Linear Equations

➤ **Complete the Example below. Then solve problems 1–9.**

Example

In the system of equations, *j* and *k* are constants. The solution of the system is (3, 1). What are the values of *j* and *k*?

$$jx - ky = 14$$

$$kx + jy = 8$$

Look at how you could use the solution of the system to find *j* and *k*.

$$j(3) - k(1) = 14 \rightarrow 3j - k = 14 \rightarrow 9j - 3k = 42$$

$$k(3) + j(1) = 8 \rightarrow 3k + j = 8 \rightarrow \underline{j + 3k = 8}$$

$$10j = 50$$

$$j = 5$$

$$3(5) - k = 14 \rightarrow k = 1$$

SOLUTION _____

CONSIDER THIS...
Substitute the *x*- and *y*-values of the solution into both equations.

PAIR/SHARE
How can you check your answer?

Apply It

1 The drama club sells tickets to their spring play. They sell 180 tickets for a total of $2,248. Adult tickets cost $14 each. Student tickets cost $10 each. How many adult tickets and how many student tickets do they sell? Show your work.

CONSIDER THIS...
What will your variables represent?

PAIR/SHARE
Suppose the drama club sells 180 tickets for $2,192. How would the problem change?

SOLUTION _____

2 Line *a* is shown. Graph line *b* in the same coordinate plane to make the following statements true.

- The solution of the system of equations is (−2, 2).

- The *y*-intercept of line *b* is positive.

- The slope of line *b* is greater than 0 and less than 1.

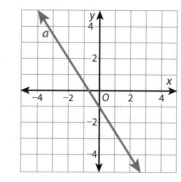

CONSIDER THIS . . .
How can you use the *y*-intercept and the point (−2, 2) to graph line *b*?

PAIR/SHARE
What *y*-intercepts are possible for line *b* to have?

3 Which system of equations can be used to solve the following problem? Reth and Allen both save money. Reth starts with $10. He then saves $7 each week. Allen starts with $16. He then saves $5 each week. After how many weeks will Reth and Allen have the same amount saved?

A $y = 5x + 10$

$y = 7x + 16$

B $y = 10x + 16$

$y = 7x + 5$

C $y = 7x + 10$

$y = 5x + 16$

D $y = 10x + 7$

$y = 16x + 5$

Elisa chose C as the correct answer. How might she have gotten that answer?

CONSIDER THIS . . .
What does each rate of change represent in this situation?

PAIR/SHARE
How many weeks does it take for Reth and Allen to have the same amount saved?

4 Evelyn knits hats and scarves for charity. She records the time it takes and the amount of yarn needed to make one of each item. Last winter Evelyn knitted for 180 hours. She used 2,520 yards of yarn. How many hats and scarves did Evelyn knit?

Hat	Scarf
5 hours	15 hours
110 yards	150 yards

a. Choose variables for the two unknown quantities in the problem and tell what each variable represents.

b. Write a system of two equations to represent the situation.

c. How many hats and scarves did Evelyn knit? Show your work.

SOLUTION _____

5 Lines *a* and *b* form a system with no solution. The points $(-3, 2)$ and $(5, -4)$ lie on line *a*. Which two points could lie on line *b*?

A $(2, 1)$ and $(6, 4)$ **B** $(1, -1)$ and $(9, -7)$

C $(-6, 4)$ and $(-2, 1)$ **D** $(3, 1)$ and $(5, -4)$

6 What are the values of *x* and *y* in the figures shown? Show your work.

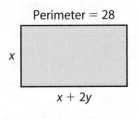

Perimeter = 28

x

x + 2*y*

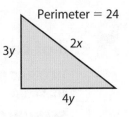

Perimeter = 24

2*x*

3*y*

4*y*

SOLUTION _____

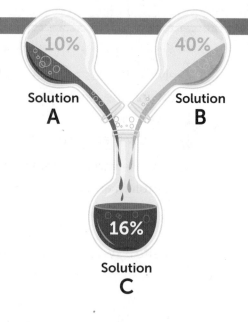

Solution A

Solution B

Solution C

7 Uma is mixing solutions in chemistry class. Solution A is 10% acid and Solution B is 40% acid. She uses both to make 10 liters of a mixture, Solution C, that is 16% acid. Explain what x and y represent in the system of equations that models this situation.

$$x + y = 10$$

$$0.10x + 0.40y = 0.16(10)$$

8 Arturo walks from school to the city library. He walks 4 miles per hour. When Arturo is 0.2 mile from school, Carson leaves school. Carson jogs 6 miles per hour. The system of equations can be used to find when Carson catches up with Arturo.

Arturo: $y = 4x + 0.2$

Carson: $y = 6x$

a. What do x and y represent?

b. How long will it take Carson to catch up with Arturo?

9 **Math Journal** Cameron buys 4 notebooks and 2 packages of pens for $16. Olivia buys 5 notebooks and 1 package of pens for $14.75. Write and solve a system of equations to find the price of each notebook and the price of each package of pens. Tell what each variable represents and what each equation represents.

✔ End of Lesson Checklist

☐ **INTERACTIVE GLOSSARY** Find the entry for *parallel lines*. Write a system of equations that represents a pair of parallel lines.

☐ **SELF CHECK** Go back to the Unit 3 Opener and see what you can check off.

Math IN **Action**

SMP 1 Make sense of problems and persevere in solving them.

Study an Example Problem and Solution

➤ **Read this problem involving systems of linear equations. Then look at one student's solution to this problem on the following pages.**

Coral Nursery

Maria is a marine biologist who grows coral in underwater nurseries to help restore coral reefs. The coral in some of the nurseries grows on reef blocks. Read her notes about a new underwater nursery location. Then write and solve a system of equations to determine the number of small reef blocks and the number of large reef blocks that Maria could use at this location.

New Nursery Location:

- Coral will grow on 16 reef blocks at this location. Some blocks will be small and some will be large.

- All the small blocks used at this location must hold the same number of samples. There are two choices.

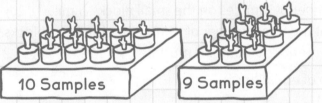

Small block choices

10 Samples   9 Samples

- All the large blocks used at this location must hold the same number of samples. There are two choices.

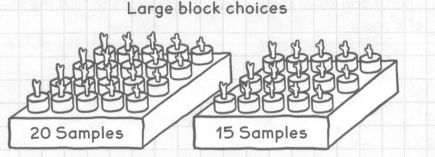

Large block choices

20 Samples   15 Samples

- This location needs to house exactly 210 samples.

There are many ways to grow coral in underwater nurseries. Some nurseries have coral samples attached to blocks or metal frames on the ocean floor. Once coral samples reach a certain size, they can be planted on coral reefs.

One Student's Solution

☑ **Problem-Solving Checklist**

- ☐ Tell what is known.
- ☐ Tell what the problem is asking.
- ☐ Show all your work.
- ☐ Show that the solution works.

NOTICE THAT...
There are only two types of blocks in this situation, so the total number of blocks is the same as the sum of the number of small blocks and the number of large blocks.

NOTICE THAT...
Multiplying the first equation by −9 results in x terms that are opposites.

First, I have to decide how many samples each small block and each large block will hold.

I know small blocks can hold 9 or 10 samples each, so I will use 9 samples for small blocks. Large blocks can hold either 15 or 20 samples each. I will use 20 samples for large blocks.

Next, I need to define the variables.

Maria needs to find the number of small blocks and the number of large blocks to put in the new location, so these are the unknown quantities in this situation.

Let x be the number of small blocks in the new nursery location.

Let y be the number of large blocks in the new nursery location.

Now, I can write a system of equations.

I know the total number of blocks must be 16. So, $x + y = 16$.

Since there will be 9 samples on each small block, $9x$ represents the total number of samples on the small blocks. Similarly, $20y$ will represent the total number of samples on the large blocks. I know the total number of samples must be 210, so $9x + 20y = 210$.

A system of equations is:

$$x + y = 16$$
$$9x + 20y = 210$$

Then, I can solve the system of equations to find the values of x and y.

I can use elimination to get a one-variable equation for y.

$$
\begin{array}{ll}
-9(x + y = 16) & {-9x - 9y = -144} \\
9x + 20y = 210 \longrightarrow & \underline{+9x + 20y = 210} \\
& 0x + 11y = 66
\end{array}
$$

Now, I can solve for y and then use substitution to solve for x.

$$11y = 66$$

$$\frac{11y}{11} = \frac{66}{11}$$

$$y = 6$$

I will substitute $y = 6$ into the equation $x + y = 16$:

$$x + 6 = 16$$

$$x + 6 - 6 = 16 - 6$$

$$x = 10$$

NOTICE THAT...
Substituting $y = 6$ into the other equation in the system, $9x + 20y = 210$, should result in the same value for x.

Finally, I can check my work by graphing both equations in the same coordinate plane.

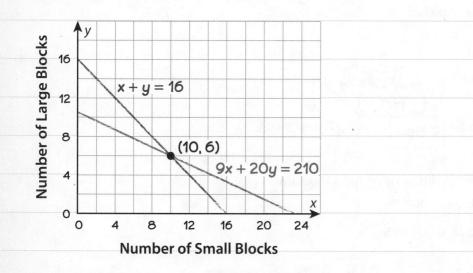

NOTICE THAT...
Since small blocks are on the x-axis and large blocks are on the y-axis, the point of intersection (10, 6) indicates that both equations are true when there are 10 small blocks and 6 large blocks.

The point of intersection of the two lines confirms that the algebraic solution is correct.

So, Maria could use 10 small blocks with 9 samples each and 6 large blocks with 20 samples each to hold 210 total samples in the new nursery location.

Try Another Approach

➤ **There are many ways to solve problems. Think about how you might solve the Coral Nursery problem in a different way.**

Coral Nursery

Maria is a marine biologist who grows coral in underwater nurseries to help restore coral reefs. The coral in some of the nurseries grows on reef blocks. Read her notes about a new underwater nursery location. Then write and solve a system of equations to determine the number of small reef blocks and the number of large reef blocks that Maria could use at this location.

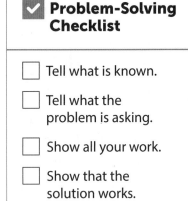

Problem-Solving Checklist

☐ Tell what is known.

☐ Tell what the problem is asking.

☐ Show all your work.

☐ Show that the solution works.

New Nursery Location:

- Coral will grow on 16 reef blocks at this location. Some blocks will be small and some will be large.

- All the small blocks used at this location must hold the same number of samples. There are two choices.

Small block choices

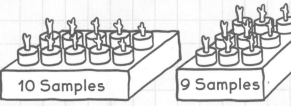

10 Samples   9 Samples

- All the large blocks used at this location must hold the same number of samples. There are two choices.

Large block choices

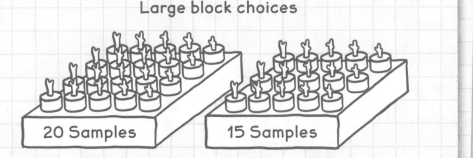

20 Samples   15 Samples

- This location needs to house exactly 210 samples.

Plan It

➤ **Answer these questions to help you start thinking about a plan.**

   a. What is another approach you could use to solve or check a system of equations?

   b. Do you expect to get the same answer or a different answer than the sample solution?

Solve It

➤ **Find a different solution for the Coral Nursery problem. Show all your work on a separate sheet of paper. You may want to use the Problem-Solving Tips to get started.**

PROBLEM-SOLVING TIPS

Math Toolkit algebra tiles, graph paper, sticky notes

Key Terms

system of equations	linear equation	elimination
substitution	variable	coefficient
constant	slope-intercept form	

Models You may want to use . . .

- inverse operations to solve an equation in one variable.
- slope-intercept form to graph an equation.
- a table, graph, or algebraic method to solve or check a system of equations.

Reflect

Use Mathematical Practices As you work through the problem, discuss these questions with a partner.

- **Make Sense of Problems** How will you reflect your choice for the number of samples each block holds in the system of equations?

- **Use Structure** How could you change one of your equations so that the system would have no solution? Infinitely many solutions?

Discuss Models and Strategies

➤ **Read the problem. Write a solution on a separate sheet of paper. Remember, there can be lots of ways to solve a problem.**

Analyzing Growth Data

Maria recorded data about the growth of several coral samples. Read Maria's notes about the branch length of the coral samples and her to-do list. Then help complete Maria's analysis.

✎   Aa   Notes   ◻   ↱   🗑

Notes ▾
Calendar
Search
Meetings
Data

Coral Growth Data

Specimen A:

Time (weeks)	Branch Length (cm)
10	12
50	28

Specimen B:
Length after 20 weeks was 17 cm.
Length after 50 weeks was 35 cm.

Specimen C:
Grew at a constant rate of 7 cm every 20 weeks.
It was 20.5 cm long after 30 weeks.

Specimen D:
Grew 0.4 cm each week to reach a length
of 21 cm after 40 weeks.

To Do: ▾   •••

◉ Make a graph showing growth over time for two specimens.

◉ Interpret the slopes, y-intercepts, and any points of intersection shown on the graph.

◉ Write a statement that compares the growth rates of the two specimens.

Plan It and Solve It

➤ **Find a solution to the Analyzing Growth Data problem.**

Write a detailed plan and support your answer. Be sure to include:

- a graph showing growth over time for two specimens. Show the data for both specimens in the same coordinate plane. Label each line with its equation.

- your interpretation of the slopes, *y*-intercepts, and any points of intersection shown on the graph.

- a statement that compares the growth rates of the two specimens.

PROBLEM-SOLVING TIPS

Math Toolkit graph paper, straightedges

Key Terms

slope	rate of change	*y*-intercept
coefficient	constant	coordinate

Models You may want to use . . .

- the coordinates of two points to make a graph and write the equation.

- the slope formula to calculate the slope of a line.

- the slope-intercept form of an equation to identify the *y*-intercept and make a graph.

Reflect

Use Mathematical Practices As you work through the problem, discuss these questions with a partner.

- **Be Precise** How will you determine what scale to use to label each of the axes on your graph?

- **Critique Reasoning** Do you agree with your partner's interpretation of the slopes, *y*-intercepts, and points of intersection shown in his or her graph? Explain.

The bright colors of many coral come from tiny algae that grow inside them. Coral depend on these algae for oxygen.

Persevere On Your Own

➤ **Read the problem. Write a solution on a separate sheet of paper.**

Designing an Experiment

Read an email from Maria's coworker about designing an experiment
to test different ideas for growing coral at an underwater nursery.
Then help her respond to the email.

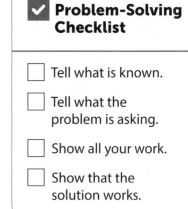

Problem-Solving Checklist

- [ ] Tell what is known.
- [ ] Tell what the problem is asking.
- [ ] Show all your work.
- [ ] Show that the solution works.

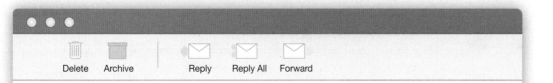

Delete   Archive   Reply   Reply All   Forward

To: Maria
Subject: Testing Wire Mesh Structures for Growing Coral

Hi Maria,

I want to do an experiment to compare how coral grows on two of the wire mesh
structures shown. Both structures need to have the same area of wire mesh and
the same length. The faces of each structure are wire mesh, except for the bottom
of each structure, which will be open.

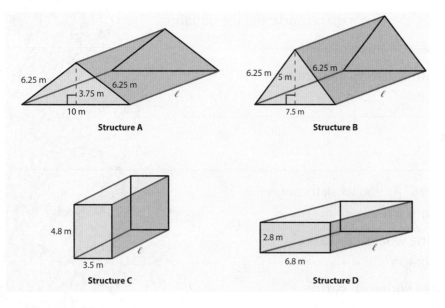

PLEASE PROVIDE:

- your suggestion of which two structures to use in the experiment.
- the length for which the two structures chosen will have the same area of mesh.

Thanks,

Vin

Solve It

➤ **Find a solution to the Designing an Experiment problem.**

- Choose two structures to use for the experiment.

- Write and solve an equation to determine the length for which the two structures have the same area of wire mesh.

Reflect

Use Mathematical Practices After you complete the problem, choose one of these questions to discuss with a partner.

- **Persevere** What was your first step? What did you do next?

- **Reason Mathematically** How do you know when to combine like terms, use the distributive property, or use inverse operations when solving a linear equation in one variable?

Coral reefs are highly biodiverse: they take up less than 1% of the ocean floor, yet they are home to more than 25% of marine life.

In this unit you learned to . . .

Skill	Lesson(s)
Define *slope* and show that the slope of a line is the same between any two points on the line.	8
Find the slope of a line and graph linear equations given in any form.	8, 9
Derive the linear equations $y = mx$ and $y = mx + b$.	9
Represent and solve one-variable linear equations with the variable on both sides of the equation.	10
Determine whether one-variable linear equations have one solution, infinitely many solutions, or no solutions, and give examples.	11
Solve systems of linear equations graphically and algebraically.	12, 13
Represent and solve systems of linear equations to solve real-world and mathematical problems.	14
Justify solutions to problems about linear equations by telling what you noticed and what you decided to do as a result.	8–14

Think about what you have learned.

➤ **Use words, numbers, and drawings.**

1 The math I could use in my everyday life is _____ because . . .

2 A mistake I made that helped me learn was . . .

3 I still need to work on . . .

Vocabulary Review

➤ **Review the unit vocabulary. Put a check mark by terms you can use in speaking and writing. Look up the meaning of any terms you do not know.**

Math Vocabulary		Academic Vocabulary
☐ **linear equation**	☐ **slope-intercept form**	☐ **eliminate**
☐ **rate of change**	☐ **systems of linear equations**	☐ **infinitely many**
☐ **slope**	☐ **y-intercept**	☐ **substitution**

➤ **Use the unit vocabulary to complete the problems.**

1 Which math or academic vocabulary terms could you use to describe ways to solve systems of linear equations?

2 Use at least three math vocabulary terms to label parts of the equation.

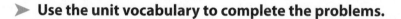

$$y = mx + b$$

3 Use two math vocabulary terms and two academic vocabulary terms to describe the system of equations. Underline each term you use.

$y = \frac{1}{2}x + 4$

$2y - x = 8$

4 Choose a math or an academic vocabulary term from the box that you have not used as an answer in problems 1–4. If you have used all the terms, choose one you only used once. Explain what the term means using your own words.

> **Use what you have learned to complete these problems.**

1 Trevor makes this graph of the amounts of bananas and strawberries to mix to make a smoothie. Which statement is true about the line?

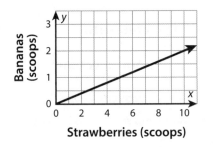

Strawberries (scoops)

A The line does not show a proportional relationship.

B The unit rate for the proportional relationship shown in the graph is 5.

C The slope tells how many scoops of banana for each scoop of strawberry.

D The $\frac{\text{rise}}{\text{run}}$ is greater than 1.

2 How many solutions does $\frac{3}{4}(8x - 4) = 3 - 6x$ have? Show your work.

SOLUTION _____

_____

3 Ciera and Bethany save money using savings accounts opened on the same day. Both deposit $20 to start and an additional $15 each week. The graph represents the total amount, *y*, in each savings account after *x* weeks. Describe the number of solutions modeled in the graph and what it means for the situation. How can you change the situation so that the graphs model a different number of solutions? Explain your reasoning.

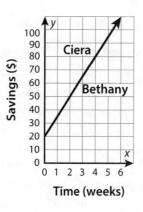

SOLUTION _____

_____

_____

_____

_____

4 Jackie runs and rides her bike. She runs 6 miles in an hour. She bikes 18 miles in an hour. Last week she ran and biked a total of 216 miles. It took her 16 hours. How many hours did Jackie run and bike last week? Show your work.

SOLUTION _____

Performance Task

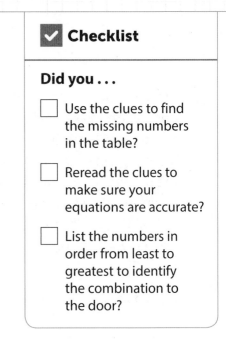
➤ **Answer the questions and show all your work on separate paper.**

You are in a space-themed escape room, trying to solve the final problem. The combination to the door is made up of four numbers in least to greatest order. Each number is the number of hours in a day on a different planet, when rounded to the nearest whole number. You are given clues to find these numbers.

Use the clues to write and solve equations that help you find each missing number. Use a calculator to make sure your solutions are correct and record them in the table. Then write the numbers in least to greatest order to identify the combination to the door.

Planet	Number of Hours in a Day
Jupiter	
Mars	
Neptune	
Saturn	

Combination to the Door: _____ _____ _____ _____

- The number of hours in a day on Mars is 2.5 times the number of hours in a day on Jupiter.

- A day on Mars lasts 15 hours longer than a day on Jupiter.

- The number of hours in a day on Saturn is 3 more than half the number of hours in a day on Neptune.

- A day on Saturn lasts 0.6875 times as long as a day on Neptune.

Reflect

Use Mathematical Practices After you complete the task, choose one of the following questions to answer.

- **Model** How do you know your equations match the information given in the clues?

- **Be Precise** How could you test your solutions to see if they satisfy the clues?

Unit 4

Functions

Linear and Nonlinear Relationships

✔ **Self Check**
Before starting this unit, check off the skills you know below.
As you complete each lesson, see how many more skills you can check off!

I can . . .	Before	After
Understand that a function is a type of rule where each input results in exactly one output.	☐	☐
Identify relationships that are functions from different representations, such as descriptions, tables, graphs, or equations.	☐	☐
Determine whether a function is linear or nonlinear.	☐	☐
Identify and interpret the rate of change and initial value for a linear function.	☐	☐
Write an equation to model a linear function.	☐	☐
Compare two functions represented in different ways, such as in words, with tables, as equations, or as graphs.	☐	☐
Use a graph to describe a function qualitatively.	☐	☐
Sketch a graph of a function from a qualitative description.	☐	☐
Make connections between different representations of functions by explaining how they are similar and different.	☐	☐

➤ **Write what you know about the equation** $y = 3x - 2$ **in the boxes. Share your ideas with a partner and add any new information you think of together.**

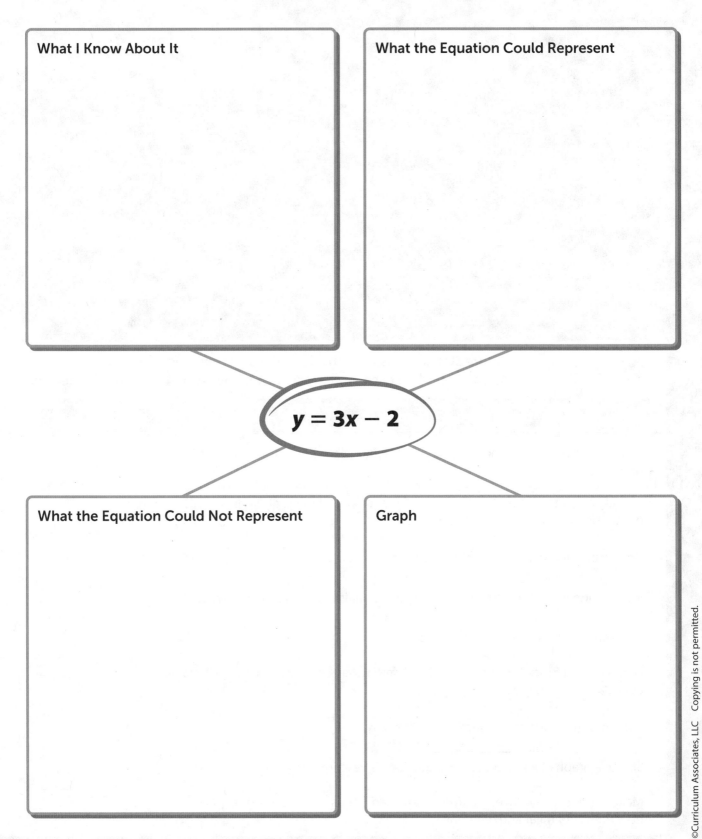

What I Know About It

What the Equation Could Represent

$$y = 3x - 2$$

What the Equation Could Not Represent

Graph

Dear Family,

This week your student is learning about **functions**. A function is a rule that defines a relationship between two quantities. When these rules are applied, one quantity, called the **input**, results in another quantity, called the **output**. For a rule to be a function, each input must have *exactly* one output.

Students will be learning to determine if relationships between two quantities are functions, such as in the problem below.

Does the equation $y = 2x + 1$ represent a function?

➤ **ONE WAY** to explore a function is to use a table.

Input (x)	−3	−2	−1	0	1	2	3
Output (y)	−5	−3	−1	1	3	5	7

The table shows that this rule produces one output for each input.

➤ **ANOTHER WAY** is to use a graph.

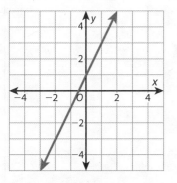

The graph shows that there is only one output, or *y*-value, for each input, or *x*-value. The graph also shows a straight line. The equation represents a **linear function**.

Using either method, the equation $y = 2x + 1$ represents a function.

 Use the next page to start a conversation about functions.

Activity Thinking About Functions

➤ **Do this activity together to investigate functions in the real world.**

You may be familiar with many real-world functions! For example, suppose cherries cost $3 a pound. A rule for finding the cost of a bag of cherries is *multiply the weight in pounds by $3*. This rule is a function because each weight has only one cost.

? Can you think of other examples of functions in the real world?

Explore Functions

Mangos
$2 each

? **UNDERSTAND:** How can you recognize a function?

Model It

➤ **Complete the problems about functions.**

1 A rule may tell you what to do to a starting value, or **input**, to get a final value, or **output**. Use the rules to complete the tables.

a. Input: number of mangos that cost $2 each
Output: total cost

Mangos	1	2	3	4
Cost	$2	$4		

b. Input: x, number of students
Output: y, least number of two-student desks needed

Students (x)	1	2	3	4	5	6
Desks (y)	1	1				

c. A **function** is a type of rule in which each input results in exactly one output. Explain why both rules above are functions.

d. In problem 1a, you can say that the total cost is *a function of* the number of mangos. Write a similar statement about the numbers of students and desks.

2 Use the rule to complete the table. Explain why y is not a function of x.

Input: x, a number; Output: y, all numbers x units from 0 on a number line

Input (x)	1	2	3	4	5
Output (y)	−1, 1				

Learning Targets SMP 1, SMP 2, SMP 3, SMP 7, SMP 8
• Understand that a function is a rule that assigns to each input exactly one output. The graph of a function is the set of ordered pairs consisting of an input and the corresponding output.
• Interpret the equation $y = mx + b$ as defining a linear function, whose graph is a straight line; give examples of functions that are not linear.

Model It

➤ **Complete the problems about showing a rule with a graph.**

3 You can make a graph of the (input, output) pairs for a rule.

a. Complete both graphs by plotting (input, output) pairs for input values of 3, 4, and 5.

Input: *x*, a whole number
Output: *y*, all factors of *x*

Input: *x*, a whole number
Output: *y*, the number of factors of *x*

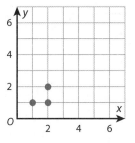 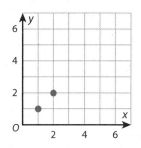

b. Look at the graph on the left. Is *y* a function of *x*? Explain how you know.

c. Look at the graph on the right. Is *y* a function of *x*? Explain how you know.

> **DISCUSS IT**
>
> *Ask:* If you extend the graph on the right to include more inputs, will you ever find an input with more than one point above it? Why?
>
> *Share:* I know that a rule is not a function if its graph . . .

4 **Reflect** How can making a table or graph help you decide whether a rule is a function?

Prepare for Functions

1. Think about what you know about rates of change. Fill in each box.
   Use words, numbers, and pictures. Show as many ideas as you can.

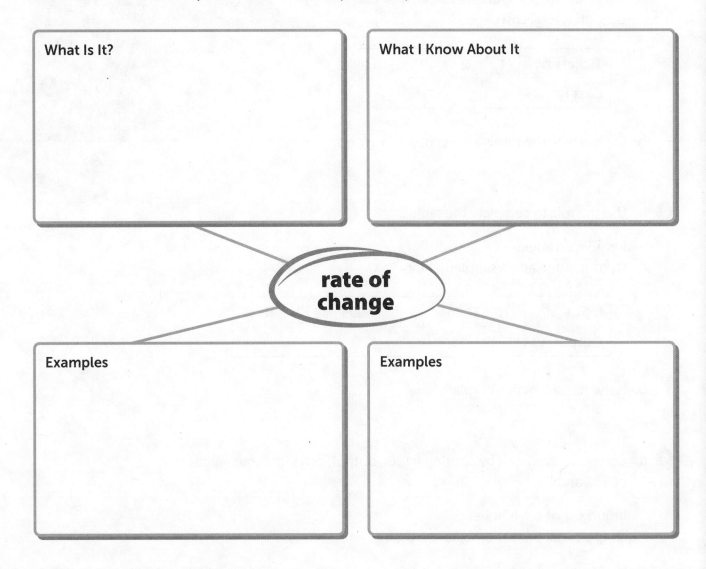

What Is It?

What I Know About It

rate of change

Examples

Examples

2. Circle the equation with a rate of change of 3.

$3y = 2x + 5$ $y = 6x - 3$ $y = 3x + 12$

➤ **Complete problems 3–5.**

3 **a.** Use the rule to complete the table.

Input: *x*, number of tickets that cost $9 each
Output: *y*, total cost

Tickets (x)	1	2	3	10
Cost (y)	$9			

b. Explain why the rule is a function.

4 **a.** Use the rule to complete the table.

Input: *x*, an angle
Output: *y*, the angle supplementary to *x*

Input (x)	10°	26°	45°	90°	112°	175°
Output (y)	170°	154°				

b. Is the rule a function? Explain.

5 **a.** Complete the graph by plotting (input, output) pairs for input values of 3, 4, and 5.

Input: *x*, a whole number
Output: *y*, all prime numbers less than or equal to *x*

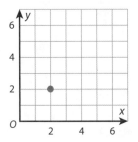

b. Is *y* a function of *x*? How can you tell by looking at the graph?

Develop Understanding of Linear and Nonlinear Functions

Model It: Graphs

➤ **Try these two problems involving linear and nonlinear functions.**

 a. Functions can be classified as linear or nonlinear. Look at this **linear function**. Then complete the table and graph.

Input: *x*, number of birdhouses Aimee paints with 0.5 pint of paint each; Output: *y*, total pints of paint she needs

Birdhouses (*x*)	Pints of Paint (*y*)
1	
2	
3	
4	
5	

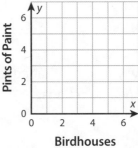

b. Look at the shape of the graph. Why do you think this function is classified as a linear function?

2 **a.** Complete the table and graph for this **nonlinear function**.

Input: *x*, an integer; Output: *y*, the square of *x*

Input (*x*)	−2	−1	0	1	2
Output (*y*)					

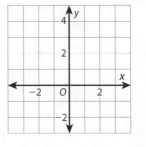

b. How is the graph different from the graph of the linear function in problem 1?

Model It: Equations

➤ **Try this problem about functions.**

3 Many functions can be represented by equations that show how to calculate the output y for the input x.

a. Determine whether each equation represents a linear function. Show your work.

$y = 2x - 1$ $\qquad\qquad$ $y = -x^2$ $\qquad\qquad$ $y = -x$

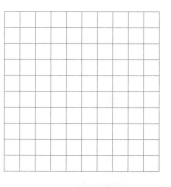

SOLUTION _____

b. Explain how you know that equations of the form $y = mx + b$ always represent linear functions.

DISCUSS IT

Ask: How do you know that equations of the form $y = x^2$ do not represent linear functions?

Share: Not all functions are linear because . . .

CONNECT IT

➤ **Complete the problems below.**

4 You want to determine whether a function is linear. How can making a graph or writing an equation help?

5 Does the rule describe a linear function? Use a model to explain.

Input: x, a number; Output: y, 6 more than 5 times x

Name:

Practice Linear and Nonlinear Functions

➤ **Study how the Example shows how to determine whether a function is linear or nonlinear. Then solve problems 1–4.**

Example

Use a graph to determine whether the function is a linear function.

Input: *x*, a number; Output: *y*, 2 more than −1 times *x*

Make a table of input and output values.

Input (*x*)	−2	−1	0	1	2
Output (*y*)	4	3	2	1	0

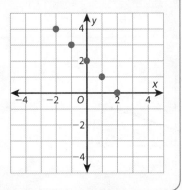

Graph the (input, output) pairs. The points lie on a straight line. Plotting more points will continue to follow the same straight line. The function is linear.

1 **a.** What is an equation that represents the rule in the Example?

b. Use the equation to explain why the rule is a linear function.

2 Complete the table and graph for the function. Tell whether the function is linear or nonlinear. Explain your reasoning.

Input: *x*, a number; Output: *y*, 6 divided by *x*

Input (*x*)	Output (*y*)
1	
2	
3	
4	

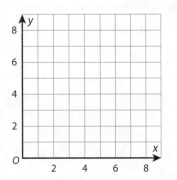

3 Each graph represents a function. Tell whether the function is *linear* or *nonlinear*.

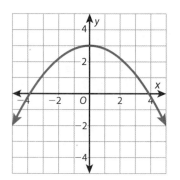

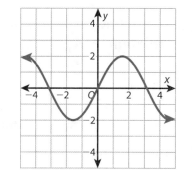

a. _____

b. _____

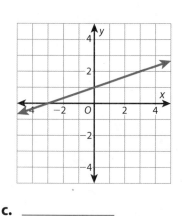

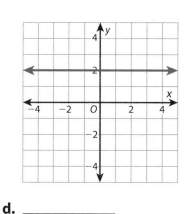

c. _____

d. _____

4 Felipe wants to figure out if the equation $y = x(x + 2)$ represents a linear function.

He finds two (x, y) pairs and plots them.

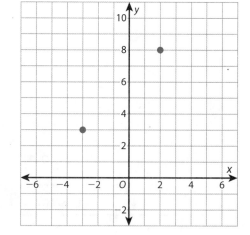

x	−3	2
y	3	8

Felipe says he can draw a line through these two points, so the equation represents a linear function.

a. Explain why Felipe's reasoning is incorrect.

b. Does the equation represent a linear function? Explain your reasoning.

Refine Ideas About Functions

Apply It

 Math Toolkit graph paper, straightedges

➤ **Complete problems 1–5.**

1 **Apply** Ana is bowling. She pays $4 per game and $7 to rent shoes. After three games, each additional game is free. Is the total cost to bowl a function of the number of games played? Use a table or graph to help explain your answer.

$4 per game
$7 shoe rental

2 **Identify** The tables show inputs and outputs for two functions. One of the functions is linear. Explain how you can tell without a graph which represents a linear function.

Table 1

Input	1	2	3	4	5
Output	6	7	9	12	16

Table 2

Input	2	4	6	8	10
Output	5	9	13	17	21

3 **Analyze** Fiona says the graph does not represent a function because inputs −1 and 1 have the same output, 3. Is Fiona correct? Explain.

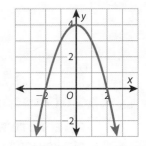

4 **PART A** Give an example of a nonlinear function. You may represent the function by giving the rule in words or by writing an equation.

PART B Make a graph or table to represent your function.

PART C Use your graph or table to help you explain why your function is nonlinear.

5 **Math Journal** How can you tell if a rule represents a function? Explain how a graph, table, or equation for a rule can help you determine whether the rule is a function.

✓ **End of Lesson Checklist**

☐ **INTERACTIVE GLOSSARY** Find the entry for *function*. Show an example of a linear function, a nonlinear function, and a relationship that is not a function.

Dear Family,

Previously, your student learned how to recognize linear functions. This week your student is learning how to use linear functions to model relationships. A linear function has a constant rate of change and can be modeled by an equation in the form of $y = mx + b$. Students will be learning to interpret linear functions that model real-world situations, such as in the problem below.

A phone company charges $25 per month for 500 minutes of talk time. If users go over 500 minutes, there is an additional charge per each minute over 500. The linear function $y = \frac{1}{2}x + 25$ gives the cost of the monthly phone plan, y, for x minutes over the first 500 minutes. What is the charge per additional minute over 500?

➤ **ONE WAY** to interpret the linear function is to graph the equation.

From the graph you can see that the slope of the line, or the rate of change of the function, is $\frac{15}{30} = \frac{1}{2}$.

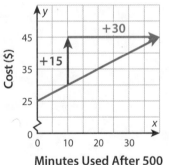

➤ **ANOTHER WAY** is to look at the different parts of the function equation.

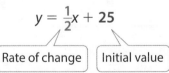

Using either method, the company charges $0.50 per additional minute over 500.

▶ Use the next page to start a conversation about linear functions.

Activity Thinking About Using Functions to Model Linear Relationships

0.2 mile per minute

➤ **Do this activity together to investigate linear functions in the real world.**

Functions can be used to model linear relationships between two quantities. You can find unknown values by writing an equation to represent a linear relationship. For example, suppose you ride your bike at a rate of 0.2 mile per minute. You can use the equation $y = 0.2x$, where y is distance in miles and x is time in minutes, to figure out that it would take you 50 minutes to travel 10 miles!

? When else might you want to use a function to think about linear relationships?

Explore Using Functions to Model Linear Relationships

Take Out — **Bill's** BrickOven — Eat Here

| Small Pie **$8.00** | Large Pie **$12.00** |
| Topping **$1.50** | Topping **$2.00** |

Previously, you learned about functions. In this lesson, you will learn about writing equations to model linear functions.

➤ **Use what you know to try to solve the problem below.**

A customer can use the menu above to call in a pizza order. He or she chooses a size and then adds toppings. The graphs and equations model the prices of the two sizes of pizza.

$y = 1.5x + 8$

$y = 2x + 12$

Which equation and which line model the price of a small pizza?
Which equation and which line model the price of a large pizza?

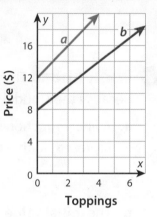

TRY IT

DISCUSS IT

Ask: Which numbers in the problem helped you answer the questions?

Share: The numbers I used were . . .

◎ **Learning Target**   SMP 1, SMP 2, SMP 3, SMP 4, SMP 5, SMP 6, SMP 7
Construct a function to model a linear relationship between two quantities. Determine the rate of change and initial value of the function from a description of a relationship or from two (x, y) values, including reading these from a table or from a graph. Interpret the rate of change and initial value of a linear function in terms of the situation it models, and in terms of its graph or a table of values.

CONNECT IT

1 **Look Back** Which equation and graph represent the price of each size pizza? How do you know?

2 **Look Ahead** The graphs and equations in the **Try It** problem are linear models because they model, or represent, linear functions.

a. A linear function has a constant rate of change. What do the rates of change represent in this situation?

b. The **initial value** of each function in the **Try It** is the value of y when $x = 0$. What do the initial values represent in this situation?

c. What quantities do the variables x and y represent in this situation? Use the phrase *is a function of* to describe the relationship between these quantities.

3 **Reflect** Look back at the equations and graphs in the **Try It** problem. Which type of model would you rather use to find the price of a pizza? Explain.

Prepare for Using Functions to Model Linear Relationships

1 Think about what you know about linear equations. Fill in each box.
Use words, numbers, and pictures. Show as many ideas as you can.

What Is It?	What I Know About It

slope-intercept form

Examples	Non-Examples

2 Write an equation for the graph in slope-intercept form.

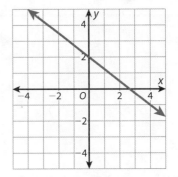

3 A poster announces a carnival is coming to town. People pay an admission fee to enter the carnival. Then they buy tickets to go on rides. The total cost of attending the carnival is a function of the number of tickets bought. The graphs and equations model the total costs for children and for adults.

$$y = 1.25x + 10$$

$$y = 0.75x + 5$$

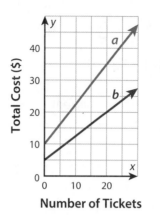

a. Which equation and which line model the total cost for a child? Which equation and line model the total cost for an adult? Show your work.

SOLUTION _____

_____

b. Check your answer to problem 3a. Show your work.

Develop Interpreting a Linear Function

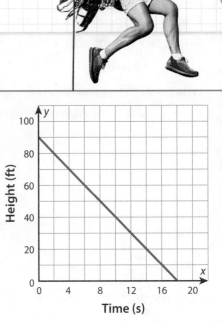

➤ **Read and try to solve the problem below.**

Aretha is rappelling down the side of a cliff. The graph shows her height above the ground in feet as a function of time in seconds as she descends.

What is Aretha's height above ground when she begins rappelling down? At what rate does she descend?

TRY IT

DISCUSS IT

Ask: How did you use the information from the graph to solve the problem?

Share: I used the graph by . . .

➤ **Explore different ways to interpret a linear function.**

Aretha is rappelling down the side of a cliff. The graph shows her height above the ground in feet as a function of time in seconds as she descends.

What is Aretha's height above ground when she begins rappelling down? At what rate does she descend?

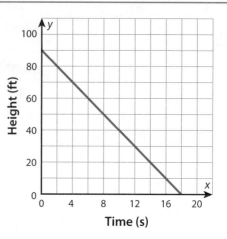

Model It

You can model the function with a linear equation.

Find the slope and y-intercept.

$$\text{slope} = \frac{90 - 0}{0 - 18}$$

$$= \frac{90}{-18}$$

$$= -5$$

The graph shows that the y-intercept is 90.

An equation of the function is $y = -5x + 90$.

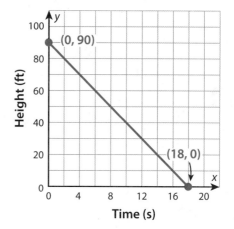

Analyze It

You can answer the questions by analyzing each part of the equation.

$$y = -5x + 90$$

rate of change   initial value

The **rate of change** shows how Aretha's height, *y*, changes over time, *x*.

The **initial value** of the function is Aretha's height at time 0.

➤ **Use the problem from the previous page to help you understand how to interpret a linear function.**

1 How can you determine what *x* and *y* represent in the equation of the function?

2 Look at **Model It** and **Analyze It**. What is Aretha's height above the ground when she starts rappelling? At what rate does she descend? How do you know?

3 **a.** Explain how to write an equation of a linear function when you know the rate of change and initial value of the function.

b. Describe how the rate of change and initial value of the linear function are represented in the graph of the function.

4 **Reflect** Think about all the models and strategies you have discussed today. Describe how one of them helped you better understand how to solve the **Try It** problem.

Apply It

➤ **Use what you learned to solve these problems.**

5 The total monthly cost of exercise classes is a linear function of the number of classes attended. The table shows costs for two different gyms.

Classes Attended	Monthly Cost Gym A	Monthly Cost Gym B
5	$75	$110
10	$150	$160
15	$225	$210
20	$300	$260

a. What is the cost per class at each gym?

b. Which gym charges a monthly fee? How do you know?

6 The graph shows distance in feet as a function of time in seconds. Write an equation for the function and describe a situation that it could represent. Include the initial value and rate of change for the function and what each quantity represents in this situation.

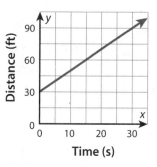

7 Mr. Seda plans a field trip for one of his classes. He rents one bus for the whole class and purchases a museum ticket for each student. The equation $y = 11x + 400$ gives the cost of the field trip as a function of the number of students who attend.

What is the initial value of the function? What is the rate of change? What do these values tell you about the field trip?

Practice Interpreting a Linear Function

➤ **Study the Example showing how to interpret a linear function. Then solve problems 1–4.**

Example

Snow falls early in the morning and stops. Then at noon snow begins to fall again and accumulate at a constant rate. The table shows the number of inches of snow on the ground as a function of time after noon. What is the initial value of the function? What does this value represent?

Hours After Noon	Inches of Snow
0	6
1	8.5
2	11

The initial value is 6, the number of inches of snow at noon, when the time value is 0. It represents the amount of snow that was already on the ground before it began snowing again.

1   **a.** What is the rate of change of the function in the Example? What does this value represent?

    b. Suppose there was no snow on the ground before it began snowing at noon. What is the equation of this function?

2   The graph shows money in dollars as a function of time in days. Write an equation for the function, and describe a situation that it could represent. Include the initial value, rate of change, and what each quantity represents in the situation.

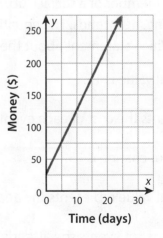

LESSON 16 Use Functions to Model Linear Relationships   **369**

3 Each day Kyle buys a cup of soup and a salad for lunch. The salad costs a certain amount per ounce. The equation below models the total cost of Kyle's lunch.

$y = 0.45x + 3.75$

a. What do the variables x and y represent? Use the phrase *is a function of* to describe how the equation relates these quantities to one another.

b. What does the value of the function for $x = 0$ represent?

c. What does the rate of change represent?

d. What is the cost of an 8-ounce salad without soup? How do you know?

4 Carmela is a member of a social club. She pays an annual membership fee and $15 for each event she attends. The equation $y = 15x + 25$ represents her total cost each year. Which statement about the function is true? Select all that apply.

A The initial value is 15.

B x represents the cost of each event.

C The rate of change is 15.

D The initial value represents the annual membership fee.

E The number of events she attends is a function of the total cost.

F The total cost is a function of the number of events she attends.

Develop Writing an Equation for a Linear Function from Two Points

➤ **Read and try to solve the problem below.**

The Duda family owns 10 acres of land. They want to buy more land and start a ranch. The amount of land they need is a linear function of the number of grazing animals they plan to have. The family decides to raise alpaca. The table gives the number of acres they need for different numbers of alpaca.

Write an equation to model the data in the table.

DUDA ALPACA RANCH

Number of Alpaca	Land Needed (acres)
10	25
20	40
30	55

TRY IT

Math Toolkit graph paper, straightedges

DISCUSS IT

Ask: How did you use the information given in the table?

Share: I used the numbers in the table to . . .

➤ **Explore different ways to write an equation for a linear function.**

The Duda family owns 10 acres of land. They want to buy more land and start a ranch. The amount of land they need is a linear function of the number of grazing animals they plan to have. The family decides to raise alpaca. The table gives the number of acres they need for different numbers of Alpaca.

Write an equation to model the data in the table.

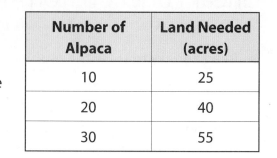

Number of Alpaca	Land Needed (acres)
10	25
20	40
30	55

Picture It

You can use a graph to find the slope and *y*-intercept.

Plot the points given in the table and graph the line.

$$\text{slope} = \frac{\text{rise}}{\text{run}}$$

$$= \frac{15}{10}$$

$$= 1.5$$

y-intercept = **10**

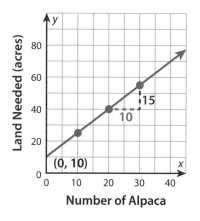

Model It

You can calculate the rate of change and initial value.

Use the values from any two rows of the table to find the rate of change.

Use (10, 25) and (30, 55): rate of change $= \frac{55 - 25}{30 - 10} = \frac{30}{20} = 1.5$

To find the initial value, substitute the rate of change and one pair of values from the table into the equation for a linear function.

Use (**10, 25**): $y = mx + b$

$25 = 1.5(10) + b$

$10 = b$

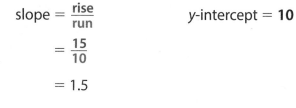

➤ **Use the problem from the previous page to help you understand how to write an equation for a linear function.**

① Look at **Picture It** and **Model It**. What is the equation for the amount of land needed as a function of the number of alpaca on the ranch? What does the equation mean in this situation?

② **a.** Look at **Model It**. What other pair of *x*- and *y*-values could you use to find the initial value? Use these values to show you get the same answer.

   b. Edward uses $x = 10$ and $y = 40$ to find the initial value. What is his mistake?

③ How do you know that there is only one possible value for the rate of change?

④ Explain how you can write the equation for a linear function when you know only two points on the line.

⑤ **Reflect** Think about all the models and strategies you have discussed today. Describe how one of them helped you better understand how to solve the **Try It** problem.

Apply It

➤ **Use what you learned to solve these problems.**

6 The cost of a cross-stitch project is a function of the number of skeins of embroidery floss it requires. The table shows the cost of projects that use different amounts of embroidery floss. What is the equation of the linear function that models this situation? Show your work.

Skeins of Embroidery Floss	Cost of Project
5	$11.25
8	$13.50
12	$16.50

SOLUTION _____

7 You are trying to find the equation of the line that passes through two points, P and Q. P is in Quadrant II and Q is in Quadrant IV. What do you know about the slope of the line? Explain.

8 What is the equation of the function shown by the graph? Show your work.

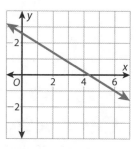

SOLUTION _____

Name:

Practice Writing an Equation for a Linear Function from Two Points

➤ **Study the Example showing how to write an equation for a linear function from two points. Then solve problems 1–4.**

Example

What is the equation of the function shown by the graph? Show your work.

The lines passes through (9, 12) and (3, 3).

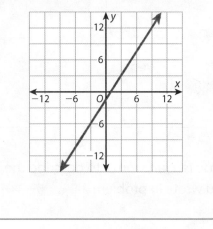

$$\text{slope} = \frac{12-3}{9-3}$$

$$= \frac{9}{6}$$

$$= \frac{3}{2}$$

$$y = mx + b$$

$$12 = \frac{3}{2}(9) + b$$

$$12 = \frac{27}{2} + b$$

$$-\frac{3}{2} = b$$

$$y = \frac{3}{2}x - \frac{3}{2}$$

---

1 What is the equation of the function shown by the graph? Show your work.

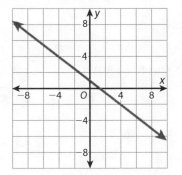

2 The graph of a linear function passes through the points (3, 19) and (5, 23). Write an equation for the function. Show your work.

SOLUTION _____

SOLUTION _____

---

3 Vinh pays a convenience fee when he reserves movie tickets on his cell phone app. The app shows him the total cost of his purchase for different numbers of tickets.

TICKETS	TOTAL COST
2	$32.00
3	$44.50
6	$82.00

a. What is the equation that models this linear function? Show your work.

SOLUTION _____

b. Use the phrase *is a function of* to describe the situation represented by the equation you wrote in problem 3a.

c. How much is each movie ticket?

d. How much is the convenience fee?

4 a. The graph of a linear function passes through the points $(-6, 26)$ and $(9, -39)$. Write an equation for the function. Show your work.

SOLUTION _____

b. What is the *y*-intercept of the line?

Develop Writing an Equation for a Linear Function from a Verbal Description

120 pages read in 3 hours

➤ **Read and try to solve the problem below.**

Kadeem spends the afternoon reading a book he started yesterday. He reads 120 pages in 3 hours. One hour after Kadeem begins reading, he is on page 80. Write an equation for the page he is on, *y*, as a function of minutes spent reading, *x*. What page number was he on when he started reading today?

TRY IT **Math Toolkit** graph paper, straightedges, tracing paper

➤ **Explore different ways to write an equation for a linear function from a verbal description.**

Kadeem spends the afternoon reading a book he started yesterday. He reads 120 pages in 3 hours. One hour after Kadeem begins reading, he is on page 80. Write an equation for the page he is on, y, as a function of minutes spent reading, x. What page number was he on when he started reading today?

Picture It

You can graph the function.

Plot the point **(60, 80)**.

Find the rate of change, which is the slope of the line.

120 pages in 3 hours is 120 pages in 180 minutes.

$$\text{slope} = \frac{120}{180} = \frac{40}{60} = \frac{2}{3}$$

Use the slope to plot another point at **(120, 120)**.

Draw a line through the points and identify the y-intercept.

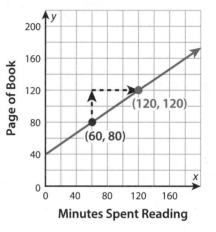

Model It

You can calculate the rate of change and initial value.

$\frac{120 \text{ pages}}{3 \text{ hours}}$ can be written as $\frac{120 \text{ pages}}{180 \text{ minutes}}$.

The rate of change is $\frac{2}{3}$ page per minute.

To find the initial value, use the equation for a linear function. Then substitute the **rate of change** and the point **(60, 80)**.

$$y = mx + b$$

$$80 = \frac{2}{3}(60) + b$$

➤ **Use the problem from the previous page to help you understand how to write an equation for a linear function from a verbal description.**

1 What does the point (60, 80) represent?

2 Use the graph in **Picture It** to estimate the y-intercept. Check your estimate by solving the equation in **Model It** to find the value of b. What does this value represent in this situation?

3 Write the equation for the page Kadeem is on as a function of minutes he spends reading.

4 What is the rate of change in pages per hour? Write an equation for the page Kadeem is on as a function of hours spent reading.

5 Use the equations you wrote in problems 3 and 4 to find the page that Kadeem was on after 3 hours, or 180 minutes, of reading. Are your answers the same?

6 Do the different equations in problems 3 and 4 represent the same function? Explain.

7 **Reflect** Think about all the models and strategies you have discussed today. Describe how one of them helped you better understand how to solve the **Try It** problem.

LESSON 16 Use Functions to Model Linear Relationships   **379**

Apply It

➤ **Use what you learned to solve these problems.**

8 A lawn mower has the given energy rating. A full tank of gas can power the lawn mower for about 6 hours. What equation can be used to find the amount of gas left in the tank, *y*, as a function of the mowing time, *x*? Show your work.

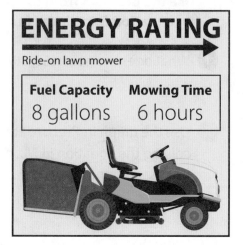

ENERGY RATING

Ride-on lawn mower

Fuel Capacity	Mowing Time
8 gallons	6 hours

SOLUTION _____

9 The graph of a linear function passes through the point (–2, –7). When the input increases by 3, the value of the function increases by 8. What is the equation that models the function?

10 Aniyah is driving home at a constant speed. After 20 minutes, she is 70 miles from home. After 1 hour, she is 40 miles from home. What equation models her distance from home, *y*, as a function of time, *x*? Show your work.

SOLUTION _____

Practice Writing an Equation for a Linear Function from a Verbal Description

➤ Study the Example showing how to write an equation for a linear function from a verbal description. Then solve problems 1–4.

Example

Dolores is making a music video using a drone. She sets the drone on a platform 1 meter above the ground. Then she uses the controls to make it rise at a constant rate. The drone reaches a height of 16 meters in 5 seconds. What is the equation for the drone's height, y, as a function of time, x?

At 0 seconds, the drone is 1 meter above the ground.

At 5 seconds, the drone is 16 meters above the ground.

rate of change: $\dfrac{16 - 1}{5 - 0} = \dfrac{15}{5} = 3$ initial value: 1

Use the equation for a linear function, $y = mx + b$.

$y = 3x + 1$

1 The drone in the Example hovers at 16 meters for a few minutes before being lowered at a constant rate. It reaches the ground after 6 seconds.

a. Why can the drone's descent be modeled by a linear function?

b. The linear model of the drone's descent gives its height as a function of time. Is the rate of change positive or negative? Explain.

c. What equation models the drone's descent as time increases? Show your work.

Vocabulary

initial value
in a linear function, the value of the output when the input is 0.

linear function
a function that can be represented by a linear equation.

rate of change
in a linear relationship between x and y, it tells how much y changes when x changes by 1.

SOLUTION _____

2 The Drama Club is selling tie-dye T-shirts as a fundraiser. They buy the dyeing materials for $60 and white T-shirts for $2.50 each. They sell the finished shirts for $10 each.

FRANKLIN MIDDLE SCHOOL DRAMA CLUB FUNDRAISER

 a. Write an equation for the money they spend, y, as a function of the number of T-shirts they buy, x.

 b. Write an equation for the money they collect, y, as a function of the number of T-shirts they sell, x.

 c. Write an equation for their profit, y, as a function of the number of T-shirts they sell, x.

3 On his first birthday, Tomás was 30 inches tall. For the next year, he grew half an inch each month. What equation models his height during that year, y, as a function of the number of months, x?

4 Write an equation for each linear function described below.

 a. The value of the function at $x = -2$ is 0. The value of the function at $x = 8$ is -25.

 b. The graph of the function has a y-intercept of 13. When x increases by 1, y decreases by 4.

 c. The graph of the function intersects the y-axis at $y = 18$ and intersects the x-axis at $x = -15$.

 d. The function describes a proportional relationship. Its graph passes through the point (3, 7).

Refine Using Functions to Model Linear Relationships

➤ **Complete the Example below. Then solve problems 1–9.**

Example

A swimming pool is being filled at a constant rate of 6 gallons per minute. After 1 minute, there are 8 gallons of water in the pool. What equation represents this function?

Look at how you could use the rate of change and a point to write the equation.

The rate of change is 6.

The 8 gallons of water in the pool after 1 minute is represented by the point (1, 8) on the graph of the function.

$$y = mx + b$$
$$8 = 6(1) + b$$
$$2 = b$$

SOLUTION _____

Apply It

1 Celsius (C) and Fahrenheit (F) are two different scales for measuring temperature. The freezing point of water is 0°C, or 32°F. The boiling point of water is 100°C, or 212°F. Write an equation that shows the temperature in degrees Fahrenheit as a function of the temperature in degrees Celsius. Show your work.

SOLUTION _____

2 What is the equation of the function shown by the graph? Show your work.

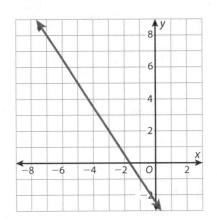

SOLUTION _____

3 Lillie uses some birthday money to open a bank account. Then she deposits the same amount into the account each week. The equation $y = 35x + 100$ represents the total amount in the account after x weeks. What does the initial value of the function represent?

A The amount deposited each week

B The amount used to open the bank account

C The total amount in the account after the first week of saving

D The total amount in the account after x weeks

Chloe chose A as the correct answer. How might she have gotten that answer?

4 Javier and Ellema both get their cars washed and fill their gas tanks at the same gas station. Javier pays $26.96 for a car wash and 5.6 gallons of gas. Ellema pays $48.62 for a car wash and 13.2 gallons of gas.

a. What is an equation for the cost of gas and a car wash as a function of the amount of gas bought? Show your work.

SOLUTION _____

b. What does each variable represent?

c. What are the initial value and the rate of change of the function? What does each one represent?

5 Which savings plan can be modeled by $y = 50x + 25$?

A Start with $50. Save $25 each week.

B Save $250 in 5 weeks for a total of $300.

C Start with $25. The total saved after 5 weeks is $275.

D The total saved is $25 the first week and $50 the second week.

6 Does the table show a linear function? Explain.

x	0	2	5	10
y	20	30	40	50

7 The equation $y = 0.15x + 0.40$ represents the cost of mailing a letter weighing 1 ounce or more. In the equation, x represents the weight of the letter in ounces and y represents the cost in dollars of mailing the letter. In this situation, the _____ is a function of the _____.

8 Tell whether the information given is enough to write an equation for the linear function.

	Yes	No
a. The initial value and the rate of change of the function	○	○
b. The slope of the line and the rate of change of the function	○	○
c. The slope of the line and one point on the line that is not the y-intercept	○	○
d. The y-intercept of the line and the value of the function at $x = 5$	○	○
e. The y-intercept of the line and the value of the function at $x = 0$	○	○

9 **Math Journal** The graph shows distance as a function of time. Write an equation for the line. Then describe a situation that could be represented by the graph. Include the initial value and rate of change for the function. Then tell what each quantity represents in this situation.

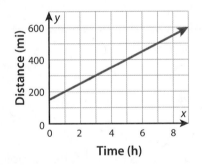

✓ **End of Lesson Checklist**

 ☐ **INTERACTIVE GLOSSARY** Find the entry for *initial value*. Give an example of a situation that can be modeled by a linear function with an initial value of 30.

 ☐ **SELF CHECK** Go back to the Unit 4 Opener and see what you can check off.

Dear Family,

This week your student is learning about comparing different representations of functions. Students will compare functions that are represented in a variety of ways, including graphs, tables, equations, and words. They will learn to use these different representations to answer questions about functions, such as in the problem below.

A museum sells adult and student day passes for its new dinosaur exhibit. The equation for the cost, C, of n student passes is $C = 12n$. The table shows the costs of adult passes. What is the difference in cost of the two types of passes?

Number of Passes	1	2	3	4
Cost ($)	20	40	60	80

➤ **ONE WAY** to find the difference is to compare costs for one pass.

Student: Substitute 1 for n in the equation: $C = 12(1) = $ **12**.

Adult: You can see from the table that 1 pass costs $**20**.

➤ **ANOTHER WAY** is to compare rates of change.

Student: Using the equation, the rate of change is **12**.

Adult: Using the table, the rate of change is $\frac{40 - 20}{2 - 1} = $ **20**.

Using either method, the difference in the cost of the two types of passes is $20 - $12 = $8.

 Use the next page to start a conversation about different representations of functions.

LESSON 17 Compare Different Representations of Functions

Compare Different Representations of Functions

Activity Thinking About Different Representations of Functions

➤ **Do this activity together to investigate different representations of functions.**

Different representations of functions can be compared to find useful information. Below are representations of the costs of three different movie streaming services as functions of the number of movies watched.

? What conclusions can you draw about each function based on its representation?

STREAMING SERVICE 1:

$C = m + 15$

C is the cost in dollars and m is the number of movies watched.

STREAMING SERVICE 2:

This service does not charge a base fee. It costs $4 per movie watched.

STREAMING SERVICE 3:

Movies Watched	0	1	2	3	4
Cost ($)	10	12	14	16	18

Explore Different Representations of Proportional Relationships

Sailfish Swim
$d = 30t$

Previously, you learned to model linear functions. In this lesson, you will learn to compare different representations of functions.

➤ **Use what you know to try to solve the problem below.**

The equation $d = 30t$ gives the distance a sailfish swims in meters as a function of time in seconds. The graph shows the distance an Olympic athlete swims over time. Does the athlete or the fish swim faster?

Olympic Athlete Swim

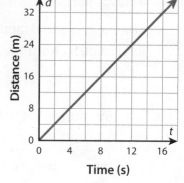

TRY IT

 Math Toolkit graph paper, straightedges

DISCUSS IT

Ask: How did you get started finding who is faster?

Share: I knew . . . so I . . .

◎ **Learning Targets** SMP 1, SMP 2, SMP 3, SMP 4, SMP 5, SMP 6
• Compare properties of two functions each represented in a different way.
• Graph proportional relationships, interpreting the unit rate as the slope of the graph.
  Compare two different proportional relationships represented in different ways.

1 Look Back Does the athlete or the sailfish swim faster? How do you know?

2 Look Ahead There are many ways to compare functions. One way is to compare their rates of change.

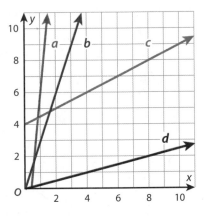

a. Lines *a, b, c,* and *d* model four different linear functions. List the lines in order from the steepest to the least steep.

b. Find the slope of each line. Complete the table.

Line	*a*	*b*	*c*	*d*
Slope	10			

c. How does the steepness of the lines relate to their slopes?

d. How can a graph help you determine which of two increasing linear functions has the greater rate of change?

3 Reflect Suppose you graph the equation for the sailfish from the **Try It** in the same coordinate plane as the athlete's line. Which line would be steeper? How do you know?

Prepare for Comparing Different Representations of Functions

1 Think about what you know about relationships between variables. Fill in each box. Use words, numbers, and pictures. Show as many ideas as you can.

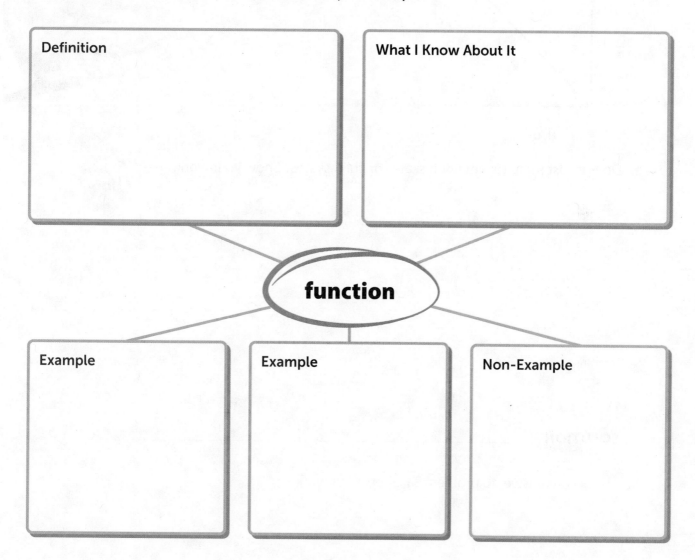

Definition

What I Know About It

function

Example

Example

Non-Example

2 Circle each model that represents a function.

$y = 4x - 23$

For every pound of dried oats purchased, the price decreases by $0.25 per pound.

Input	3	3	3	3
Output	4	5	6	7

3 An ice rink rents skates by the hour. The equation $C = 8h$ gives the cost in dollars for renting adult skates. The cost is a function of time in hours. The graph shows the cost for renting child skates.

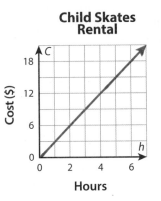

Child Skates Rental

a. Does it cost more to rent adult skates or child skates? Show your work.

SOLUTION _____

b. Check your answer to problem 3a. Show your work.

Develop Comparing Increasing and Decreasing Linear Functions

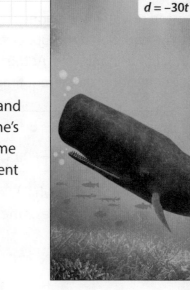

$d = -30t$

➤ **Read and try to solve the problem below.**

A two-person research submarine starts at the ocean surface and begins to descend. The equation $d = -30t$ gives the submarine's elevation in meters as a function of time in minutes. At the same time, a whale begins to ascend. The whale's elevation at different times is given in the table.

Time (min)	0	4	8	10
Whale's Elevation (m)	−800	−560	−320	−200

What is the difference in the submarine's elevation and the whale's elevation at 0 minutes? Is the submarine or the whale traveling at a faster speed?

TRY IT

Math Toolkit graph paper, straightedges

LESSON 17 Compare Different Representations of Functions   **393**

➤ **Explore different ways to compare linear functions.**

A two-person research submarine starts at the ocean surface and begins to descend. The equation $d = -30t$ gives the submarine's elevation in meters as a function of time in minutes. At the same time, a whale begins to ascend. The whale's elevation at different times is given in the table.

Time (min)	0	4	8	10
Whale's Elevation (m)	−800	−560	−320	−200

What is the difference in the whale's elevation and the submarine's elevation at 0 minutes? Is the submarine or the whale traveling at a faster speed?

Analyze It

You can compare initial values to find the difference in elevation at 0 minutes.

The initial value is the elevation when $t = 0$.

Use the table. When $t = 0$, the whale is at -800 meters, or 800 meters below the surface of the water.

Use the equation $d = -30t$. When $t = 0$, the submarine's elevation is 0 meters.

Analyze It

You can compare rates of change to find the faster traveling speed.

whale:
$$\frac{y_1 - y_2}{x_1 - x_2} = \frac{-560 - (-320)}{4 - 8}$$
$$= \frac{-240}{-4}$$
$$= 60$$

submarine: $d = -30t$, so the rate of change is -30.

Compare the absolute values of the rates.

➤ **Use the problem from the previous page to help you understand how to compare linear functions.**

1 Look at the first **Analyze It**. What is the difference between the whale's elevation and the submarine's elevation at 0 minutes?

2 **a.** Look at the second **Analyze It**. Speed is never negative. The whale's rate of change is positive, but the submarine's is negative. What does the sign of each rate represent in this situation?

b. Write an inequality statement comparing the absolute values of the rates. Is the submarine or the whale traveling at a faster speed?

c. Suppose the submarine's rate changes to −72 meters per minute. The whale's rate stays the same. Describe the direction each is moving. Which is traveling faster? Explain.

d. Suppose the whale is traveling at an average rate of −30 meters per minute and the submarine is traveling at an average rate of −25 meters per minute. Describe the direction each is moving. Which is traveling faster? Explain.

3 Why do you compare the absolute values of rates of change when comparing increasing and decreasing linear functions?

4 **Reflect** Think about all the models and strategies you have discussed today. Describe how one of them helped you better understand how to compare linear functions.

Apply It

➤ **Use what you learned to solve these problems.**

5 A small-business owner has two bank accounts. The first is a payroll account. The equation $P = 45,000 - 2,500w$ represents the dollar amount in the payroll account as a function of time in weeks. The second account has $8,000 at Week 0, and the business owner deposits $1,500 each week. What is the total amount in the two accounts at Week 0?

6 Which statement is true? Select all that apply.

A The initial value of an increasing function is always less than the initial value of a decreasing function.

B You can use rate of change to compare functions.

C A line representing an increasing function will always be steeper than a line representing a decreasing function.

D Absolute value can help you compare rates of change when at least one of the functions is decreasing.

E The initial value of a proportional relationship is always 1.

7 The table shows the amount of water in a large pool as it drains. The graph shows the rate at which a small pool fills. Does the large pool drain or the small pool fill at a faster rate? Show your work.

Water in Small Pool

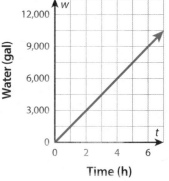

Time (h)	0	40	80
Water in Large Pool (gal)	200,000	104,000	8,000

SOLUTION _____

Practice Comparing Increasing and Decreasing Linear Functions

➤ **Study the Example showing how to compare increasing and decreasing linear functions. Then solve problems 1–3.**

Example

Starting at 5:00 AM, the temperature is 63°F and rises at an average rate of 1.5°F each hour for the next 5 hours. The table shows the average rate that the temperature falls starting at 5:00 PM. Does the temperature change at a greater average rate in the morning or the evening?

5:00 PM	6:00 PM	7:00 PM	8:00 PM	9:00 PM
80°F	78°F	76°F	74°F	72°F

rate of change in the morning: 1.5

rate of change in the evening: $\dfrac{y_1 - y_2}{x_1 - x_2} = \dfrac{78 - 80}{6 - 5} = \dfrac{-2}{1} = -2$

$|-2| > |1.5|$

The temperature changes at a greater average rate in the evening.

① What is the difference in the initial values of the functions in the Example?

② Demi teaches drum classes. The equation $B = 50t$ gives the dollar amount she earns as a function of the time in hours she teaches. Demi also takes spin classes. The graph shows how much she has left on a gift card as a function of the time in hours Demi is in class. Does Demi earn more teaching 1 hour of drum class or spend more taking 1 hour of spin class? Show your work.

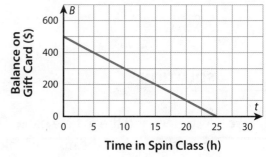

Money on Gift Card

SOLUTION _____

3 A marine biologist and her colleague are scuba diving. The marine biologist begins to ascend. At the same time, her coworker begins to descend. The graph shows the marine biologist's change in elevation over time. The table shows the colleague's elevation at different times.

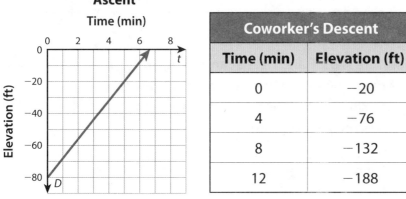

Marine Biologist's Ascent

Coworker's Descent	
Time (min)	**Elevation (ft)**
0	−20
4	−76
8	−132
12	−188

a. How far apart are the marine biologist and her coworker at $t = 0$?

b. Is the marine biologist or her coworker moving faster? Show your work.

SOLUTION _____

c. A student and the marine biologist are together at $t = 0$. The student ascends more slowly than the marine biologist. Write an equation of a function that could represent the student's ascent.

Develop Comparing Functions at Different Values

➤ **Read and try to solve the problem below.**

A silversmith compares the prices of jewelry-making classes at two Native American studios. He finds prices at Studio A on his phone. The table shows the prices at Studio B.

Number of Classes	1	5	10	15	20	25
Studio B Total Cost ($)	80	200	350	500	650	800

Navajo and Hopi
Silver Jewelry Class
$100 Initial fee $25 per class

Which studio should the silversmith attend if he has exactly $200 to spend? Which studio should the silversmith attend if he plans to take 15 or more classes?

TRY IT

Math Toolkit graph paper, straightedges

DISCUSS IT

Ask: How does your work show how many classes the silversmith can take for $200?

Share: In my solution . . . represents . . .

➤ **Explore different ways to compare functions at different values.**

A silversmith compares the prices of jewelry-making classes at two Native American studios. Studio A charges a $100 initial fee and $25 per class. The table shows the prices at Studio B.

Number of Classes	1	5	10	15	20	25
Studio B Total Cost ($)	80	200	350	500	650	800

Which studio should the silversmith attend if he has exactly $200 to spend? Which studio should the silversmith attend if he plans to take 15 or more classes?

Analyze It

You can use the description to find the Studio A information for each question.

Studio A charges a $100 initial fee and $25 per class.

For $200, Studio A offers four classes: $100 + $25 + $25 + $25 + $25.

15 classes cost $100 + 15($25) = $475.

20 classes cost $100 + 20($25) = $600.

25 classes cost $100 + 25($25) = $725.

Analyze It

You can use the table to find the Studio B information for each question.

The second column shows that for $200, the silversmith can take 5 classes.

The fourth through sixth columns show that 15, 20, and 25 classes cost $500, $650, and $800, respectively.

➤ **Use the problem from the previous page to help you understand how to compare functions at different values.**

1 Look at both **Analyze Its**. For each question, decide whether the silversmith should choose Studio A or Studio B.

2 **a.** What is the initial value of the Studio A function? What is the initial value of the Studio B function? What does the initial value represent?

b. What is the rate of change of the Studio A function? What is the rate of change of the Studio B function? What does the rate of change represent?

3 Look at the graph of the Studio A and Studio B functions.

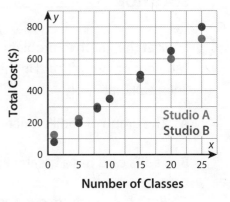

a. For what numbers of classes is Studio B the better choice?

b. For what number of classes are the studios the same price?

c. For what numbers of classes is Studio A the better choice?

4 Studio A offers less expensive classes. Why is it not always the better choice?

5 Do rates of change and initial values always provide enough information to compare two linear functions? Explain.

6 **Reflect** Think about all the models and strategies you have discussed today. Describe how one of them helped you better understand how to compare functions.

Apply It

➤ **Use what you learned to solve these problems.**

7 Fadil and Luke have gift cards to their favorite diner. Fadil starts with $50 on his card. He spends $4.50 each day. The graph shows the amount Luke starts with on his card, and the amount he has remaining each day.

Who has more money left on his card between Day 0 and Day 4? Show your work.

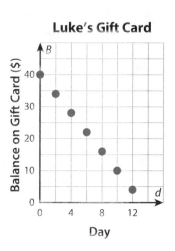

Luke's Gift Card

SOLUTION _____

8 Look at the graph in problem 7. Suppose you graph the amount of money Fadil has on his gift card in this same coordinate plane. Which statement is true? Select all that apply.

A The graph of Fadil's function is steeper than Luke's since $|-4.50| > |-3.00|$.

B Fadil's card has a greater initial value than Luke's card.

C Both functions are decreasing.

D Each day, Fadil spends more of his card's money than Luke does.

E There is a day when the cards have the same value greater than 0.

9 Look at problem 7. Who spends all of the money on his gift card first, Fadil or Luke? Show your work.

SOLUTION _____

Practice Comparing Functions at Different Values

➤ **Study the Example showing two decreasing functions. Then solve problems 1–3.**

Example

Pedro and Naomi begin to hike down a mountain at the same time. They begin at different elevations and descend at different speeds. The equation $E = 4,200 - 800h$ gives Pedro's elevation in feet as a function of time in hours. The table shows Naomi's elevation as she hikes at a constant rate. Who has greater elevation at 1 hour?

Time (h)	0	1	3	5.5
Naomi's Elevation (ft)	3,500	2,900	1,700	200

Pedro: $4,200 - 800(1) = 3,400$; **3,400 ft**

Naomi: The table shows that Naomi has elevation **2,900 ft** at 1 hour.

Pedro has greater elevation because **3,400 > 2,900.**

1 Look at the Example.

    a. Does Pedro or Naomi have greater elevation at $h = 0$? How much greater?

    b. Who descends at a greater speed? How do you know?

    c. The base of the mountain has 0 feet elevation. Does Pedro or Naomi reach the base of the mountain first? Show your work.

SOLUTION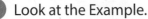

2 An internet store advertises your favorite sneakers with a special promotion. The price decreases at the steady rate shown in the table. Sneakers may someday be free, if they do not sell out first. A nearby store always charges $45 for the same sneakers.

Day	1	2	3	4
Internet Store Price ($)	65	62	59	56

a. What is the difference in price at the stores on Day 1? on Day 4?

b. Which store's price changes at a greater rate? Explain.

c. What is the first day the internet store's price is less than the nearby store's price?

3 A fashion designer checks the price of a certain fabric. Manufacturer A charges $7.50 per yard. The graph shows the price that Manufacturer B charges.

Manufacturer B

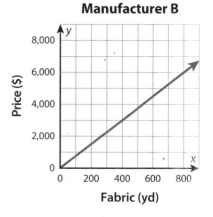

a. What is the initial value of each function?

b. How much does 400 yd of fabric cost at each manufacturer? How much does 800 yd of fabric cost at each manufacturer?

c. What can you conclude about the two functions? Explain.

d. Manufacturer C offers the fabric for $5.50/yd but you have to buy at least 500 yd. What should the designer do if she needs 400 yd? Explain.

Refine Comparing Different Representations of Functions

▶ **Complete the Example below. Then solve problems 1–7.**

Example

Compare the nonlinear function $y = x^2$ and the linear function shown in the table. Where do the functions intersect? For what inputs does the linear function have greater outputs than $y = x^2$?

Input (x)	−2	−1	0	1	2
Output (y)	4	3	2	1	0

Look at how you could use a graph to compare the functions.

Graph the functions using the same inputs. The functions intersect at (1, 1) and (−2, 4). The linear function has greater outputs between these two points.

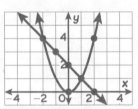

SOLUTION _____

Apply It

1 Dalila runs a 5K race at a steady rate of 11 kilometers per hour. Lulu starts a 10K race at the same time. She runs at the steady rate shown in the table. Who runs at a faster rate? How far has Lulu run when Dalila crosses her finish line? Show your work.

Time (h)	0	0.25	0.5	0.75	1	1.11
Lulu's Distance Run (km)	0	2.25	4.5	6.75	9	10

SOLUTION _____

2 Scientists release a drone and a turtle with a tracker on its shell from the surface of the ocean at the same time. The turtle immediately dives for jellyfish. The equation $D = -6t$ gives the turtle's elevation in feet as a function of time in seconds. The drone rises at an average rate of 7 feet per second.

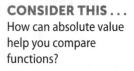

CONSIDER THIS . . .
How can absolute value help you compare functions?

a. What is the difference in elevation between the turtle and the drone at $t = 0$?

b. Is the turtle or the drone traveling faster? How much faster?

c. How deep is the turtle when the drone is 35 ft above the water? Show your work.

SOLUTION _____

3 The graph shows the acres of corn a farmer has left to plant. The equation $A = 4{,}000 - 180d$ gives the acres of soybeans a neighbor has left to plant as a function of time in days. Which statement is true?

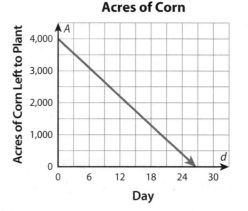

Acres of Corn

CONSIDER THIS . . .
What does 4,000 mean in this context?

A Both farmers have 4,000 acres to plant on Day 0.

B The corn farmer plants more acres per day than the soybean farmer.

C The corn farmer will finish planting first.

D From days 1–20, the soybean farmer always has more to plant.

Bianca chose B as the correct answer. How might she have gotten that answer?

4 The graph shows a nonlinear function.

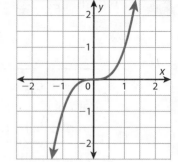

a. Write the equation of a second function that has a constant rate of change of 0 and passes through (2, 1). What does its graph look like?

b. What is the difference in outputs of the two functions at $x = 0$? Explain.

c. How many times do the graphs of the functions intersect? Explain.

d. For inputs between -1 and 0.5, which function has greater outputs? Explain.

5 Teff is a small grain. A traditional recipe for Ethiopian flatbread calls for $1\frac{1}{2}$ cups of water to 1 cup of teff flour. An online search shows the proportion used in a modern recipe. Which recipe has a greater rate of water to teff flour?

A   Traditional recipe

B   Modern recipe

C   The recipes have the same rate.

D   Not enough information is provided.

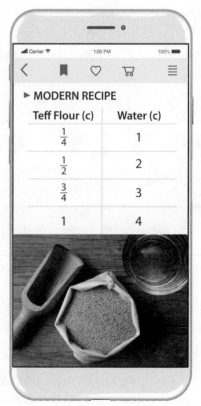

▶ MODERN RECIPE

Teff Flour (c)	Water (c)
$\frac{1}{4}$	1
$\frac{1}{2}$	2
$\frac{3}{4}$	3
1	4

6 Tell whether each statement is *Always*, *Sometimes*, or *Never* true.

	Always	Sometimes	Never
a. If two increasing linear functions have the same rate of change and different initial values, their graphs will intersect.	○	○	○
b. If the graphs of two linear functions intersect, one function has a positive rate of change and one function has a negative rate of change.	○	○	○
c. If two proportional relationships have the same rate of change, they are the same function.	○	○	○
d. The graphs of a linear function and a nonlinear function intersect exactly once.	○	○	○

7 **Math Journal** Represent the same linear function in two different ways. Explain how you know your functions are the same.

✓ **End of Lesson Checklist**

☐ **INTERACTIVE GLOSSARY** Write a new entry for *ascend*. Tell what it means when an object *ascends*. How are *ascend* and *descend* related?

☐ **SELF CHECK** Go back to the Unit 4 Opener and see what you can check off.

Dear Family,

This week your student is learning how to analyze and interpret graphs of functions. Students will learn to write descriptions of functions based on their graphs. These **qualitative descriptions** of functions use the shapes and directions of the graphs, and often do not rely on exact numbers or quantities.

Many of the graphs in this lesson represent a quantity that changes over time. By analyzing the graph from left to right, students learn the *story* of that change. Students will solve problems like the one below.

The graph shows the temperature for a day in a city. Write a qualitative description of the temperature throughout the day.

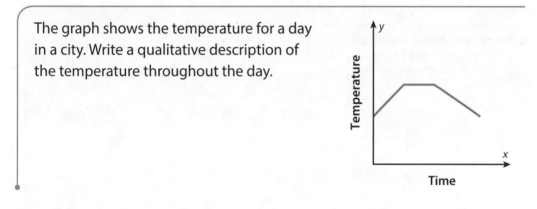

➤ **ONE WAY** to describe the function is to break it into sections.

The graph is made up of three line segments. The first segment slants up from left to right. This shows that the temperature increased at a constant rate early in the day. The second segment is horizontal. So, in the middle of the day, the temperature did not change. The third segment slants downward, so the temperature decreased at a constant rate at the end of the day.

➤ **ANOTHER WAY** is to write a description as you *read* the graph from left to right.

The graph shows the temperature increasing steadily for the first part of the day. Then the temperature stays the same for a little while, and then it drops at a consistent rate later in the day.

Using either method, the descriptions explain temperature rising, staying the same, and then falling over the course of the day.

 Use the next page to start a conversation about functional relationships.

Activity Thinking About Analyzing Functional Relationships Qualitatively

➤ **Do this activity together to investigate functional relationships in the real world.**

Qualitative descriptions of functional relationships tell stories about how two quantities change in relation to each other. This graph models how one quantity increases rapidly at a constant rate, then stays the same, and then increases more slowly, with respect to the other quantity. One example of a situation this could represent is distance traveled as a function of time, where a person sprints at a constant rate, stops to rest, and then jogs at a slower pace.

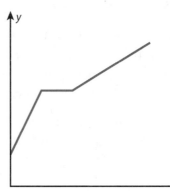

 Can you think of another situation, or story, that the graph could represent?

Explore Analyzing Graphs of Functions

Runner's Routine

Stretch   Walk   Run

Previously, you learned how to interpret the slope and *y*-intercept of the graph of a linear function. In this lesson, you will analyze and interpret the overall shape of the graph of a function.

➤ **Use what you know to try to solve the problem below.**

Efia warms up and goes for a run. The graph shows her distance from home as a function of time. Which sections of the graph represent Efia stretching, walking, or running?

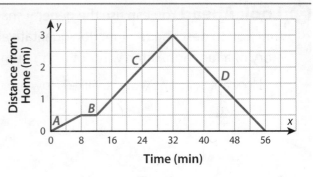

TRY IT

DISCUSS IT

Ask: How did you use the graph to answer the question?

Share: I used the graph by . . .

◎ **Learning Target**   SMP 1, SMP 2, SMP 3, SMP 4, SMP 5, SMP 6, SMP 7
Describe qualitatively the functional relationship between two quantities by analyzing a graph (e.g., where the function is increasing or decreasing, linear or nonlinear). Sketch a graph that exhibits the qualitative features of a function that has been described verbally.

CONNECT IT

1 Look Back What activity does each section of the graph represent? Explain.

2 Look Ahead You can use the general shape and direction of a graph of a function to describe the function qualitatively. A **qualitative description** tells the story of a function, often without using numbers or exact quantities.

a. How are sections A and C alike? How are they different?

b. How are sections C and D alike? How are they different?

c. Section A represents Efia's distance for times from 0 to 8 minutes. You can write these times as $0 < x < 8$. This interval includes every value of x that is both greater than 0 *and* less than 8. Is Efia running toward home or away from home in the interval $32 < x < 56$? How do you know?

3 Reflect Explain why you do not need to know Efia's exact speed in order to determine when she is stretching, walking, or running.

Prepare for Analyzing Functional Relationships Qualitatively

1 Think about what you know about nonlinear functions. Fill in each box. Use words, numbers, and pictures. Show as many ideas as you can.

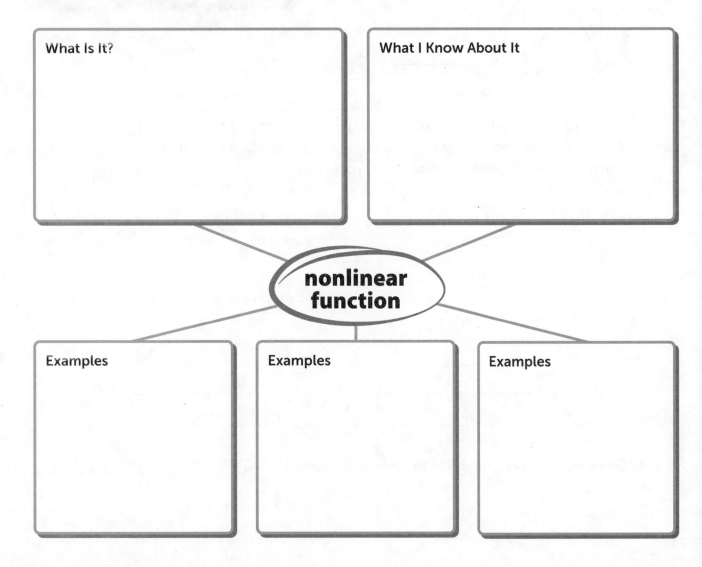

What Is It?

What I Know About It

nonlinear function

Examples

Examples

Examples

2 Tell whether each function is *linear* or *nonlinear*.

a.

x	y
1	2
2	4
3	8

b.

c. $y = 3x^2$

3 Carissa rents a motorboat to fish in a local lake. The graph shows her distance from the dock where she rented the boat as a function of time.

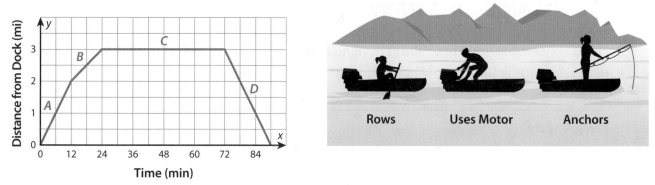

Rows   Uses Motor   Anchors

a. Carissa rows the boat part of the time and uses the motor part of the time. When she fishes, she anchors the boat in one place. Describe what Carissa is doing in each section of the graph. Show your work.

SOLUTION _____

_____

b. Check your answer to problem 3a. Show your work.

Develop Using Graphs to Describe Functions Qualitatively

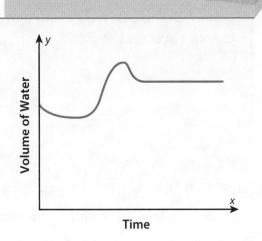

dam

➤ **Read and try to solve the problem below.**

Dara is tracking the amount of water in a lake. The lake is formed by a dam across a river. The graph shows the volume of water in the lake as a function of time since the beginning of the month. Tell a story about how the volume of water changes over time.

Volume of Water

Time

TRY IT

DISCUSS IT

Ask: What words did you use to describe the change in the volume of water?

Share: I used the words . . .

➤ **Explore different ways to use graphs to describe functions qualitatively.**

Dara is tracking the amount of water in a lake. The lake is formed by a dam across a river. The graph shows the volume of water in the lake as a function of time since the beginning of the month. Tell a story about how the volume of water changes over time.

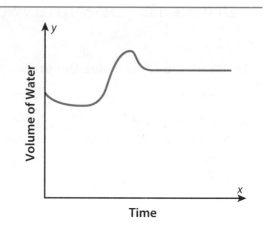

Analyze It

You can analyze each change in **direction** and **shape** of the graph.

The graph starts as a **downward curve**. The volume of water **decreases at a varying rate**.

The graph then **curves upward** more steeply, almost linear. The volume of water **increases at a varying rate**.

The graph **curves downward** again, showing a **decrease** in volume, again **at a varying rate**.

The graph ends with a **horizontal line segment**. The volume of water **does not change**.

Solve It

You can use your analysis to tell a story for the situation.

You can use personal knowledge to add details and make a richer story.

At the beginning of the month, the volume of water in the lake decreases slowly as the dam allows water to drain. Then, there is a storm and volume increases almost steadily as it rains. After the storm, the dam allows water to drain faster than it did earlier. Finally, the dam stops draining and the volume remains constant.

➤ **Use the problem from the previous page to help you understand how to use graphs to describe functions qualitatively.**

1 **a.** Look at **Analyze It**. How can you describe the graph when the function is increasing, decreasing, or constant?

b. How does the rate of change of a function differ between a linear section and a nonlinear section?

2 Which function increases slowly at first and then gets faster? Which function increases quickly at first and then slows down? Explain.

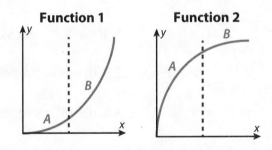

Function 1

Function 2

3 Describe how you can use the graph of a function to help tell a story about the function. What else can help you tell a story?

4 **Reflect** Think about all the models and strategies you have discussed today. Describe how one of them helped you better understand how to use graphs to describe functions qualitatively.

Apply It

➤ **Use what you learned to solve these problems.**

5 Use the graph to write a qualitative description of the function.

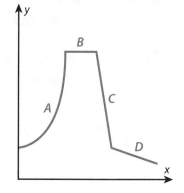

6 The graph shows the effectiveness of a dose of medication as a function of time. Which statements are true? Select all that apply.

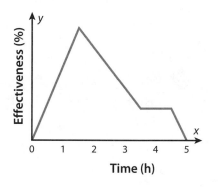

A For $0 < x < 1.5$, the effectiveness increases at a constant rate.

B For $2.5 < x < 3.5$, the effectiveness decreases at a varying rate.

C For $3.5 < x < 4.5$, the effectiveness stays the same.

D For $0 < x < 3.5$, the effectiveness is increasing.

E For $2 < x < 5$, the effectiveness is decreasing.

7 The graph shows a driver's distance from home as a function of time. Oliver wrote this description: A driver drives away from home at a constant rate. She then drives at a slightly slower constant rate for a short time before gradually slowing down and stopping. Does Oliver's story match the graph? Explain.

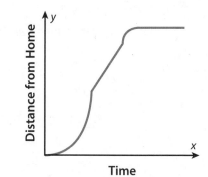

Practice Using Graphs to Describe Functions Qualitatively

➤ **Study the Example showing how to use a graph to describe a function qualitatively. Then solve problems 1–7.**

Example

The graph shows Mora's height above the ground as a function of time as she climbs up to a platform and rides a zip line down. Describe what the graph shows.

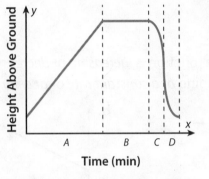

Mora's height from the ground increases at a constant rate as she climbs up to the zipline platform. Her height above ground stays constant while she waits on the platform. Then, her height above ground decreases slowly at first and then more quickly as her speed increases as she rides the zip line down. Her height above ground slows down again as she finishes her ride and ends up at the height at which she started.

1 How does the graph in the Example show that Mora's height above ground stays constant for a while?

2 How does the graph in the Example show that Mora's height above ground decreases at a varying rate rather than a constant rate?

3 For each section, tell whether the graph in the Example is *increasing*, *decreasing*, or *neither*. Then tell whether the section of the graph is *linear* or *nonlinear*.

a. Section *A*

b. Section *B*

c. Section *C*

d. Section *D*

> **Vocabulary**
>
> **rate**
> a ratio that tells the number of units of one quantity for 1 unit of another quantity.

④ Describe the graph of the function for each interval shown by the dashed lines.

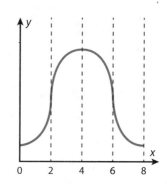

⑤ Tell whether the function is *increasing* or *decreasing*. Then tell whether the function is changing *at a constant rate* or *at a varying rate*.

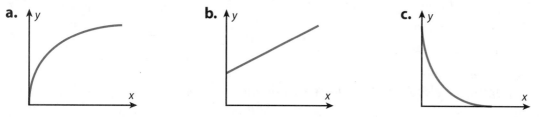

a. **b.** **c.**

⑥ This graph shows the weight of a puppy over a 6-month period. Deon says that the puppy's weight increased at a faster rate at first than it did at the end of the 6 months. Do you agree? Explain.

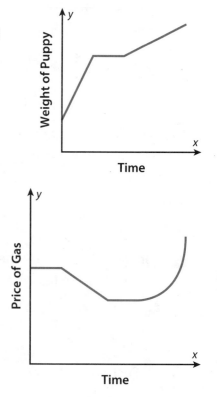

⑦ The graph shows gasoline prices over time. Tell a story about how gas prices change over time.

Develop Sketching Graphs of Functions from Qualitative Descriptions

➤ **Read and try to solve the problem below.**

Ellie rides her skateboard along a curved ramp. She starts at one end and moves down the ramp at a quick constant rate. She then rides up to the other end of the ramp at a slower constant rate. She stops to change direction before riding back down the ramp to where she began, moving at the fastest constant rate of the ride. Sketch a graph representing Ellie's distance from her starting point on the ramp as a function of time.

Half pipe skateboard ramp

TRY IT   **Math Toolkit** graph paper, straightedges

DISCUSS IT

Ask: How do you know your graph is reasonable?

Share: I know it is reasonable because . . .

➤ **Explore different ways to sketch graphs of functions from qualitative descriptions.**

Ellie rides her skateboard along a curved ramp. She starts at one end and moves down the ramp at a quick constant rate. She then rides up to the other end of the ramp at a slower constant rate. She stops to change direction before riding back down the ramp to where she began, moving at the fastest constant rate of the ride. Sketch a graph representing Ellie's distance from her starting point on the ramp as a function of time.

Analyze It

You can break the story into sections and analyze each.

Section A: Ellie starts at a quick **constant** rate, **increasing** the distance from her starting point. This section is **linear** with a **positive slope**.

Section B: Ellie rides up the other end of the ramp at a slower **constant** rate than in section A, **increasing** her distance from the starting point. This section is **linear**. It has a **positive slope** but is not as steep as in section A.

Section C: Ellie stops. Her distance from where she started **does not change**. This section is horizontal. It has a **slope of zero**. She is at the farthest distance from where she started.

Section D: Ellie rides back at the fastest **constant** rate of the ride, **decreasing** her distance from where she started. This is a **linear** section with a steep **negative slope**. Ellie ends back at her starting point.

Model It

You can use your analysis to sketch a graph.

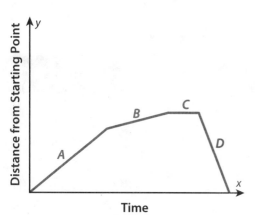

➤ **Use the problem from the previous page to help you understand how to sketch graphs of functions from qualitative descriptions.**

1 Look at **Analyze It**. Why is section *B* described as less steep than section *A*?

2 Look at **Model It**. Why does the graph start and end on the horizontal axis?

3 Suppose the rates of change in the problem were not constant. How would this affect the graph?

4 A classmate sketches the graph shown to model Ellie's ride. Can his sketch and the sketch in **Model It** both be right? Explain.

5 **Reflect** Think about all the models and strategies you have discussed today. Describe how one of them helped you better understand how to sketch graphs of functions from qualitative descriptions.

Apply It

➤ **Use what you learned to solve these problems.**

6 A function is decreasing at a constant rate. Then it keeps decreasing but starts to slow down. Then it stops decreasing and remains constant. Sketch a graph of the function.

7 Ayana starts driving home from work at a constant speed. She stops on the way to pick up a friend. At her friend's house, she realizes she forgot her cell phone. She drives back to work at a constant speed, parks her car, and goes in to get her phone. Why is the graph of the situation incorrect? Sketch a correct graph to model the story.

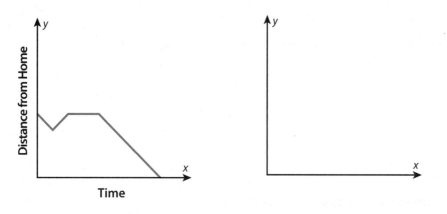

8 Josephine gives her dog a bath. She puts the dog in the tub and then adds water to the tub. The height of the water in the tub is a function of time, x. For $0 < x < 10$, Josephine fills the tub at a constant rate and then turns off the water. For $10 < x < 25$, she washes her dog. When Josephine finishes, she opens the drain. For $25 < x < 30$, the water drains at a constant rate. Sketch what a graph of this function could look like.

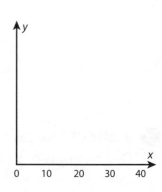

©Curriculum Associates, LLC Copying is not permitted.

Practice Sketching Graphs of Functions from Qualitative Descriptions

➤ **Study the Example showing how to sketch a graph of a function from a qualitative description. Then solve problems 1–5.**

Example

Salvador leaves home and walks to the store at a constant rate. He is at the store for a short time and then starts back home at a constant rate. On the way home, he stops at a friend's house for a few minutes. Then he walks home at a varying rate, quickly at first and then more slowly. Sketch a graph of Salvador's distance from home as a function of time.

Break the story into sections.

A Salvador walks from his home to the store at a constant rate.

B He is at the store for a short time.

C He heads back toward home at a constant rate.

D He stops at a friend's house.

E He walks the rest of the way at a varying rate. He walks quickly at first and then gets slower.

1. **a.** In the Example graph, why are sections B and D horizontal segments?

   b. In the Example graph, why is section E a curve?

2. A function is decreasing at a varying rate. It decreases slowly at first and then gets faster before it slows down again. Sketch a graph of the function.

3 Sketch a graph of a function that matches the qualitative description.

a. Increasing at a varying rate first slowly, then faster

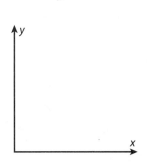

b. Decreasing at a varying rate first quickly, then more slowly

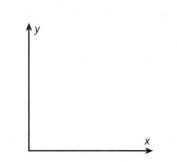

c. Decreasing at a varying rate first slowly, then faster

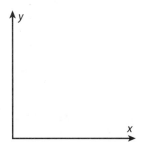

d. Increasing at a varying rate first quickly, then more slowly

4 Charles and Carlota are riding bikes up a hill. The first part of the trail is rough, so they ride at a slow constant rate for 20 minutes. Halfway up, they stop and rest for 5 minutes. Then they continue at a slightly faster constant rate for 15 minutes. After reaching the highest part of the trail, they immediately ride down at a constant rate and reach the bottom in only 15 minutes. Sketch a graph of Charles and Carlota's distance from the bottom of the hill as a function of time.

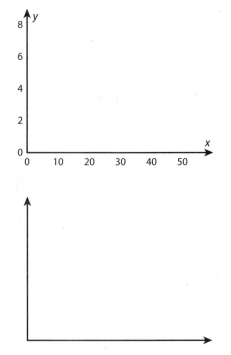

5 As students enter an empty classroom, the noise level rises at a varying rate, slowly at first and gradually rising faster. When all the students have arrived, the noise remains at the same level. Then when the teacher arrives, the noise decreases at a very quick constant rate, until it is silent again. Sketch a graph that shows the noise level as a function of time.

Refine Analyzing Functional Relationships Qualitatively

➤ **Complete the Example below. Then solve problems 1–9.**

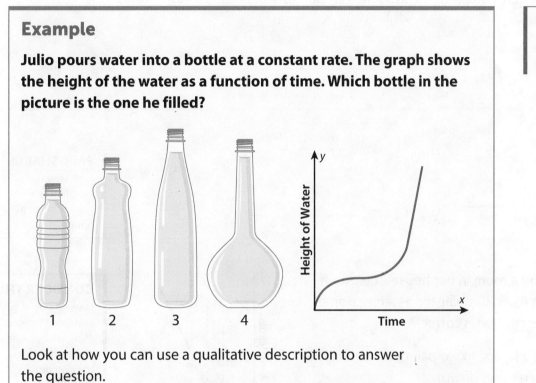

Example

Julio pours water into a bottle at a constant rate. The graph shows the height of the water as a function of time. Which bottle in the picture is the one he filled?

Look at how you can use a qualitative description to answer the question.

The height of the water rises at a varying rate. It rises quickly at first, then more slowly, then quickly again. Then it rises very quickly at a constant rate.

SOLUTION _____

CONSIDER THIS . . .
Would water rise faster or slower as a bottle gets wider?

PAIR/SHARE
How does the width of the bottle Julio filled change from bottom to top?

Apply It

1 Write a qualitative description of the function.

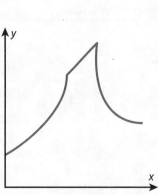

CONSIDER THIS . . .
Remember to consider both the direction and shape of each section of the graph.

PAIR/SHARE
How would your description change if the linear section was horizontal?

2 The temperature of food in a slow cooker starts at room temperature. It then increases at a constant rate for 4 hours. The slow cooker then keeps the food at the same temperature for the next hour. Then the food is put into the refrigerator. Its temperature decreases quickly at first. Then it decreases more slowly. After 3 hours in the refrigerator, the food is colder than it was before it was cooked. Sketch a graph that shows the temperature of the food as a function of time.

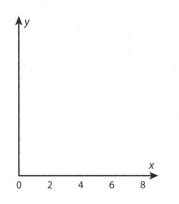

CONSIDER THIS...
For $5 < x < 8$, is the function increasing or decreasing? Is it linear or nonlinear?

PAIR/SHARE
How would your graph be different if the food cooled down to room temperature?

3 Akiko is painting a room in her house. The graph shows the area Akiko has painted as a function of time. Which description is correct?

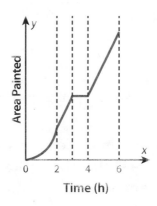

A For the first 2 hours, Akiko paints very quickly at first, but then slows down.

B For $2 < x < 3$, Akiko paints at a constant rate.

C For $3 < x < 4$, Akiko continues painting at the same rate.

D For the last 2 hours, Akiko paints at a constant rate, but much more slowly than earlier in the day.

Andres chose A as the correct answer. How might he have gotten that answer?

CONSIDER THIS...
Look closely at each section of the graph. Make sure you think about all the details in the description.

PAIR/SHARE
How would you change the other answers to make them correct?

4 What information about a function should a qualitative description provide? Select all that apply.

A The equation for the function

B The direction of the graph in each interval or section

C The rate of change for each linear section of the graph

D The shape of the graph (linear or nonlinear)

E The value of the function at any given point

F Whether the function is changing at a constant rate

5 The graphs represent parts of Jesse's trip to or from school on different days. Next to each graph, write the number (I, II, III, IV) of the description that *best* matches the graph. Assume both Jesse and the bus are moving at constant rates.

I. Jesse walks to the bus stop, waits for the bus, and then takes the bus to school.

II. Jesse waits for his father to pick him up after school, and his father drives him home.

III. After school, Jesse walks to a friend's house, which is on the way home. He stays there until he takes a bus home.

IV. Jesse walks from home to the bus stop. He pauses to check in his bag for his notebook. He runs back home to get his notebook.

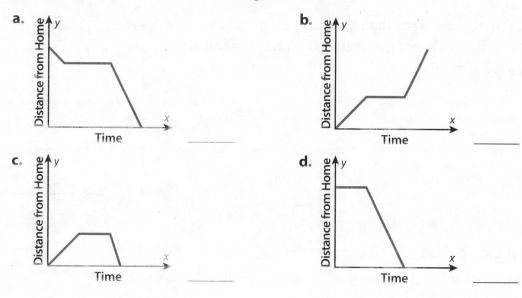

a. Distance from Home / Time _____

b. Distance from Home / Time _____

c. Distance from Home / Time _____

d. Distance from Home / Time _____

6 In a graph that shows the distance a boat travels as a function of time, why would a vertical section not make sense?

7 Write the correct word in each blank to describe the function at the right.

When $4 < x < 6$, the function is _____ at a _____ rate.

8 Sketch the graph of a function that fits the description.

- Over the interval $0 < x < 4$, the value of the function does not change.

- Over the interval $4 < x < 6$, the function is decreasing at a varying rate, first very quickly and then more slowly.

- Over the interval $6 < x < 8$, the function increases at a constant rate.

9 **Math Journal** Think about a situation in which your distance from a starting point changes over time. Sketch a graph of the situation and write a qualitative description.

End of Lesson Checklist

☐ **INTERACTIVE GLOSSARY** Find the entry for *qualitative description*. Tell what it means to describe a function qualitatively.

☐ **SELF CHECK** Go back to the Unit 4 Opener and see what you can check off.

SMP 1 Make sense of problems and persevere in solving them.

Study an Example Problem and Solution

➤ **Read this problem involving a functional relationship. Then look at one student's solution to this problem on the following pages.**

Planning a Car Chase

Luis and Akiko are stunt coordinators for a new action movie. Their next task is to plan a car chase scene. Read this email from Luis, and help Akiko come up with a response.

Delete   Archive   Reply   Reply All   Forward

To: Akiko
Subject: Car Chase Scene at the Port

Hi Akiko,

We need to start planning the car chase scene that will take place at the port. This scene is pretty short and will only take about 4 minutes of screen time.

Here are some stunts we might want to include.

Stunt Type	Notes
Barrel roll	Car does spiral rotation in mid-air; starts by going off a ramp at 40 miles per hour
Fast acceleration	Start from a full stop; increase speed to 80 miles per hour
Handbrake turn	Slow down to 25 miles per hour; pull handbrake to do a 180° turn and drive away in opposite direction
J-turn	Go into reverse and increase speed to 35 miles per hour; do a 180° turn; then drive away in forward direction
Swerving	Swerve while keeping a constant speed

HERE'S WHAT I NEED FROM YOU:
· Choose at least three stunts from the list. Arrange them in a logical sequence.
· Sketch a graph that approximates how the speed of the car will change over time as the stunts are performed. For now, estimates are fine.
· Write a description of what each section of the graph represents.

Thanks!

Luis

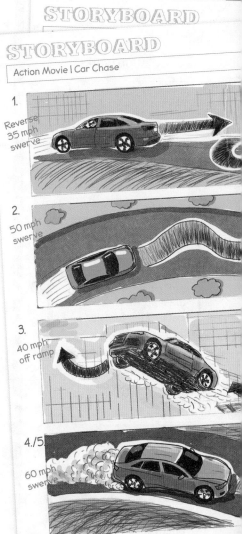

STORYBOARD
STORYBOARD
Action Movie | Car Chase

1. Reverse 35 mph swerve

2. 50 mph swerve

3. 40 mph off ramp

4./5. 60 mph swerve

Storyboards are graphics that tell a story. For a car chase scene, a storyboard shows the sequence of the car's movements.

One Student's Solution

Problem-Solving Checklist ✓

☐ Tell what is known.

☐ Tell what the problem is asking.

☐ Show all your work.

☐ Show that the solution works.

First, I have to choose some stunts and arrange them in a logical order.

I need at least three stunts from Luis's list. I choose a barrel roll, a J-turn, and swerving.

Since the chase is at a port, I think it would also be cool to have the car drive up a ramp and onto a ship.

I will use this order: (1) J-turn, (2) swerving, (3) barrel roll, (4) more swerving, and (5) ramp to ship.

Next, I will sketch and describe a graph for the first stunt, the J-turn.

For this stunt, the driver starts from a stop, and the car's speed increases to 35 miles per hour in reverse. The car's speed probably stays constant while the 180° turn occurs. Then I want the car's speed to increase from 35 to 50 miles per hour as it pulls away from the turn.

NOTICE THAT . . .
You can show that the car is speeding up by using an interval on the graph in which the value of the function increases.

Now, I will add the second stunt, swerving, to the graph.

The car will stay at a constant speed of 50 miles per hour while it swerves around other cars.

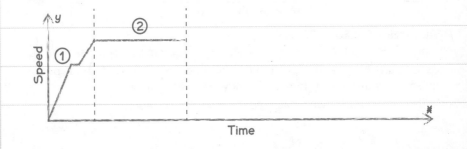

NOTICE THAT . . .
A horizontal segment on the graph shows that the car is traveling at a constant speed.

Then, I will describe the third stunt, the barrel roll, and add it to the graph.

For this stunt, I will have the car slow down to 20 miles per hour and then speed up to jump off the ramp at 40 miles per hour. The car's speed probably stays constant while the barrel roll occurs. Then I want the car to speed up to 60 miles per hour after it lands.

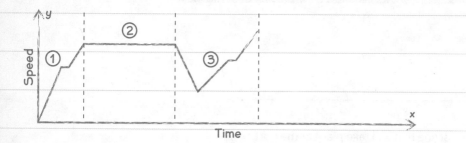

Finally, I will add and describe the last two stunts: more swerving and driving onto the ship.

This time, the car will stay at a constant speed of 60 miles per hour while it swerves around cargo containers.

Next, I will have the car slow down to 35 miles per hour and keep this speed as it approaches and goes up the ramp to the ship. Once the car is on the ship, its speed quickly drops to 0 miles per hour when the driver hits the brakes.

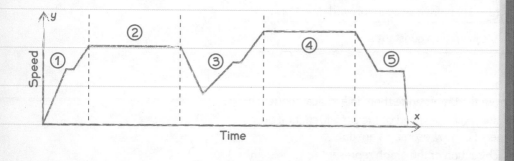

Try Another Approach

➤ **There are many ways to solve problems. Think about how you might solve the Planning a Car Chase problem in a different way.**

Planning a Car Chase

Luis and Akiko are stunt coordinators for a new action movie. Their next task is to plan a car chase scene. Read this email from Luis, and help Akiko come up with a response.

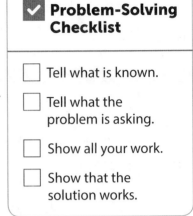

To: Akiko
Subject: Car Chase Scene at the Port

Hi Akiko,

We need to start planning the car chase scene that will take place at the port. This scene is pretty short and will only take about 4 minutes of screen time.

Here are some stunts we might want to include.

Stunt Type	Notes
Barrel roll	Car does spiral rotation in mid-air; starts by going off a ramp at 40 miles per hour
Fast acceleration	Start from a full stop; increase speed to 80 miles per hour
Handbrake turn	Slow down to 25 miles per hour; pull handbrake to do a 180° turn and drive away in opposite direction
J-turn	Go into reverse and increase speed to 35 miles per hour; do a 180° turn; then drive away in forward direction
Swerving	Swerve while keeping a constant speed

HERE'S WHAT I NEED FROM YOU:
• Choose at least three stunts from the list. Arrange them in a logical sequence.
• Sketch a graph that approximates how the speed of the car will change over time as the stunts are performed. For now, estimates are fine.
• Write a description of what each section of the graph represents.

Thanks!

Luis

Plan It

➤ **Answer these questions to help you start thinking about a plan.**

a. Which stunts will you use for the car chase, and how will you sequence them?

b. How will you use a graph to show the changes in speed for each stunt?

Solve It

➤ **Find a different solution for the Planning a Car Chase problem. Show all your work on a separate sheet of paper. You may want to use the Problem-Solving Tips to get started.**

PROBLEM-SOLVING TIPS

Math Toolkit graph paper, straightedges

Key Terms

| function | interval |
| qualitative description | rate of change |

Sentence Starters

- My graph shows that the car is speeding up fastest when . . .

- I can use the graph to show times when the car is slowing down by . . .

- I can use the graph to show times when the car is traveling at a constant speed by . . .

Reflect

Use Mathematical Practices

As you work through the problem, discuss these questions with a partner.

- **Use Models** How does your graph show that the relationship between time and the car's speed is a function?

- **Reason Mathematically** What does the steepness of the graph in different intervals indicate about how the car's speed is changing?

Discuss Models and Strategies

➤ **Read the problem. Write a solution on a separate sheet of paper. Remember, there can be lots of ways to solve a problem.**

Budgeting for Background Actors

Andres is an assistant director working on the new action movie. He needs some information about the movie's extras, or background actors. Read this email Andres sent to Fernando, a production assistant, and help Fernando respond.

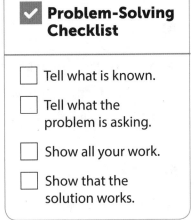
| Delete | Archive | | Reply | Reply All | Forward |

To: Fernando
Subject: Background actors

Hey Fernando,

I just finished the casting call notice for our background (BG) actors. It gives the regular and holiday pay rates. Now I am working on the filming schedule, and I could use some help. Our total budget for paying the BG actors is $351,800.

The director wants a core group of 27 BG actors for the scenes filmed inside the bank. These actors will work a total of 7 days for 8 hours each day. One of these days is a holiday.

We will also have another group of 150 BG actors for the crowd scenes. These actors can work up to 8 hours a day. Assume that none of them will work holidays.

Casting Call

Background Actors Needed for Action Movie!

$21.75/hr

Double pay rate for Holidays!

WHAT I NEED YOU TO DO:

- Decide how many hours the BG actors for the crowd scenes will work each day. Use your best judgment.
- Write an equation that shows how the total amount we will pay BG actors depends on the number of days we film crowd scenes.
- Explain what each number or variable in your equation represents.
- Finally, determine the greatest number of days we can afford to film crowd scenes, based on our budget.

Thanks so much for your help!

Andres

Plan It and Solve It

➤ **Find a solution to the Budgeting for Background Actors problem.**

Write a detailed plan and support your answer. Be sure to include:

- your suggestion for the number of hours the background actors for the crowd scenes will work each day.

- an equation that models the total amount paid to the background actors based on the number of days filming crowd scenes.

- an explanation of what each number or variable in your equation represents.

- the greatest number of days the film crew can afford to film crowd scenes.

PROBLEM-SOLVING TIPS

Math Toolkit graph paper, straightedges

Key Terms

function	initial value	input
linear function	nonlinear function	output
rate of change	slope	y-intercept

Questions

- How much does a background actor get paid for working 8 hours on a holiday?

- What is the total amount the core group of background actors gets paid for filming the scenes in the bank?

Reflect

Use Mathematical Practices As you work through the problem, discuss these questions with a partner.

- **Use Structure** Does your equation represent a linear or nonlinear function? How do you know?

- **Be Precise** Should you round up or round down to the nearest whole number when determining the greatest number of days the film crew can afford to film crowd scenes? Explain.

Persevere On Your Own

➤ **Read the problem. Write a solution on a separate sheet of paper.**

Choosing a VFX Company

Kazuko is the visual effects (VFX) supervisor for the new action movie. She is considering bids from two visual effects companies: Moonshot and Lemon Cloud. Read this email from Kazuko to her assistant, Xavier. Then help Xavier respond to Kazuko's request.

Delete   Archive   Reply   Reply All   Forward

To: Xavier
Subject: VFX bids for museum chase sequence

Hi Xavier,

The companies bidding on the VFX for the museum chase sequence have sent us their pricing information. Unfortunately, the companies have used different formats to show their pricing. This makes it a little difficult to compare them.

Moonshot VFX

Medium Difficulty Pricing	
VFX Time (s)	Price ($)
10	54,000
20	104,000
30	154,000
40	204,000

Lemon Cloud VFX
Medium Difficulty VFX Pricing

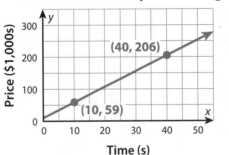

We estimate that we will probably need between 120 seconds and 130 seconds of medium-difficulty VFX for the chase sequence.

WHAT I NEED FROM YOU:

• Convert the pricing information from each company to the same format (table, graph, or equation).

• Recommend a company for the VFX, and explain your choice.

• In case we go over our original time estimate, calculate the cost per second of VFX for each company.

Thank you!

Kazuko

Solve It

➤ **Find a solution to the Choosing a VFX Company problem.**

- Use the same representation (table, graph, or equation) to model the pricing information from each VFX company.

- Recommend a VFX company for the museum chase sequence, and explain why you chose that company.

- Determine how much each company charges for each additional second of VFX.

Reflect

Use Mathematical Practices After you complete the problem, choose one of these questions to discuss with a partner.

- **Use Models** Which representation did you use to model the pricing functions, and why did you choose that representation?

- **Make an Argument** Would your recommendation for the choice of VFX company change if only 50 seconds of VFX were needed for the chase sequence? Explain.

Computer-generated imagery, or CGI, is often used to create visual effects in movies. CGI is easier to control and of a higher quality than visual effects created in other ways, such as by using miniatures.

In this unit you learned to . . .

Skill	Lesson(s)
Understand that a function is a type of rule where each input results in exactly one output.	**15, 16**
Identify relationships that are functions from different representations, such as descriptions, tables, graphs, or equations.	**15, 16**
Determine whether a function is linear or nonlinear.	**15, 16**
Identify and interpret the rate of change and initial value for a linear function.	**16**
Write an equation to model a linear function.	**16**
Compare two functions represented in different ways, such as in words, with tables, as equations, or as graphs.	**17**
Use a graph to describe a function qualitatively.	**18**
Sketch a graph of a function from a qualitative description.	**18**
Make connections between different representations of functions by explaining how they are similar and different.	**15–18**

Think about what you have learned.

➤ **Use words, numbers, and drawings.**

1 Two important things I learned are . . .

2 I worked hardest to learn how to . . .

3 One thing I could do better is . . .

Vocabulary Review

➤ **Review the unit vocabulary. Put a check mark by terms you can use in speaking and writing. Look up the meaning of any terms you do not know.**

Math Vocabulary		Academic Vocabulary
☐ function	☐ output (of a function)	☐ ascend
☐ initial value	☐ qualitative description	☐ constant
☐ input (of a function)		☐ descend
☐ linear function		☐ respectively
☐ nonlinear function		☐ varying

➤ **Use the unit vocabulary to answer these questions.**

1 Antonyms are words that mean the opposite of a given word.
What pairs of academic terms in the list are antonyms? What do the terms mean?

2 Sketch and label a graph of a linear function and a graph of a nonlinear function. Then, use at least four unit math or academic vocabulary words to explain the similarities and differences between a linear function and a nonlinear function. Underline each term you use.

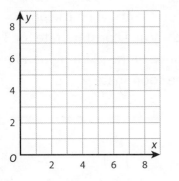

3 Rephrase this sentence in your own words: Daria, her mother, and her brother ran 5, 4, and 3 miles, respectively.

➤ **Use what you have learned to complete these problems.**

1 Brianna says that the graph represents a function. Is Brianna correct? Explain your reasoning.

SOLUTION _____

_____

_____

2 Two friends are biking. Greta starts at mile marker 5 on a bike trail and is biking at a speed of 12 miles per hour. The table shows the mile marker Shayla reaches after biking x hours. What is the difference in the initial values of the functions? Record your answer on the grid. Then fill in the bubbles.

Hours Biking	0	0.5	1	1.5	2
Mile Marker	8	15	22	29	36

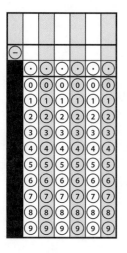

3 Javier goes to the county fair. He pays to enter the fair and also pays for each ticket he needs for games, rides, and food. The equation $y = 1.75x + 5$ represents how much Javier spends at the county fair. Which statements about the function are true? Choose all the correct answers.

A The total amount Javier spends is a function of the number of tickets Javier purchases.

B The initial value represents the cost of one ticket.

C The rate of change is 5.

D The variable x represents the number of tickets Javier purchases for games, rides, and food.

E The initial value is 5.

4 Karina buys a painting. The price of the painting slowly starts to decrease at a constant rate for 3 years. It then increases faster during the next 2 years and stays the same price for 2 years. Then the price increases slowly at a constant rate for 3 years. Sketch the price of the painting as a function of time in the coordinate plane.

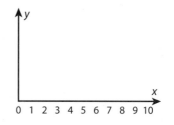

5 The graph shows a function. The equation that represents the function is $y = x^2 + 1$. Tell whether the function is linear or nonlinear. Explain your reasoning.

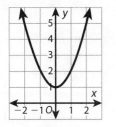

SOLUTION _____

_____

_____

_____

_____

6 Miles and kilometers are two different scales for measuring distances. A 5-kilometer race is approximately 3.1 miles, and a 10-kilometer race is approximately 6.2 miles. Write an equation that shows the approximate distance in kilometers as a function of the distance in miles. Show your work.

7 The manager of a juice bar checks the price of a certain fruit. Company A charges $10.50 per pound. The graph shows the price that Company B charges.

Company B

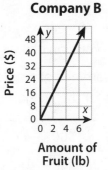

Amount of Fruit (lb)

Decide if each statement about the two functions is true or false. Select *True* or *False* for each statement.

	True	False
a. It costs $80 to buy 10 pounds of fruit from Company B.	○	○
b. The initial value for each function is different.	○	○
c. Company B charges $2.50 more per pound than Company A.	○	○
d. It costs $84 to buy 8 pounds from Company A.	○	○

SOLUTION _____

Performance Task

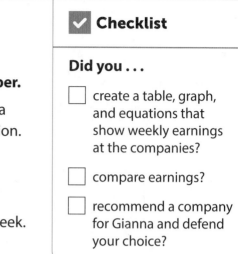
➤ **Answer the questions and show all your work on separate paper.**

Gianna receives job offers from three companies for a position as a salesperson. Each company offers a weekly salary plus a commission. The commission is the amount of money she earns based on weekly sales.

- Company A pays its employees a weekly salary of $830. Each employee earns a commission of 0.03 times their sales for the week.

- The table shows the earnings of employees at Company B as a function of their sales for the week.

Sales ($)	0	500	1,000	1,500	2,000
Earnings ($)	?	840	865	890	915

- The graph shows the earnings of employees at Company C as a function of their sales for the week.

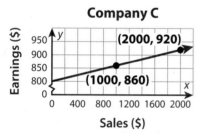

Company C

Gianna needs to choose one of these job offers. To make her decision, she predicts that she will have $0, $500, $1,000, $1,500, or $2,000 in sales each week.

Help Gianna choose Company A, B, or C. Write an equation for each company to represent her earnings as a function of her sales for the week. Then create a table and graph comparing her weekly earnings at Companies A, B, and C. Recommend a company for Gianna. Explain your reasoning.

Reflect

Use Mathematical Practices After you complete the task, choose one of the following questions to answer.

- **Use Reasoning** How did you use the different information to determine Gianna's predicted weekly earnings at each company?

- **Model** Was your table, graph, or equation most helpful to compare weekly earnings at each company?

Set 1 Find Unit Rates Involving Ratios of Fractions

➤ **Find the unit rate. Show your work.**

1 A horse travels $3\frac{1}{4}$ miles in $\frac{1}{4}$ hour. What is the horse's speed in miles per hour?

2 A park has an area of $\frac{1}{6}$ mi². On a map, the park has an area of $1\frac{1}{4}$ cm². On the map, how many square centimeters represent 1 mi²?

Set 2 Proportional Relationships

➤ **Solve the problems. Show your work.**

1 Show whether x and y are in a proportional relationship.

x	1	2	3	6
y	2.5	5	7.5	12

2 Find the constant of proportionality for the line shown on the graph.

3 The amount of money Luana earns for tutoring is proportional to the time she spends tutoring. She earns $24 for tutoring $1\frac{1}{2}$ hours. What is the constant of proportionality for the relationship between dollars earned and number of hours?

Set 3 Add and Subtract with Negative Numbers

➤ **Add or subtract. Show your work.**

1 $6 + (-14)$

2 $-6.1 + 2.4$

3 $-5 - (-3)$

4 $1\frac{2}{3} + \left(-3\frac{1}{3}\right)$

5 $-1\frac{3}{4} - \left(2\frac{1}{4}\right)$

6 $-2.6 - (-3.1)$

Set 4 Multiply and Divide with Rational Numbers

➤ **Multiply or divide for problems 1–3. Show your work.**

1 $1.9(-6)$

2 $-\frac{2}{5} \div (-4)$

3 $-3.2(-1.5) \div 2$

➤ **Express each fraction as a decimal for problems 4–6. Show your work.**

4 $\frac{2}{5}$

5 $\frac{4}{9}$

6 $3\frac{1}{12}$

Set 5 Use the Four Operations with Negative Numbers

➤ **Evaluate the expressions. Show your work.**

1 $-1.2 + 6.5 + (-5.2)$

2 $\left(-\frac{5}{4}\right)^2 - 2$

3 $\frac{7(4 - 6 - 2)}{4}$

Set 6 Equivalent Linear Expressions

➤ **Tell whether the expressions are equivalent. Show your work.**

1 $(6b - 12 + 4) - (2b - 3b + 3)$ and $4(2b - 3) - b + 1$

2 $\frac{1}{3}(2x + 1) - \frac{1}{2}(x - 1)$ and $\frac{1}{6}(x - 1)$

Set 7 Solve Multi-Step Problems

➤ **Solve the problems. Show your work.**

1 Eric buys 5 bus tickets. He gets $0.50 off the regular price of each ticket. In total, he spends $12.50. What is the regular price of a bus ticket?

2 Mila buys some bananas and 2 bottles of juice. Each banana costs $0.75. Each bottle of juice costs $2.10. The total cost is $7.95. How many bananas does Mila buy?

Set 8 Write and Solve Equations and Inequalities

➤ **Solve each equation or inequality for problems 1–3. Show your work.**

1 $3x + 4 + 16$

2 $\frac{3}{4}(x + 5) + 3 = 21$

3 $-2(3x - 2) < 16$

➤ **Write an inequality to represent and solve problem 4. Show your work.**

4 The product of 8 and a number, n, is no greater than 60. What are all possible values of n?

Set 9 Solve Problems with Percents

➤ **Solve the problems. Show your work.**

1 Felipe pays $20.70 for a meal at a restaurant. The amount includes a 15% tip. How much is the meal without the tip?

2 The price of a movie ticket increases from $8 to $10. What is the percent change in the price?

3 Ava estimates it will take her about 40 minutes to complete her run. She times her run and it actually takes 50 minutes. What is the percent error in her estimate?

Set 1 Rigid Transformations of Line Segments

➤ **Fill in the blanks to complete the statements.**

1 Figure *JKLMN* is a translation of figure *ABCDE*.

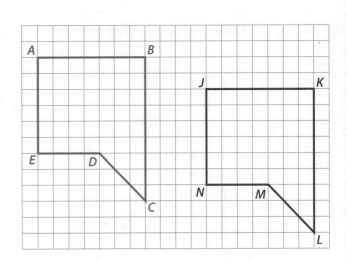

$\overline{JK}$ corresponds to _____.

$\overline{JK}$ is the same length as _____.

$\overline{MN}$ corresponds to _____.

$\overline{KL}$ is the same length as _____.

$\overline{LM}$ is the same length as _____.

Set 2 Rigid Transformations of Angles

➤ **Fill in the blanks to complete the statements.**

1 Figure *VWXYZ* is a reflection of figure *ABCDE*.

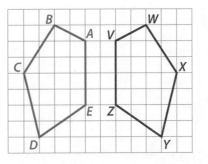

∠*V* corresponds to _____.

∠*Y* has the same measure as _____.

∠*W* has the same measure as _____.

∠*W* corresponds to _____.

2 Figure *PQRS* is a rotation of figure *DEFG*.

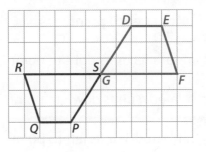

_____ corresponds to ∠*D*.

_____ corresponds to ∠*F*.

_____ has the same measure as ∠*F*.

_____ has the same measure as ∠*G*.

Set 3 Rigid Transformations of Parallel Lines

➤ **Fill in the blanks to complete the statements.**

1 Figure *PQRS* is a rotation of figure *ABCD*.

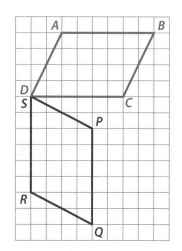

$\overline{SP}$ corresponds to _____.

$\overline{RQ}$ corresponds to _____.

$\overline{AB}$ is parallel to _____.

$\overline{SR}$ is parallel to _____.

2 Figure *UVWXYZ* is a reflection of figure *HIJKLM*.

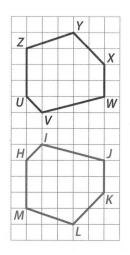

_____ corresponds to $\overline{HM}$.

_____ corresponds to $\overline{JK}$.

Since $\overline{JK}$ is parallel to $\overline{HM}$,

_____ is parallel to _____.

Set 4 Translations

➤ **Write the coordinates of each point.**

1 Point *Q*(3, 2) is translated 3 units right to point *Q'*.　　　　*Q'* _____

2 Point *P*(*x*, *y*) is translated 4 units down to point *P'*.　　　　*P'* _____

3 Point *S*(2, −2) is translated 5 units left to point *S'*.　　　　*S'* _____

4 Point *T*(*x*, *y*) is translated 1 unit right to point *T'*.　　　　*T'* _____

5 Point *W*(−2, −2) is translated 3 units up to point *W'*.　　　　*W'* _____

6 Point *A*(*x*, *y*) is translated 5 units left to point *A'*.　　　　*A'* _____

Set 5 Rotations

➤ **Write the coordinates of each point.**

1 Triangle *ABC* is rotated 90° counterclockwise around the origin to form the image triangle *A'B'C'*. Draw triangle *A'B'C'*.

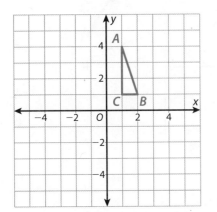

A' _____

B' _____

C' _____

2 Quadrilateral *KLMN* is rotated 180° clockwise around the origin to form the image quadrilateral *K'L'M'N'*. Draw quadrilateral *K'L'M'N'*.

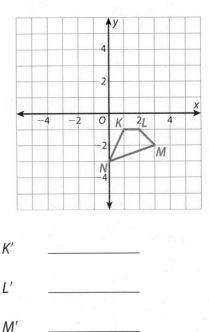

K' _____

L' _____

M' _____

N' _____

3 Point *R*(4, 2) is rotated 90° clockwise around the origin to point *R'*.

R' _____

4 Point *P*(*x, y*) is rotated 180° counterclockwise around the origin to point *P'*.

P' _____

5 Point *S*(*x, y*) is rotated 270° counterclockwise around the origin to point *S'*.

S' _____

6 Point *T*(3, −2) is rotated 270° clockwise around the origin to point *T'*.

T' _____

Set 6 Reflections

➤ **Solve the problems.**

1 Reflect △DEF across the y-axis to form △LMN. Draw △LMN.

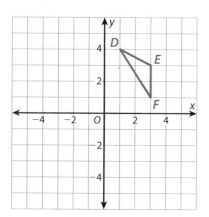

2 Reflect figure ABCD across the x-axis to form figure QRST. Draw figure QRST.

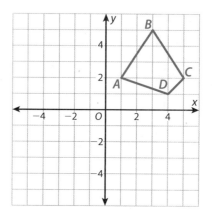

3 △JKL is reflected across the x-axis to form △J'K'L'. The coordinates of J are (−4, 3).

What are the coordinates of J'? _____

4 Point S(x, y) is reflected across the y-axis to point S'.

What are the coordinates of S'? _____

Set 7 Sequences of Transformations and Congruence

➤ **Fill in the blanks to complete the statement.**

1 △GHI ≅ △KLM because a reflection across the _____-axis

and then a translation _____ units _____ maps

△GHI onto △KLM.

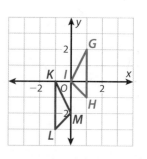

2 △ABC ≅ △DEF because a translation _____ units

_____ and then a rotation of _____° clockwise

around the origin maps △ABC onto △DEF.

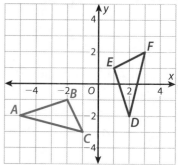

Cumulative Practice

Name: _____

Set 1 Dilations and Similarity

➤ **Fill in the blanks.**

1 $\triangle AB'C'$ is a dilation of $\triangle ABC$.

$m\angle B = m$ _____ $m\angle C = m$ _____

$B'C' =$ _____ $\times BC$ $AB' =$ _____ $\times AB$

$AC' =$ _____ $\times AC$ $\triangle ABC \sim$ _____

2 Quadrilateral $P'Q'R'S'$ is a dilation of quadrilateral $PQRS$ with a scale factor of $\frac{1}{3}$.

$m\angle R = m$ _____ $m\angle S = m$ _____

$S'P' =$ _____ $\times SP$ $QR =$ _____ $\times Q'R'$

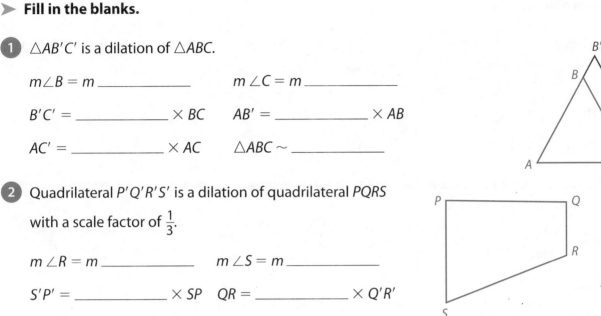

Set 2 Transformations Involving Dilations

➤ **Perform the transformation.**

1 Dilate the parallelogram with a scale factor of $\frac{3}{2}$ and the center of dilation at the origin.

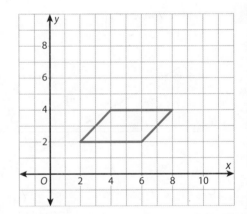

➤ **Describe the sequence of transformations that maps $\triangle ABC$ on to $\triangle A'B'C'$.**

2 A dilation with a scale factor of _____ with center of dilation at vertex _____ and then a reflection across the _____ -axis.

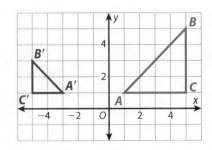

Set 3 Angle Relationships in Triangles

➤ **Solve the problems.**

1. Fill in the blanks.

   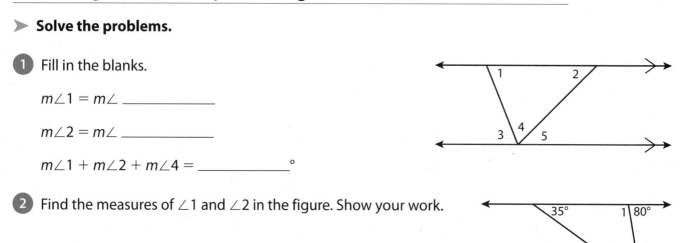

   $m\angle 1 = m\angle$ _____

   $m\angle 2 = m\angle$ _____

   $m\angle 1 + m\angle 2 + m\angle 4 =$ _____°

2. Find the measures of $\angle 1$ and $\angle 2$ in the figure. Show your work.

Set 4 Angle Relationships

➤ **Use the parallel lines cut by a transversal to solve. Show your work.**

1. Find the value of x.

   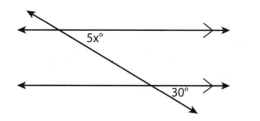

2. Find the value of x.

   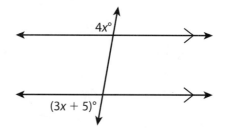

Set 5 Triangle Similarity

➤ **Compare angles to show whether the triangles are similar. Show your work.**

1 Are the triangles similar?

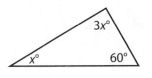
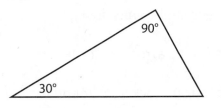

2 Are the triangles similar?

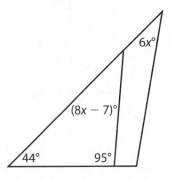

Set 6 Properties of Rigid Transformations

➤ **Fill in the blanks to compare the figures.**

1 Figure *PQRS* is a rotation of figure *ABCD*.

_____ corresponds to ∠*A*.

_____ has the same measure as ∠*B*.

_____ has the same length as $\overline{BC}$.

_____ is parallel to $\overline{DC}$.

_____ corresponds to $\overline{AB}$ and _____ corresponds to $\overline{DC}$,

so _____ is parallel to $\overline{SR}$.

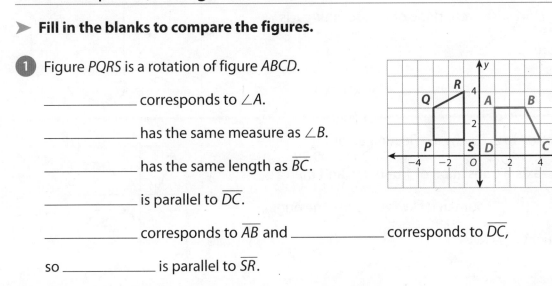

Set 7 Single Transformations

➤ **Write the coordinates of each point.**

1 Point $T(x, y)$ is translated 2 units right. T' _____

2 Point $G(2, -2)$ is translated 4 units down. G' _____

3 Point $A(-4, 2)$ is reflected across the x-axis. A' _____

4 Point $S(3, 2)$ is rotated 90° clockwise around the origin. S' _____

5 Point $W(x, y)$ is rotated 180° counterclockwise around the origin. W' _____

➤ **Identify the transformation.**

6 $\triangle A$ and its image $\triangle A'$ are shown in the coordinate plane. What single transformation maps $\triangle A$ onto $\triangle A'$?

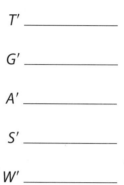

Set 8 Sequences of Transformations and Congruence

➤ **Fill in the blanks to describe the sequences of transformations.**

1 Figure F can be mapped onto Figure G by a translation of

_____ units _____ and then a rotation

of _____° clockwise around the origin, so Figure F is

congruent to Figure G.

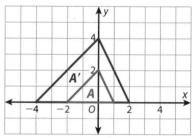

2 $\triangle PQR$ can be mapped to $\triangle TUV$ by a reflection across

the _____-axis, a translation of 1 unit left, and then a

rotation of _____° counterclockwise around the origin,

so $\triangle PQR$ is congruent to $\triangle TUV$.

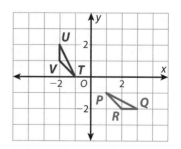

Set 1 Graph Proportional Relationships and Calculate Slope

➤ **Solve the problems. Show your work.**

1 A polar bear swims at a constant speed. It swims 12 meters in 8 seconds. Complete the graph to show the change in the polar bear's distance over time. How far does the polar bear swim in 1 second?

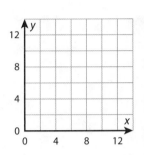

2 Two points on a line are (10, 55) and (15, 82.5). What is the slope of the line?

Set 2 Write and Graph Linear Equations

➤ **Write the equation of the line for problems 1 and 2. Show your work.**

1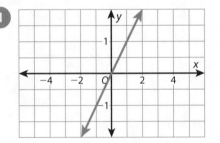

2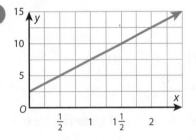

➤ **Graph the line for the linear equation for problems 3 and 4.**

3 $y = -2x$

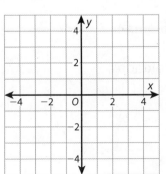

4 $y = \frac{1}{2}x - 3$

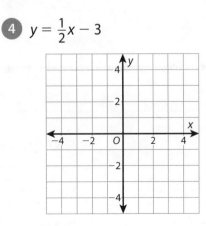

Set 3 Solve Linear Equations in One Variable

➤ **Solve the equations. Show your work.**

1 $\frac{1}{4}(3x + 2) = x - \frac{1}{3}$

2 $2.5x + 0.6 = \frac{x}{2}$

3 $9(x + 2) = 24$

4 $3x + 2 - \frac{1}{4}x = \frac{1}{2}(x - 5)$

5 $\frac{1}{5}(2x + 1) = \frac{1}{2}(4 - x)$

6 $3x - 3 = 4(x - 9)$

Set 4 Determine the Number of Solutions to One-Variable Equations

➤ **Solve the equations and tell how many solutions there are for problems 1–3. Show your work.**

1 $4x - 2 = 6x - 3$

2 $3(3 + x) = 3x - 3$

3 $9x = 7(x - 2) + 2(x + 7)$

➤ **Write a single term in each blank to make true statements for problems 4–7.**

4 $15(x - 3) + 3 =$ _____ + _____ has infinitely many solutions.

5 $11.5(2.3 - 3x) + 2 =$ _____ + 3 has no solution.

6 $4(x + 1) + 2x =$ _____ + _____ has infinitely many solutions.

7 $6(x - 2) + 3x =$ _____ + 19 has no solution.

Set 5 Systems of Linear Equations in Two Variables

➤ **Tell how many solutions each system of equations has.**

1 $y = -x$

$y = x + 3$

2 $y - 2 = -x$

$y = -x - 2$

3 $y = \frac{1}{2}x$

$2y = x$

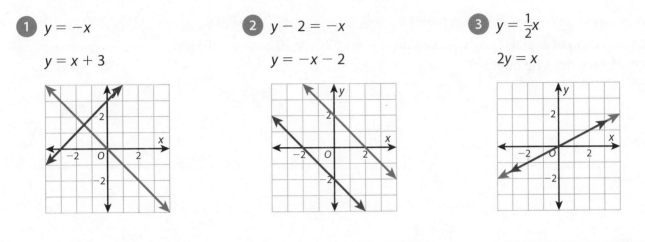

Set 6 Solve Systems of Linear Equations

➤ **Solve the systems of linear equations. Show your work.**

1 $2x + 4y = 12$

$x = y$

2 $3x - y = 4$

$x + y = 9$

3 $4x - 2 = 3y$

$y = 3x$

4

5 $3x + y = 0$

$x + y = 4$

6 $y = x - 2$

$3y = 2x$

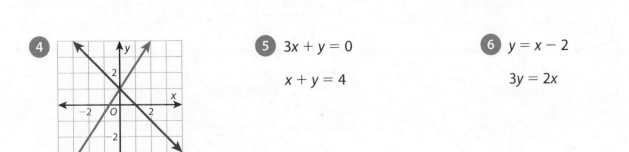

Set 7 Solve Problems with Systems of Linear Equations

➤ **Write a system of linear equations to solve each problem. Show your work.**

1 Leyton buys bags of popcorn and bags of pretzels for a party. A bag of popcorn costs $2. A bag of pretzels costs $3. Leyton spends $24 for 10 bags in all. How many of each does he buy?

2 Kacey spends 30 minutes studying for her math and history tests. She spends twice as long studying math as studying history. How much time does she spend on each subject?

Set 8 Angle Relationships

➤ **Find the value of x. Show your work.**

1

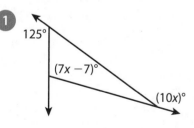

125°

$(7x - 7)°$

$(10x)°$

2

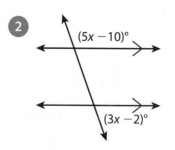

$(5x - 10)°$

$(3x - 2)°$

Interactive Glossary/Glosario interactivo

English/Español	Example/Ejemplo	Notes/Notas

Aa

acute angle an angle that measures more than 0° but less than 90°.

ángulo agudo ángulo que mide más de 0° pero menos de 90°.

acute triangle a triangle that has three acute angles.

triángulo acutángulo triángulo que tiene tres ángulos agudos.

additive inverses two numbers whose sum is zero. The additive inverse of a number is the opposite of that number, i.e., the additive inverse of a is $-a$.

-2 and 2

$\frac{1}{2}$ and $-\frac{1}{2}$

inverso aditivo dos números cuya suma es cero. El inverso aditivo de un número es el opuesto de ese número; por ejemplo, el inverso aditivo de a es $-a$.

adjacent angles two non-overlapping angles that share a vertex and a side.

ángulos adyacentes dos ángulos que no se superponen y que comparten un vértice y un lado.

$\angle ADB$ and $\angle BDC$ are adjacent angles.

algorithm a set of routine steps used to solve problems.

```
      17 R 19
31)546
    -31↓
     236
    -217
      19
```

algoritmo conjunto de pasos rutinarios que se siguen para resolver problemas.

English/Español	Example/Ejemplo	Notes/Notas

alternate exterior angles when two lines are cut by a transversal, a pair of angles on opposite sides of the transversal and outside the two lines. When the two lines are parallel, alternate exterior angles are congruent.

ángulos alternos externos cuando a dos rectas se cortan con una transversal, par de ángulos en lados opuestos de la transversal y fuera de las dos rectas. Cuando las dos rectas son paralelas, los ángulos alternos externos son congruentes.

∠1 and ∠7
∠4 and ∠6

alternate interior angles when two lines are cut by a transversal, a pair of angles on opposite sides of the transversal and between the two lines. When the two lines are parallel, alternate interior angles are congruent.

ángulos alternos internos cuando a dos rectas se cortan con una transversal, par de ángulos en lados opuestos de la transversal y entre las dos rectas. Cuando las dos rectas son paralelas, los ángulos alternos internos son congruentes.

∠2 and ∠8
∠3 and ∠5

angle a geometric shape formed by two rays, lines, or line segments that meet at a common point.

ángulo figura geométrica formada por dos semirrectas, rectas o segmentos de recta que se encuentran en un punto común.

area the amount of space inside a closed two-dimensional figure. Area is measured in square units such as square centimeters.

área cantidad de espacio dentro de una figura bidimensional cerrada. El área se mide en unidades cuadradas, como los centímetros cuadrados.

6 units
Area = 30 units² 5 units

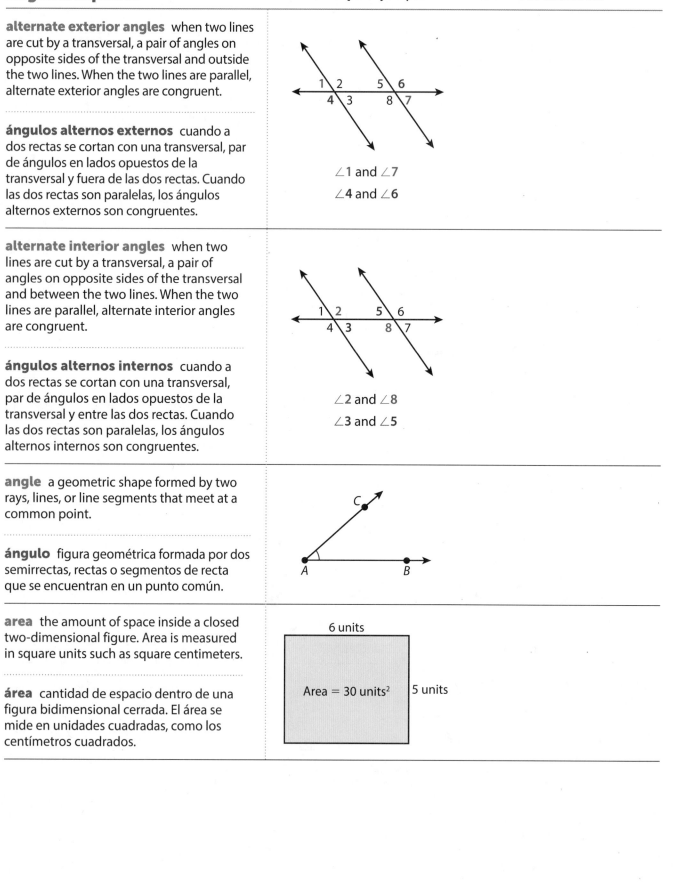

association (between two variables)
a relationship between two variables. Two variables can be described as having a *linear association*, a *nonlinear association*, or *no association*. Linear associations can be described as *positive* or *negative*.

asociación (entre dos variables)
relación que existe entre dos variables. Dos variables se pueden describir como que tienen una *asociación lineal, no lineal*, o *ninguna asociación*. Las asociaciones lineales se pueden describir como *positivas* o *negativas*.

There is a positive association between *x* and *y*.

associative property of addition
regrouping the terms does not change the value of the expression.

propiedad asociativa de la suma
reagrupar los términos no cambia el valor de la expresión.

$(a + b) + c = a + (b + c)$

$(2 + 3) + 4 = 2 + (3 + 4)$

associative property of multiplication
regrouping the terms does not change the value of the expression.

propiedad asociativa de la multiplicación reagrupar los términos no cambia el valor de la expresión.

$(a \cdot b) \cdot c = a \cdot (b \cdot c)$

$(2 \cdot 3) \cdot 4 = 2 \cdot (3 \cdot 4)$

axis a horizontal or vertical number line that determines a coordinate plane. The plural form is *axes*.

eje recta numérica horizontal o vertical que determina un plano de coordenadas.

Bb

balance point the point that represents the center of a data set. In a two-variable data set, the coordinates of the balance point are the mean of each variable.

punto de equilibrio punto que representa el centro de un conjunto de datos. En un conjunto de datos de dos variables, las coordenadas del punto de equilibrio son la media de cada variable.

Data set: (1, 1), (3, 4), (5, 6), (7, 8)

$$\frac{1 + 3 + 5 + 7}{4} = 4$$

$$\frac{1 + 4 + 6 + 8}{4} = 4.75$$

Balance point: (4, 4.75)

---

base (of a parallelogram) a side of a parallelogram from which the height is measured.

base (de un paralelogramo) lado de un paralelogramo desde el que se mide la altura.

---

base (of a power) in a power, the number that is used as a repeated factor.

base (de una potencia) en una potencia, el número que se usa como factor que se repite.

$$8^2$$

base

---

base (of a three-dimensional figure) a face of a three-dimensional figure from which the height is measured.

base (de una figura tridimensional) cara de una figura tridimensional desde la que se mide la altura.

---

base (of a triangle) a side of a triangle from which the height is measured.

base (de un triángulo) lado de un triángulo desde el que se mide la altura.

English/**Español**	**Example**/Ejemplo	**Notes**/Notas

bivariate involving two variables.

bivariante que tiene dos variables.

Car Data	
Years Old	**Color**
3	Red
4	Blue

box plot a visual display of a data set on a number line that shows the minimum, the lower quartile, the median, the upper quartile, and the maximum. The sides of the box show the lower and upper quartiles and the line inside the box shows the median. Lines connect the box to the minimum and maximum values.

diagrama de caja representación visual de un conjunto de datos en una recta numérica que muestra el mínimo, el cuartil inferior, la mediana, el cuartil superior y el máximo. Los lados de la caja muestran los cuartiles inferior y superior y la recta del centro muestra la mediana. Las rectas conectan la caja con los valores mínimo y máximo.

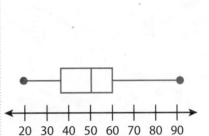

20 30 40 50 60 70 80 90

Cc

categorical data data that are divided into categories, such as characteristics of the population.

Car color: red, blue, white, black

datos por categorías datos que se dividen en categorías, como las características de la población.

---

center (of a circle) the point inside a circle that is the same distance from every point on the circle.

centro (de un círculo) punto dentro de un círculo que está a la misma distancia de todos los puntos del círculo.

center

---

center of dilation a fixed point from which a figure is dilated.

centro de dilatación punto fijo desde el que se dilata una figura.

center of dilation

A   B′   B

C′

C

---

center of rotation a fixed point around which a figure is rotated.

centro de rotación punto fijo alrededor del que se rota una figura.

B

A

center of rotation

---

circle a two-dimensional shape in which every point is the same distance from the center.

círculo figura bidimensional en que todos los puntos están a la misma distancia del centro.

---

circumference the distance around the outside of a circle. It can be thought of as the perimeter of the circle.

circunferencia distancia alrededor del exterior de un círculo. Se puede considerar como el perímetro del círculo.

circumference

English/Español	Example/Ejemplo	Notes/Notas
closed figure a two-dimensional figure that begins and ends at the same point. **figura cerrada** figura bidimensional que comienza y termina en el mismo punto.	Closed figure Open figure	
cluster a group of data points that are close to each other. **agrupación** conjunto de datos que están cerca unos de otros.	cluster 0 1 2 3 4	
coefficient a number that is multiplied by a variable. **coeficiente** número que se multiplica por una variable.	$5x + 3$ coefficient	
commission a fee paid for services, often a percent of the total cost. A salesperson who earns a commission often gets a percent of the total sale. **comisión** tarifa que se paga por servicios, que suele ser un porcentaje del costo total. Un vendedor que gana una comisión por lo general recibe un porcentaje de la venta total.	A 5% commission on $4,000 is 0.05($4,000), or $200.	
common denominator a number that is a common multiple of the denominators of two or more fractions. **denominador común** número que es múltiplo común de los denominadores de dos o más fracciones.	A common denominator for $\frac{1}{2}$ and $\frac{3}{5}$ is 10 because $2 \cdot 5 = 10$.	
commutative property of addition changing the order of the addends does not change the sum. **propiedad conmutativa de la suma** cambiar el orden de los sumandos no cambia el total.	$a + b = b + a$ $4.1 + 7.5 = 7.5 + 4.1$	

English/Español	Example/Ejemplo	Notes/Notas
commutative property of multiplication changing the order of the factors does not change the product. **propiedad conmutativa de la multiplicación** cambiar el orden de los factores no cambia el producto.	$ab = ba$ $4(7.5) = 7.5(4)$	
compare to describe the relationship between the value or size of two numbers or quantities. **comparar** describir la relación que hay entre el valor o el tamaño de dos números o cantidades.	$-4 < 8.5$	
complementary angles two angles whose measures sum to 90°. **ángulos complementarios** dos ángulos cuyas medidas suman 90°.	$\angle AEB$ and $\angle BEC$	
complex fraction a fraction in which the numerator is a fraction, the denominator is a fraction, or both the numerator and the denominator are fractions. **fracción compleja** fracción en la que el numerador es una fracción, el denominador es una fracción, o tanto el numerador como el denominador son fracciones.	$\dfrac{\frac{1}{2}}{\frac{3}{4}}$	
compose to make by combining parts. You can put together numbers to make a greater number or put together shapes to make a new shape. **componer** formar al combinar partes. Se pueden unir números para hacer un número mayor o unir figuras para formar una figura nueva.		
composite number a number that has more than one pair of whole number factors. **número compuesto** número que tiene más de un par de números enteros como factores.	16 is a composite number because 1 • 16, 2 • 8, and 4 • 4 all equal 16.	

English/Español	Example/Ejemplo	Notes/Notas
compound event an event that consists of two or more simple events.	Rolling a number cube twice	
evento compuesto evento que consiste en dos o más eventos simples.		
cone a three-dimensional figure with one circular base and one vertex, connected by a curved surface.		
cono figura tridimensional que tiene una base circular y un vértice, conectados por una superficie curva.		
congruent (≅) same size and shape. Two figures are congruent if there is a sequence of rigid transformations that maps one figure onto the second.	Figure *C′* is congruent to Figure *C*.	
congruente (≅) del mismo tamaño y forma. Dos figuras son congruentes si hay una secuencia de transformaciones rígidas que hace coincidir una figura con la segunda.		
constant of proportionality the unit rate in a proportional relationship.	Unit rate: $10 per hour Constant of proportionality for dollars per hours: 10.	
constante de proporcionalidad tasa unitaria en una relación proporcional.		
converse of the Pythagorean Theorem in a triangle, if the square of the length of the longest side is equal to the sum of the squares of the lengths of the other two sides, then the triangle is a right triangle.	If $c^2 = a^2 + b^2$, the triangle is a right triangle.	
recíproco del teorema de Pitágoras en un triángulo, si el cuadrado de la longitud del lado más largo es igual a la suma de los cuadrados de las longitudes de los otros dos lados, entonces el triángulo es un triángulo rectángulo.		
convert to write an equivalent measurement using a different unit.	60 in. is the same as 5 ft.	
convertir escribir una medida equivalente usando una unidad diferente.		

English/Español	**Example**/Ejemplo	**Notes**/Notas

coordinate plane a two-dimensional space formed by two perpendicular number lines called *axes*.

plano de coordenadas espacio bidimensional formado por dos rectas numéricas perpendiculares llamadas ejes.

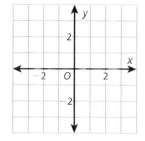

corresponding angles
(1) angles in the same relative position in figures. When figures are similar or congruent, corresponding angles are congruent.
(2) angles in the same relative position when two lines are cut by a transversal. When the two lines are parallel, corresponding angles are congruent.

ángulos correspondientes
(1) ángulos que están en la misma posición relativa en las figuras. Cuando las figuras son semejantes o congruentes, los ángulos correspondientes son congruentes.
(2) ángulos que están en la misma posición relativa cuando se cortan dos rectas con una transversal. Cuando las dos rectas son paralelas, los ángulos correspondientes son congruentes.

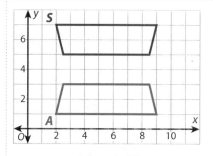

∠A and ∠S

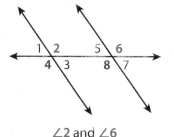

∠2 and ∠6
∠4 and ∠8

corresponding sides sides in the same relative position in figures. When figures are congruent, corresponding sides are the same length.

lados correspondientes lados que están en la misma posición relativa en las figuras. Cuando las figuras son congruentes, los lados correspondientes tienen la misma longitud.

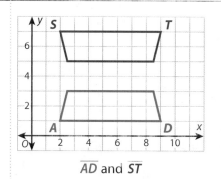

$\overline{AD}$ and $\overline{ST}$

corresponding terms terms that have the same position in two related patterns. For example, the second term in one pattern and the second term in a related pattern are corresponding terms.

términos correspondientes términos que tienen la misma posición en dos patrones relacionados. Por ejemplo, el segundo término en un patrón y el segundo término en un patrón relacionado son términos correspondientes.

Pattern A: 12, **18**, 24, **30**
Pattern B: 6, **9**, 12, **15**

cross-section a two-dimensional shape that is exposed by making a straight cut through a three-dimensional figure.

sección transversal figura bidimensional que se forma al hacer un corte recto a través de una figura tridimensional.

cube a rectangular prism in which each face of the prism is a square.

cubo prisma rectangular en el que cada cara del prisma es un cuadrado.

1 unit
1 unit
1 unit

cube root of x the number that when cubed is equal to x.

raíz cúbica de x número que cuando se eleva al cubo es igual a x.

$$\sqrt[3]{8} = \sqrt[3]{2\cdot2\cdot2}$$
$$= 2$$

2 is the cube root of 8.

cylinder a three-dimensional figure with two parallel curved bases that are the same size. The bases are connected by a curved surface.

cilindro figura tridimensional que tiene dos bases curvas paralelas que tienen el mismo tamaño. Las bases están conectadas por una superficie curva.

Interactive Glossary/Glosario interactivo

Dd

data a set of collected information. Often numerical information such as a list of measurements.

datos conjunto de información reunida. Con frecuencia, información numérica como una lista de medidas.

Commute length (mi):

15, 22, 10.5, 21, 9.5

---

decimal a number containing a decimal point that separates a whole from fractional place values (tenths, hundredths, thousandths, and so on).

decimal número que tiene un punto decimal que separa un entero de los valores posicionales fraccionarios (décimas, centésimas, milésimas, etc.).

1.293

---

decompose to break into parts. You can break apart numbers and shapes.

descomponer separar en partes. Se puede separar en partes números y figuras.

---

degree (°) a unit used to measure angles.

grado (°) unidad que se usa para medir ángulos.

There are 360° in a circle.

---

denominator the number below the line in a fraction that tells the number of equal parts in the whole.

denominador número debajo de la línea en una fracción que indica el número de partes iguales que hay en el entero.

$\frac{3}{4}$

---

dependent variable a variable whose value depends on the value of a related independent variable.

variable dependiente variable cuyo valor depende del valor de una variable independiente relacionada.

$y = 5x$

The value of y depends on the value of x.

English/Español	Example/Ejemplo	Notes/Notas
diameter a line segment that goes through the center of a circle and has endpoints on the circle. Also, the distance across a circle through the center. **diámetro** segmento de recta que pasa por el centro de un círculo y tiene extremos en el círculo. También, la distancia de un lado al otro del círculo a través del centro.	 diameter	
difference the result of subtraction. **diferencia** resultado de la resta.	$$\begin{array}{r}16.75\\-\ 15.70\\\hline 1.05\end{array}$$	
digit a symbol used to write numbers. **dígito** símbolo que se usa para escribir números.	The digits are 0, 1, 2, 3, 4, 5, 6, 7, 8, and 9.	
dilation a transformation that makes a scale copy of a figure. A dilation is a proportional shrinking or enlargement of a figure. **dilatación** transformación que produce una copia a escala de una figura. Una dilatación es una reducción o ampliación proporcional de una figura.	 Figure B is a dilation of Figure A.	
dimension length in one direction. A figure may have one, two, or three dimensions. **dimensión** longitud en una dirección. Una figura puede tener una, dos o tres dimensiones.	 5 in. 2 in. 3 in.	
distribution a representation that shows how often values in a data set occur. **distribución** representación que muestra la frecuencia con la que ocurren los valores en un conjunto de datos.		Pet	Frequency
---	---
Bird	7
Cat	12
Dog	8
Snake	3	

English/Español	Example/Ejemplo	Notes/Notas
distributive property multiplying each term in a sum or difference by a common factor does not change the value of the expression.		
propiedad distributiva multiplicar cada término de una suma o diferencia por un factor común no cambia el valor de la expresión.	$a(b + c) = ab + ac$ $5(4 + 2) = 5(4) + 5(2)$	
dividend the number that is divided by another number.		
dividendo número que se divide por otro número.	$22.5 \div 3 = 7.5$	
divisor the number by which another number is divided.		
divisor número por el que se divide otro número.	$22.5 \div 3 = 7.5$	
dot plot a data display that shows data as dots above a number line. A dot plot may also be called a *line plot*.		
diagrama de puntos representación de datos que muestra datos como puntos sobre una *recta numérica*.		

Ee

edge a line segment where two faces meet in a three-dimensional shape.

arista segmento de recta en el que dos caras se unen en una figura tridimensional.

edge

---

equal having the same value, same size, or same amount.

igual que tiene el mismo valor, el mismo tamaño o la misma cantidad.

$50 - 20 = 30$

$50 - 20$ is equal to 30.

---

equation a mathematical statement that uses an equal sign (=) to show that two expressions have the same value.

ecuación enunciado matemático que tiene un signo de igual (=) para mostrar que dos expresiones tienen el mismo valor.

$x + 4 = 15$

---

equilateral triangle a triangle that has all three sides the same length.

triángulo equilátero triángulo que tiene los tres lados de la misma longitud.

---

equivalent having the same value.

equivalente que tiene el mismo valor.

4 is equivalent to $\frac{8}{2}$.

---

equivalent expressions two or more expressions in different forms that always name the same value.

expresiones equivalentes dos o más expresiones en diferentes formas que siempre nombran el mismo valor.

$2(x + 4)$ is equivalent to $2x + 2(4)$ and $2x + 8$.

English/Español	Example/Ejemplo	Notes/Notas
equivalent fractions two or more different fractions that name the same part of a whole or the same point on the number line. **fracciones equivalentes** dos o más fracciones diferentes que nombran la misma parte de un entero o el mismo punto en la recta numérica.	$-\dfrac{5}{10}$ $\dfrac{4}{8}$ $-\dfrac{1}{2}$ $\dfrac{1}{2}$ ←—+——●——+——●——+——→ −1 0 1	
equivalent ratios two ratios that express the same comparison. Multiplying both numbers in the ratio $a : b$ by a nonzero number n results in the equivalent ratio $na : nb$. **razones equivalentes** dos razones que expresan la misma comparación. Multiplicar ambos números en la razón $a : b$ por un número distinto de cero n da como resultado la razón equivalente $na : nb$.	$6 : 8$ is equivalent to $3 : 4$	
estimate (noun) a close guess made using mathematical thinking. **estimación** suposición aproximada que se hace por medio del razonamiento matemático.	$28 + 21 = ?$ $30 + 20 = 50$ 50 is an estimate of $28 + 21$.	
estimate (verb) to give an approximate number or answer based on mathematical thinking. **estimar** dar un número o respuesta aproximada basados en el razonamiento matemático.	$28 + 21$ is about 50.	
evaluate to find the value of an expression. **evaluar** hallar el valor de una expresión.	The expression $4.5 \div (1 + 8)$ has a value of 0.5.	

English/Español	Example/Ejemplo	Notes/Notas
event a set of one or more outcomes of an experiment. **evento** conjunto de uno o más resultados de un experimento.	Experiment: rolling a number cube once Possible events: rolling an even number, rolling a 1	
experiment a repeatable procedure involving chance that results in one or more possible outcomes. **experimento** procedimiento repetible en el que se hacen pruebas y da uno o más resultados posibles.	Experiment: rolling a number cube once	
experimental probability the probability of an event occurring based on the results from an experiment. **probabilidad experimental** probabilidad de que un evento ocurra con base en los resultados de un experimento.	A coin is flipped **30** times and lands heads up **17** times. The experimental probability of the coin landing heads up is $\frac{17}{30}$.	
exponent in a power, the number that shows how many times the base is used as a factor. **exponente** en una potencia, el número que muestra cuántas veces se usa la base como factor.	8^2 exponent	
exponential expression an expression that includes an exponent. **expresión exponencial** expresión que tiene un exponente.	$3x^3$	

expression a group of numbers, variables, and/or operation symbols that represents a mathematical relationship. An expression without variables, such as $3 + 4$, is called a *numerical expression*. An expression with variables, such as $5b^2$, is called an *algebraic expression*.

$$\frac{32 - 4}{7}$$

$$3x + y - 9$$

expresión grupo de números, variables y/o símbolos de operaciones que representa una relación matemática. Una expresión sin variables, como $3 + 4$, se llama *expresión numérica*. Una expresión con variables, como $5b^2$, se llama *expresión algebraica*.

exterior angle when you extend one side of a polygon, the angle between the extended side and the adjacent side. This angle forms a linear pair with the adjacent interior angle of the polygon.

ángulo externo cuando se amplía un lado de un polígono, se forma un ángulo entre el lado ampliado y el lado adyacente. Este ángulo forma un par lineal con el ángulo interno adyacente del polígono.

Ff

face a flat surface of a solid shape.

cara superficie plana de una figura sólida.

face

---

factor (noun) a number, or expression with parentheses, that is multiplied.

factor número, o expresión entre paréntesis, que se multiplica.

$4 \times 5 = 20$

factors

---

factor (verb) to rewrite an expression as a product of factors.

descomponer volver a escribir una expresión como producto de factores.

$12x + 42 = 6(2x + 7)$

---

factor pair two numbers that are multiplied together to give a product.

par de factores dos números que se multiplican para dar un producto.

$4 \times 5 = 20$

factor pair

---

factors of a number whole numbers that multiply together to get the given number.

factores de un número números enteros que se multiplican para obtener el número dado.

$4 \times 5 = 20$

4 and 5 are factors of 20.

---

formula a mathematical relationship that is expressed in the form of an equation.

fórmula relación matemática que se expresa en forma de ecuación.

$A = \ell w$

Interactive Glossary/Glosario interactivo

fraction a number that names equal parts of a whole. A fraction names a point on the number line and can also represent the division of two numbers.

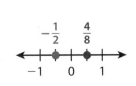

fracción número que nombra partes iguales de un entero. Una fracción nombra un punto en la recta numérica y también puede representar la división de dos números.

---

frequency a numerical count of how many times a data value occurs in a data set.

Data set: 12, 13, 12, 15, 12, 13, 15, 14, 12, 12

frecuencia conteo numérico de cuántas veces ocurre un valor en un conjunto de datos.

Data Value	Frequency
12	5
13	2
14	1
15	2

---

function a rule in which each input results in exactly one output.

Rule: $y = \frac{3}{2}x$

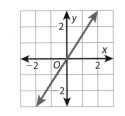

función regla en la que cada entrada resulta en exactamente una salida.

Gg

gap an interval of the number line for which a distribution has no data values.

espacio intervalo de la recta numérica para el que una distribución no tiene valores.

gratuity an amount added on to the cost of a service, often a percent of the total cost. Gratuity is often referred to as a *tip*.

propina cantidad que se suma al costo de un servicio; suele ser un porcentaje del costo total.

A gratuity of 18% on a $20 bill is 0.18($20), or $3.60.

greatest common factor (GCF) the greatest factor two or more numbers have in common.

máximo común divisor (M.C.D.) el mayor factor que dos o más números tienen en común.

GCF of 20 and 30: $2 \cdot 5$, or 10

$20 = 2 \cdot 2 \cdot 5$

$30 = 2 \cdot 3 \cdot 5$

grouping symbol a symbol, such as braces {}, brackets [], or parentheses (), used to group parts of an expression that should be evaluated before others.

símbolo de agrupación símbolo, como las llaves {}, los corchetes [] o los paréntesis (), que se usa para agrupar partes de una expresión que deben evaluarse antes que otras.

$3 \div (7 - 2) = 3 \div 5$

$\frac{3}{7-2} = \frac{3}{5}$

Hh

height (of a parallelogram) the perpendicular distance from a base to the opposite side.

altura (de un paralelogramo) distancia perpendicular desde una base hasta el lado opuesto.

height (of a prism) the perpendicular distance from a base to the opposite base.

altura (de un prisma) distancia perpendicular desde una base hasta la base opuesta.

height (of a triangle) the perpendicular distance from a base to the opposite vertex.

altura (de un triángulo) distancia perpendicular desde una base hasta el vértice opuesto.

hexagon a polygon with exactly 6 sides and 6 angles.

hexágono polígono que tiene exactamente 6 lados y 6 ángulos.

histogram a data display similar to a bar graph. A histogram groups the data into equal-size intervals. The height of each bar represents the number of data points in that group.

histograma presentación de datos parecida a una gráfica de barras. Un histograma agrupa los datos en intervalos de igual tamaño. La altura de cada barra representa el número de datos que hay en ese grupo.

English/Español	Example/Ejemplo	Notes/Notas
hypotenuse the side of a right triangle opposite the right angle.	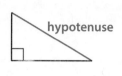	
hipotenusa lado de un triángulo rectángulo opuesto al ángulo recto.		

Ii

identity property of multiplication any number multiplied by 1 is itself.	$3 \cdot 1 = 3$	
propiedad de identidad de la multiplicación cualquier número multiplicado por 1 es el mismo número.		
image a figure that results from a transformation or sequence of transformations. **imagen** figura que resulta de una transformación o secuencia de transformaciones.	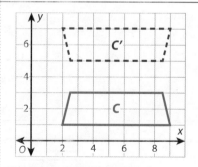 Figure *C′* is the image of Figure *C* after a reflection.	

English/Español	Example/Ejemplo	Notes/Notas
independent variable a variable whose value is used to find the value of another variable. An independent variable determines the value of a dependent variable. **variable independiente** variable cuyo valor se usa para hallar el valor de otra variable. Una variable independiente determina el valor de una variable dependiente.	$y = 5x$ The value of x is used to find the value of y.	
inequality a mathematical statement that uses an inequality symbol $(<, >, \leq, \geq)$ to show the relationship between values of expressions. **desigualdad** enunciado matemático que muestra con un signo de desigualdad $(<, >, \leq, \geq)$ la relación que existe entre los valores de las expresiones.	$4,384 > 3,448$ $x \geq -2$	
initial value in a linear function, the value of the output when the input is 0. **valor inicial** en una función lineal, el valor de la salida cuando la entrada es 0.	$y = \frac{1}{2}x + \mathbf{25}$ initial value	
input (of a function) the independent variable of a function. **entrada (de una función)** variable independiente de una función.	$y = 2x + 1$ 	Input (x)	0	2	3
---	---	---	---
Output (y)	1	5	7		
integers the set of whole numbers and their opposites. **enteros (positivos y negativos)** conjunto de números enteros y sus opuestos.	$-3, -1, 0, 2, 3$	
interquartile range (IQR) the difference between the upper quartile and lower quartile. **rango entre cuartiles (REC)** diferencia entre el cuartil superior y el cuartil inferior.	interquartile range 20 30 40 50 60 70 80 90 IQR: $60 - 35 = 25$	

inverse operations operations that undo each other. For example, addition and subtraction are inverse operations, and multiplication and division are inverse operations.

operaciones inversas operaciones que se cancelan entre sí. Por ejemplo, la suma y la resta son operaciones inversas, y la multiplicación y la división son operaciones inversas.

$$300 \div 10 = 30$$
$$30 \times 10 = 300$$

---

irrational number a number that cannot be expressed as a quotient of two integers. The decimal expansion of an irrational number never repeats or terminates.

número irracional número que no se puede expresar como el cociente de dos enteros. La expansión decimal de un número irracional nunca se repite o termina.

$$1.12112111211112\ldots$$
$$\sqrt{2}$$

---

isosceles triangle a triangle that has at least two sides the same length.

triángulo isósceles triángulo que tiene al menos dos lados de la misma longitud.

8 in.   8 in.
6 in.

Ll

least common multiple (LCM) the least multiple shared by two or more numbers.

mínimo común múltiplo (m.c.m.) el menor múltiplo que comparten dos o más números.

LCM of 20 and 30: $2 \cdot 2 \cdot 3 \cdot 5$, or 60

$20 = 2 \cdot 2 \cdot 5$

$30 = 2 \cdot 3 \cdot 5$

---

legs (of a right triangle) the two sides of a right triangle that form the right angle.

catetos (de un triángulo rectángulo) los dos lados de un triángulo rectángulo que forman el ángulo recto.

---

like terms two or more terms that have the same variable factors.

términos semejantes dos o más términos que tienen los mismos factores variables.

$2x^2$ and $4x^2$

1.2 and 5.1

$6xy$ and xy

---

line a straight row of points that goes on forever in both directions.

recta línea recta de puntos que continúa infinitamente en ambas direcciones.

---

line of fit a line drawn on a scatter plot to approximately model the relationship between the two sets of data.

recta de aproximación línea que se dibuja en un diagrama de dispersión para representar de manera aproximada la relación que existe entre los dos conjuntos de datos.

---

line of reflection a line across which a figure is reflected.

eje de reflexión línea a través de la que se refleja una figura.

English/Español	Example/Ejemplo	Notes/Notas

line of symmetry a line that divides a shape into two mirror images.

eje de simetría línea que divide a una figura en dos imágenes reflejadas.

line segment a straight row of points between two end points.

segmento de recta fila recta de puntos entre dos extremos.

linear association an association in which the relationship between the two variables can be generally approximated using a line.

asociación lineal asociación en la que la relación que existe entre las dos variables se puede aproximar de manera general usando una recta.

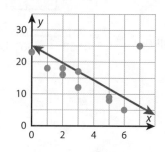

linear equation an equation whose graph is a straight line.

ecuación lineal ecuación cuya gráfica es una línea recta.

Equation: $y = \frac{3}{2}x$

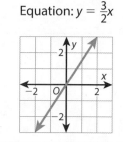

linear function a function that can be represented by a linear equation. The graph of a linear function is a nonvertical straight line.

función lineal función que se puede representar con una ecuación lineal. La gráfica de una función lineal es una recta no vertical.

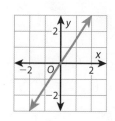

English/Español	Example/Ejemplo	Notes/Notas

linear pair two angles that are adjacent and supplementary.

par lineal dos ángulos que son adyacentes y suplementarios.

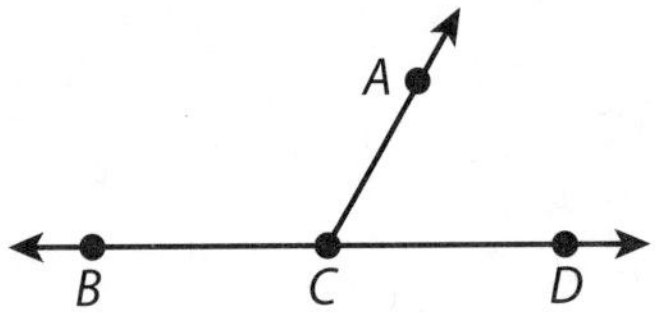

$\angle BCA$ and $\angle ACD$ form a linear pair.

---

lower quartile the middle number between the minimum and the median in an ordered set of numbers. The lower quartile is also called the 1st quartile or Q1.

cuartil inferior el número del medio entre el mínimo y la mediana en un conjunto ordenado de números. El cuartil inferior también se llama primer cuartil, o Q1.

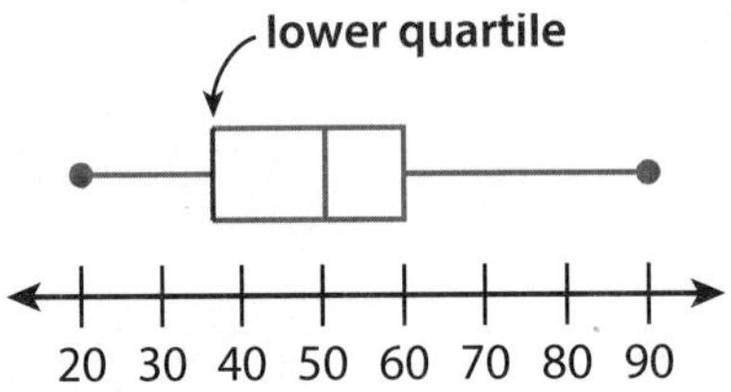

lower quartile

20 30 40 50 60 70 80 90

Mm

markdown an amount subtracted from the cost of an item to determine the final price. The amount subtracted is often a percent of the cost.

reducción de precio cantidad que se resta al costo de un artículo para determinar el precio final. La cantidad que se resta suele ser un porcentaje del costo.

A discount of $20 is the same as a markdown of $20.

markup an amount added to the cost of an item to determine the final price. The amount added is often a percent of the cost.

margen de ganancia cantidad que se suma al costo de un artículo para determinar el precio final. La cantidad que se suma suele ser un porcentaje del costo.

A price increase of $25 is the same as a markup of $25.

maximum (of a data set) the greatest value in a data set.

máximo (de un conjunto de datos) mayor valor en un conjunto de datos.

Data set: 9, 10, 8, 9, 7

mean the sum of a set of values divided by the number of values. This is often called the *average*.

media suma de un conjunto de valores dividida por el número de valores. Suele llamarse *promedio*.

Data set: 9, 10, 8, 9, 7

Mean: $\dfrac{9 + 10 + 8 + 9 + 7}{5} = 8.6$

mean absolute deviation (MAD) the sum of the distances of each data point from the mean of the data set divided by the number of data points. It is always positive.

desviación media absoluta (DMA) suma de las distancias de cada dato desde la media del conjunto de datos dividido por el número de datos. Siempre es positiva.

Data set: 9, 10, 8, 9, 7

Mean: 8.6

MAD:

$\dfrac{0.4 + 1.4 + 0.6 + 0.4 + 1.7}{5} = 0.9$

English/Español	Example/Ejemplo	Notes/Notas
measure of center a single number that summarizes what is typical for all the values in a data set. Mean and median are measures of center. **medida de tendencia central** único número que resume qué es típico para todos los valores en un conjunto de datos. La media y la mediana son medidas de tendecia central.	Data set: 9, 10, 8, 9, 7 Mean: 8.6 Median: 9	
measure of variability a single number that summarizes how much the values in a data set vary. Mean absolute deviation and interquartile range are measures of variability. **medida de variabilidad** único número que resume cuánto varían los valores en un conjunto de datos. La desviación media absoluta y el rango entre cuartiles son medidas de variabilidad.	Data set: 9, 10, 8, 9, 7 MAD: 0.9 IQR: 1	
median the middle number, or the halfway point between the two middle numbers, in an ordered set of values. **mediana** el número del medio, o punto intermedio entre los dos números del medio, de un conjunto ordenado de valores.	Data set: 9, 10, 8, 9, 7 7, 8, 9, 9, 10	
minimum (of a data set) the least value in a data set. **mínimo (de un conjunto de datos)** valor mínimo en un conjunto de datos.	Data set: 9, 10, 8, 9, **7**	
multiple the product of a given number and any other whole number. **múltiplo** producto de un número dado y cualquier otro número entero.	4, 8, 12, 16 are multiples of 4.	

English/Español	Example/Ejemplo	Notes/Notas
multiplicative comparison a comparison that tells how many times as many.	$\frac{1}{2} \times 6 = 3$ tells that 3 is $\frac{1}{2}$ times as many as 6 and that 3 is 6 times as many as $\frac{1}{2}$.	
comparación multiplicativa comparación que indica cuántas veces más.		
multiplicative inverse a number is the multiplicative inverse of another number if the product of the two numbers is 1.	3 and $\frac{1}{3}$	
inverso multiplicativo un número es el inverso multiplicativo de otro número si el producto de los dos números es 1.		

Nn

negative association a linear association in which as the value of one variable increases, generally the other variable decreases.	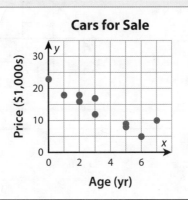 **Cars for Sale**	
asociación negativa asociación lineal en la que el valor de una variable por lo incrementa, generalmente cuando el valor de la otra variable disminuye.		

English/Español	Example/Ejemplo	Notes/Notas
negative numbers numbers that are less than 0. They are located to the left of 0 on a horizontal number line and below 0 on a vertical number line.		
números negativos números que son menores que 0. Se ubican a la izquierda del 0 en una recta numérica horizontal y debajo del 0 en una recta numérica vertical.		
net a flat, "unfolded" representation of a three-dimensional shape.		
modelo plano representación plana "desplegada" de una figura tridimensional.		
no association when two variables have no relationship or association.		
sin asociación cuando dos variables no tienen relación o asociación.		
nonlinear association an association in which no line can reasonably describe the relationship between two variables.		
asociación no lineal asociación en la que ninguna recta puede describir razonablemente la relación que existe entre dos variables.		
nonlinear function a function with a graph that is not a straight line.		
función no lineal función que tiene una gráfica que no es una línea recta.		

English/Español	Example/Ejemplo	Notes/Notas
numerator the number above the line in a fraction that tells the number of equal parts that are being described.	$\dfrac{3}{4}$	
numerador número que está sobre la línea en una fracción y que indica el número de partes iguales que se describen.		

Oo

obtuse angle an angle that measures more than 90° but less than 180°.		
ángulo obtuso ángulo que mide más de 90° pero menos de 180°.		
obtuse triangle a triangle that has one obtuse angle.		
triángulo obtusángulo triángulo que tiene un ángulo obtuso.		

English/Español	Example/Ejemplo	Notes/Notas

opposite numbers numbers that are the same distance from 0 on the number line but in opposite directions. Opposite numbers have the same numeral, but opposite signs. The opposite of a number is also called the *additive inverse* of that number.

números opuestos números que están a la misma distancia del 0 en la recta numérica pero en direcciones opuestas. Los números opuestos son el mismo número, pero con el signo opuesto. El opuesto de un número también se llama *inverso de suma* de ese número.

−3 and 3

$-\frac{8}{15}$ and $\frac{8}{15}$

Order of Operations a set of rules that state the order in which operations should be performed to evaluate an expression.

orden de las operaciones conjunto de reglas que establecen el orden en el que deben hacerse las operaciones para evaluar una expresión.

Working from left to right:

1. Grouping symbols
2. Exponents
3. Multiplication/Division
4. Addition/Subtraction

---

ordered pair a pair of numbers, (x, y), that describes the location of a point in the coordinate plane. The *x*-coordinate gives the point's horizontal distance from the *y*-axis, and the *y*-coordinate gives the point's vertical distance from the *x*-axis.

par ordenado par de números, (x, y), que describen la ubicación de un punto en el plano de coordenadas. La coordenada *x* da la distancia horizontal del punto desde el eje *y*, y la coordenada *y* da la distancia vertical del punto desde el eje *x*.

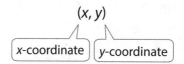

---

origin the point (0, 0) on the coordinate plane where the *x*-axis and *y*-axis intersect.

origen el punto (0, 0) en el plano de coordenadas donde el eje *x* y el eje *y* se intersecan.

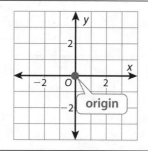

English/Español	Example/Ejemplo	Notes/Notas
outcome one of the possible results of a chance experiment.	Experiment: Rolling a number cube once	
resultado uno de los efectos posibles de un experimento aleatorio.	All possible outcomes: 1, 2, 3, 4, 5, 6	
outlier a data value that is much greater or much less than most of the other values in the data set. An outlier seems to not quite fit with the rest of the data points.		
valor atípico dato que es mucho mayor o mucho menor que la mayoría de los otros valores del conjunto de datos. Un valor atípico parece no ajustarse al resto de los datos.		

outlier →

0 1 2 3 4

| **output (of a function)** the dependent variable of a function. | $y = 2x + 1$ | |
| **salida (de una función)** variable dependiente de una función. | | |

Input (x)	0	2	3
Output (y)	1	5	7

Pp

parallel (∥) always the same distance apart and never meeting.

paralelos (∥) que están siempre a la misma distancia y nunca se encuentran.

$\overline{AB} \parallel \overline{CD}$ and $\overline{AD} \parallel \overline{BC}$

parallel lines lines that are always the same distance apart and never intersect.

rectas paralelas rectas que siempre están a la misma distancia y nunca se intersecan.

parallelogram a quadrilateral with opposite sides parallel and equal in length.

paralelogramo cuadrilátero que tiene lados opuestos paralelos y de la misma longitud.

partial products the products you get in each step of the partial-products strategy. You use place value to find partial products.

productos parciales productos que se obtienen en cada paso de la estrategia de productos parciales. Se usa el valor posicional para hallar productos parciales.

218×6
Partial products:
6×200, or 1,200,
6×10, or 60, and
6×8, or 48

partial quotients the quotients you get in each step of the partial-quotient strategy. You use place value to find partial quotients.

cocientes parciales cocientes que se obtienen en cada paso de la estrategia de cocientes parciales. Se usa el valor posicional para hallar cocientes parciales.

$2,124 \div 4$
Partial quotients:
$2,000 \div 4$, or 500,
$100 \div 4$, or 25, and
$24 \div 4$, or 6

partial sums the sums you get in each step of the partial-sums strategy. You use place value to find partial sums.

sumas parciales totales que se obtienen en cada paso de la estrategia de sumas parciales. Se usa el valor posicional para hallar sumas parciales.

$124 + 234$
Partial sums:
$100 + 200$, or 300,
$20 + 30$, or 50, and
$4 + 4$, or 8

English/Español	Example/Ejemplo	Notes/Notas
partial-products strategy a strategy used to multiply multi-digit numbers. **estrategia de productos parciales** estrategia que se usa para multiplicar números de varios dígitos.	218 $\times$ 6 48 (6 × 8 ones) 60 (6 × 1 ten) + 1,200 (6 × 2 hundreds) 1,308	
partial-quotients strategy a strategy used to divide multi-digit numbers. **estrategia de cocientes parciales** estrategia que se usa para dividir números de varios dígitos.	6 25 500 4)2,125 − 2,000 125 − 100 25 − 24 1 The quotient 531 is the sum of partial quotients (6, 25, and 500) and the remainder (1).	
partial-sums strategy a strategy used to add multi-digit numbers. **estrategia de sumas parciales** estrategia que se usa para sumar números de varios dígitos.	312 + 235 Add the hundreds. 500 Add the tens. 40 Add the ones. + 7 547	
peak in a distribution, the shape formed when many data points are at one value or group of values. **pico** en una distribución, la figura que se forma cuando los puntos de muchos datos están en un valor o grupo de valores.	peak 0 1 2 3 4	
pentagon a polygon with exactly 5 sides and 5 angles. **pentágono** polígono que tiene exactamente 5 lados y 5 ángulos.		
per *for each* or *for every*. The word *per* can be used to express a rate, such as $2 per pound. **por** *por cada*. La palabra *por* se puede usar para expresar una tasa, como $2 por libra.	A price of $2 per pound means for every pound, you pay $2.	

English/Español	Example/Ejemplo	Notes/Notas
percent per 100. A percent is a rate per 100. A percent can be written using the percent symbol (%) and represented as a fraction or decimal.	15% can be represented as $\frac{15}{100}$ or 0.15.	
porcentaje por cada 100. Un porcentaje es una tasa por cada 100. Un porcentaje se puede escribir usando el símbolo de porcentaje (%) y se representa como fracción o decimal.		
percent change the amount of change compared to the original (or starting) amount, expressed as a percent. Percent change $= \frac{\text{amount of change}}{\text{original amount}} \times 100$	Saturday: 250 people Sunday: 300 people Change from Saturday to Sunday: $300 - 250 = 50$ Percent change: $\frac{50}{250} \times 100 = 20\%$	
cambio porcentual cantidad de cambio en comparación con la cantidad original (o inicial) que se expresa como porcentaje. Cambio porcentual $=$ $\frac{\text{cantidad de cambio}}{\text{cantidad original}} \times 100$		
percent decrease the percent change when a quantity decreases from its original amount. Percent decrease $=$ $\frac{\text{amount of decrease}}{\text{original amount}} \times 100$	Saturday: 250 people Sunday: 200 people Change from Saturday to Sunday: $250 - 200 = 50$ Percent change: $\frac{50}{250} \times 100 = 20\%$ There is a 20% decrease from Saturday to Sunday.	
disminución porcentual cambio porcentual cuando una cantidad disminuye desde su cantidad original. Disminución porcentual $=$ $\frac{\text{cantidad de disminución}}{\text{cantidad original}} \times 100$		
percent error the difference between the correct value and the incorrect value compared to the correct value, expressed as a percent. Percent error $= \frac{\text{amount of error}}{\text{correct value}} \times 100$	A bag of flour weighs 4.5 lb. It should weigh 5 lb. Percent error: $\frac{5 - 4.5}{5} \times 100 = 10\%$	
error porcentual diferencia que hay entre el valor correcto y el valor incorrecto en comparación con el valor correcto, expresada como porcentaje. Error porcentual $= \frac{\text{cantidad de error}}{\text{valor correcto}} \times 100$		

percent increase the percent change when a quantity increases from its original amount.

Percent increase =

$\dfrac{\text{amount of increase}}{\text{original amount}} \times 100$

incremento porcentual cambio porcentual cuando una cantidad se incrementa desde su cantidad original.

Aumento porcentual =

$\dfrac{\text{cantidad de incremento}}{\text{cantidad original}} \times 100$

Saturday: 250 people

Sunday: 300 people

Change from Saturday to Sunday: $300 - 250 = 50$

Percent change:

$\dfrac{50}{250} \times 100 = 20\%$

There is a 20% increase from Saturday to Sunday.

---

perfect cube the product when an integer is used as a factor three times.

cubo perfecto producto cuando se usa un entero como factor tres veces.

$27 = 3^3$

---

perfect square the product of an integer and itself.

cuadrado perfecto producto de un entero por sí mismo.

$9 = 3^2$

---

perimeter the distance around a two-dimensional shape. The perimeter is equal to the sum of the lengths of the sides.

perímetro distancia alrededor de una figura bidimensional. El perímetro es igual a la suma de las longitudes de los lados.

Perimeter: 200 yd
(60 yd + 40 yd + 60 yd + 40 yd)

---

perpendicular (⊥) meeting to form right angles.

perpendicular (⊥) unión donde se forman ángulos rectos.

$\overline{AD} \perp \overline{CD}$

---

perpendicular lines two lines that meet to form a right angle, or a 90° angle.

rectas perpendiculares dos rectas que se encuentran y forman un ángulo recto, o ángulo de 90°.

English/Español	Example/Ejemplo	Notes/Notas
pi (π) in a circle, the quotient $\frac{circumference}{diameter}$. Common approximations are 3.14 and $\frac{22}{7}$.		
	$\pi \approx 3.14$ or $\frac{22}{7}$	
pi (π) en un círculo, el cociente de $\frac{circumferencia}{diámetro}$. Las aproximaciones communes son 3.14 y $\frac{22}{7}$.		
place value the value of a digit based on its position in a number.		
	The 2 in 3.52 is in the hundredths place and has a value of 2 hundredths or 0.02.	
valor posicional valor de un dígito que se basa en su posición en un número. Por ejemplo, el 2 en 3.52 está en la posición de las centésimas y tiene un valor de 2 centésimas, o 0.02.		
plane figure a two-dimensional figure, such as a circle, triangle, or rectangle.		
figura plana figura bidimensional, como un círculo, un triángulo o un rectángulo.		
plane section a two-dimensional shape that is exposed by making a straight cut through a three-dimensional figure.		
	plane section	
sección plana figura bidimensional que se expone al hacer un corte recto a través de una figura tridimensional.		
point a single location in space.		
	A •	
punto ubicación única en el espacio.		
polygon a two-dimensional closed figure made with three or more straight line segments that meet only at their endpoints.		
polígono figura bidimensional cerrada formada por tres o más segmentos de recta que se encuentran solo en sus extremos.		

population the entire group of interest. Samples are drawn from populations.

población grupo entero de interés. Las muestras se obtienen de las poblaciones.

Sample: 10 students from each Grade 8 homeroom in a school

Population: All Grade 8 students in the school

---

positive association a linear association in which as the value of one variable increases, generally the value of the other variable increases.

asociación positiva asociación lineal en la que el valor de una variable aumenta, generalmente cuando el valor de la otra variable aumenta.

Baseball Pitch and Hit

---

positive numbers numbers that are greater than 0. They are located to the right of 0 on a horizontal number line and above 0 on a vertical number line.

números positivos números que son mayores que 0. Se ubican a la derecha del 0 en una recta numérica horizontal y sobre el 0 en una recta numérica vertical.

---

power an expression with a base and an exponent.

potencia expresión que tiene una base y un exponente.

8^2

---

power of 10 a number that can be written as a product of 10s.

potencia de 10 número que se puede escribir como el producto de 10.

100 and 1,000 are powers of 10 because $100 = 10 \times 10$ and $1,000 = 10 \times 10 \times 10$.

---

prime number a whole number greater than 1 whose only factors are 1 and itself.

número primo número entero mayor que 1 cuyos únicos factores son 1 y sí mismo.

2, 3, 5, 7, 11, 13

---

prism a three-dimensional figure with two parallel bases that are the same size and shape. The other faces are parallelograms. A prism is named by the shape of the base.

prisma figura tridimensional que tiene dos bases paralelas que tienen el mismo tamaño y la misma forma. Las otras caras son paralelogramos. La base determina el nombre del prisma.

probability a number between 0 and 1 that expresses the likelihood of an event occurring.

probabilidad número entre 0 y 1 que expresa la posibilidad de que ocurra un evento.

unlikely   likely

0 $\frac{1}{2}$ 1

impossible   equally   certain
              likely as not

product the result of multiplication.

producto resultado de la multiplicación.

$$3 \cdot 5 = 15$$

proportional relationship the relationship between two quantities where one quantity is a constant multiple of the other quantity. If the quantities x and y are in a proportional relationship, you can represent that relationship with the equation $y = kx$, where the value of k is constant (unchanging).

relación proporcional relación que existe entre dos cantidades en la que una cantidad es un múltiplo constante de la otra. Si las cantidades x y y están en una relación proporcional, esa relación se puede representar con la ecuación $y = kx$, en la que el valor de k es constante (no cambia).

$y = 8x$

pyramid a three-dimensional figure whose base is a polygon and whose other faces are triangles. A pyramid is named by the shape of its base.

pirámide figura tridimensional cuya base es un polígono y cuyas otras caras son triángulos. La base determina el nombre de la pirámide.

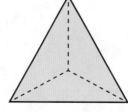

English/Español	Example/Ejemplo	Notes/Notas

Pythagorean Theorem in any right triangle, the sum of the squares of the lengths of the legs, a and b, is equal to the square of the length of the hypotenuse, c. So, $a^2 + b^2 = c^2$.

Teorema de Pitágoras en un triángulo rectángulo cualquiera, la suma del cuadrado de las longitudes de los catetos, a y b, es igual al cuadrado de la longitud de la hipotenusa, c. Por lo tanto, $a^2 + b^2 = c^2$.

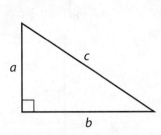

If the triangle is a right triangle, then $a^2 + b^2 = c^2$

Qq

quadrants the four regions of the coordinate plane that are formed when the x-axis and y-axis intersect at the origin.

cuadrantes las cuatro regiones del plano de coordenadas que se forman cuando los ejes x y y se intersecan en el origen.

Quadrant II · Quadrant I · Quadrant III · Quadrant IV

quadrilateral a polygon with exactly 4 sides and 4 angles.

cuadrilátero polígono que tiene exactamente 4 lados y 4 ángulos.

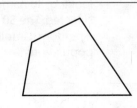

English/Español	Example/Ejemplo	Notes/Notas
qualitative description a description that focuses on the general relationship between quantities, often without using specific values.	Gas prices stay steady, then drop, then increase.	
descripción cualitativa descripción que se enfoca en la relación general que existe entre las cantidades, con frecuencia sin usar valores específicos.		

quotient the result of division.	$22.5 \div 3 = 7.5$	
cociente resultado de la división.		

Rr

radius (of a circle) a line segment from the center of a circle to any point on the circle. Also, the distance from the center to any point on a circle.	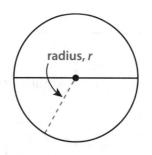	
radio (de un círculo) segmento de recta desde el centro de un círculo hasta cualquier punto en el círculo. Además, la distancia desde el centro hasta cualquier punto en un círculo.		

random sample a sample in which every element in the population has an equal chance of being selected.	The names of all of the students in the school are placed in a hat. Without looking, 30 names are selected. The 30 students are a random sample of the population.	
muestra aleatoria muestra en la que todos los elementos de la población tienen la misma probabilidad de ser elegidos.		

English/Español	**Example/Ejemplo**	**Notes/Notas**
range the difference between the greatest value (maximum) and the least value (minimum) in a data set.	Data set: 9, 10, 8, 9, 7 Range: $10 - 7 = 3$	
rango diferencia entre el mayor valor (máximo) y el menor valor (mínimo) en un conjunto de datos.		
rate a ratio tells the number of units of one quantity for 1 unit of another quantity. Rates are often expressed using the word *per*.	5 miles per hour 2 cups for every 1 serving	
tasa razón que indica el número de unidades de una cantidad para 1 unidad de otra cantidad. Las razones suelen expresarse usando la palabra *por*.		
rate of change in a linear relationship between *x* and *y*, it tells how much *y* changes when *x* changes by 1.	$y = \frac{1}{2}x + 25$ rate of change	
tasa de cambio en una relación lineal entre *x* y *y*, indica cuánto cambia *y* cuando *x* cambia en 1.		
ratio a way to compare two quantities when there are *a* units of one quantity for every *b* units of the other quantity. You can write the ratio in symbols as *a* : *b* and in words as *a* to *b*.	4 circles : 2 triangles	
razón manera de comparar dos cantidades cuando hay *a* unidades de una cantidad por cada *b* unidades de la otra cantidad. Se puede escribir la razón en símbolos como *a* : *b* y en palabras como *a* a *b*.		
rational number a number that can be expressed as the fraction $\frac{a}{b}$ where *a* and *b* are integers and $b \neq 0$. Rational numbers include integers, fractions, repeating decimals, and terminating decimals.	$\frac{3}{4}, -\frac{1}{8}, -3, 0, 1.2$	
número racional número que se puede expresar como la fracción $\frac{a}{b}$ en la que *a* y *b* son enteros y $b \neq 0$. Los números racionales incluyen los enteros, las fracciones, los decimales periódicos y los decimales finitos.		

ray a part of a line that has one end point and goes on forever in one direction.

semirrecta parte de una recta que tiene un extremo y continúa infinitamente en una dirección.

A   B

---

real numbers the set of rational and irrational numbers.

números reales conjunto de números racionales e irracionales.

Real Numbers

Rational Numbers	Irrational Numbers
27	$\sqrt{8}$
0.25	π
$\frac{1}{3}$	1.46829903...

---

reciprocal for any nonzero number a, the reciprocal is $\frac{1}{a}$. The reciprocal of any fraction $\frac{a}{b}$ is $\frac{b}{a}$. Zero does not have a reciprocal. The reciprocal of a number is also called the *multiplicative inverse* of that number.

recíproco para cualquier número a distinto de cero, el recíproco es $\frac{1}{a}$. El recíproco de cualquier fracción $\frac{a}{b}$ es $\frac{b}{a}$. El cero no tiene recíproco. El recíproco de un número también se llama *inverso multiplicativo* de ese número.

The reciprocal of $\frac{5}{4}$ is $\frac{5}{4}$.

The reciprocal of $\frac{1}{6}$ is 6.

The reciprocal of -8 is $-\frac{1}{8}$.

---

rectangle a quadrilateral with 4 right angles. Opposite sides of a rectangle are the same length.

rectángulo cuadrilátero que tiene 4 ángulos rectos. Los lados opuestos de un rectángulo tienen la misma longitud.

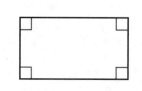

---

rectangular prism a prism where the bases are rectangles.

prisma rectangular prisma en el que las bases son rectángulos.

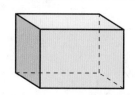

---

reflection a transformation that flips (reflects) a figure across a line to form a mirror image. This line is called the *line of reflection*.

reflexión transformación que gira (refleja) una figura del otro lado de una línea para formar una imagen reflejada. Esta línea se llama *eje de reflexión*.

relative frequency the quotient that compares the number of times a data value occurs and the total number of data values. This can be expressed as a fraction, decimal, or percent.

frecuencia relativa cociente que compara el número de veces que ocurre un valor y el número total de valores. Esto se puede expresar como fracción, decimal o porcentaje.

Data set: red, green, red, red, blue, yellow, blue, white

Frequency of *blue:* 2

Total data values: 8

Relative frequency of *blue:* $\frac{2}{8}$, or $\frac{1}{4}$, or 0.25, or 25%

remainder the amount left over when one number does not divide another number a whole number of times.

residuo cantidad que queda cuando un número no divide a otro un número entero de veces.

$7 \div 2 = 3 \text{ R } 1$

remainder

repeating decimals decimals that repeat the same digit or sequence of digits forever. A repeating decimal can be written with a bar over the repeating digits.

decimal periódico decimales que repiten el mismo dígito o secuencia de dígitos infinitamente. Un decimal periódico se puede escribir con una barra sobre los dígitos que se repiten.

$0.\overline{3}$

$2.\overline{51}$

rhombus a quadrilateral with all sides the same length.

rombo cuadrilátero que tiene todos los lados de la misma longitud.

right angle an angle that measures 90°.

ángulo recto ángulo que mide 90°.

---

right prism a prism where each base is perpendicular to the other faces. In a right prism, the faces that are not bases are rectangles.

prisma recto prisma en el que cada base es perpendicular a las otras caras. En un prisma recto, las caras que no son bases son rectángulos.

---

right rectangular prism a right prism where the bases and other faces are all rectangles.

prisma rectangular recto prisma recto en el que las bases y las otras caras son rectángulos.

---

right triangle a triangle with one right angle.

triángulo rectángulo triángulo que tiene un ángulo recto.

---

right triangular prism a right prism where the bases are triangles and the other faces are rectangles.

prisma triangular recto prisma recto en el que las bases son triángulos y las otras caras son rectángulos.

English/Español	Example/Ejemplo	Notes/Notas

rigid transformation a transformation in which the size and the shape of the figure does not change. *Translations*, *reflections*, and *rotations* are examples of rigid transformations.

transformación rígida transformación en la que el tamaño y la forma de la figura no cambian. Las *traslaciones*, las *reflexiones* y las *rotaciones* son ejemplos de transformaciones rígidas.

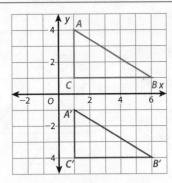

$\triangle A'B'C'$ is a rigid transformation of $\triangle ABC$.

rotation a transformation that turns (rotates) a figure through a given angle and in a given direction around a fixed point. This point is called the center of rotation.

rotación transformación que gira (rota) una figura a través de un ángulo dado y en una dirección dada alrededor de un punto fijo. Este punto se llama centro de rotación.

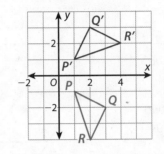

$\triangle P'Q'R'$ is a rotation of $\triangle PQR$.

round to approximate the value of a number by finding the nearest ten, hundred, or other place value.

redondear aproximar el valor de un número hallando la decena, la centena u otro valor posicional más cercano.

48 rounded to the nearest ten is 50.

Ss

same-side exterior angles when two lines are cut by a transversal, a pair of angles on the same side of the transversal and outside the two lines. When the two lines are parallel, same-side exterior angles are supplementary.

ángulos externos del mismo lado cuando dos rectas se cortan con una transversal, par de ángulos del mismo lado de la transversal y fuera de las dos rectas. Cuando las dos rectas son paralelas, los ángulos externos del mismo lado son suplementarios.

∠1 and ∠6
∠4 and ∠7

same-side interior angles when two lines are cut by a transversal, a pair of angles on the same side of the transversal and between the two lines. When the two lines are parallel, same-side interior angles are supplementary.

ángulos internos del mismo lado cuando dos rectas se cortan con una transversal, par de ángulos del mismo lado de la transversal y entre de las dos rectas. Cuando las dos rectas son paralelas, los ángulos internos del mismo lado son suplementarios.

∠2 and ∠5
∠3 and ∠8

sample a part of a population.

muestra parte de una población.

Population: All students in the school

Sample: Three students in each homeroom

sample space the set of all possible unique outcomes for an experiment.

espacio muestral conjunto de todos los resultados posibles de un experimento.

Experiment: Rolling a number cube

Sample space: 1, 2, 3, 4, 5, 6

scale tells the relationship between a length in a drawing, map, or model to the actual length.

escala indica la relación que hay entre una longitud en un dibujo, un mapa o un modelo y la longitud real.

Scale from a map to actual distances in a town:

1 in. to 20 mi

scale (on a graph) the value represented by the distance between one tick mark and the next on a number line.

escala (en una gráfica) valor representado por la distancia que hay entre una marca y la siguiente en una recta numérica.

$$\text{scale} = 5$$

scale drawing a drawing in which the measurements correspond to the measurements of the actual object by the same scale.

dibujo a escala dibujo en el que las medidas se corresponden con las medidas del objeto real según la misma escala.

3 in.   *A*   6 in.   *B*
2 in.   4 in.

$\triangle A : \triangle B$ is $1 : 2$.

scale factor the factor you multiply all the side lengths in a figure by to make a scale copy.

factor de escala factor por el que se multiplican todas las longitudes laterales en una figura para hacer una copia a escala.

Scale from a map to the actual distance: 1 in. to 20 mi

Scale factor from distances on the map to the actual distances: 20

scalene triangle a triangle that has no sides the same length.

triángulo escaleno triángulo que no tiene lados de la misma longitud.

scatter plot a graph of two-variable data displayed as ordered pairs.

diagrama de dispersión gráfica de datos de dos variables que se muestran como pares ordenados.

Talking on the Phone

Time (min) / Age (yr)

English/Español	Example/Ejemplo	Notes/Notas
scientific notation a way of expressing a number as a product in the form $n \times 10^a$, where a is an integer and n is a decimal number such that $1 \le n < 10$.	$5{,}900{,}000 = 5.9 \times 10^6$	
notación científica manera de expresar un número como producto con la forma $n \times 10^a$, en la que a es un entero y n es un número decimal tal que $1 \le n < 10$.		
sequence of transformations one or more transformations performed in a certain order.	A reflection followed by a rotation	
secuencia de transformaciones una o más transformaciones llevadas a cabo en un orden determinado.		
side a line segment that forms part of a two-dimensional shape.	side	
lado segmento de recta que forma parte de una figura bidimensional		
similar (≈) having the same shape. Two figures are similar if there is a sequence of rigid transformations and/or dilations that maps one figure onto the second.	Figures *A* and *B* are similar.	
semejante (≈) que tienen la misma forma. Dos figuras son semejantes si hay una secuencia de transformaciones rígidas y/o dilataciones que hacen coincidir una figura con la segunda.		
similar triangles triangles that are scale drawings of one another. Similar triangles have the same shape but may have a different size.	3 3 2.75 6 6 5.5	
triángulos semejantes triángulos que son dibujos a escala unos de otros. Los triángulos semejantes tienen la misma forma pero pueden tener diferente tamaño.		

English/Español	Example/Ejemplo	Notes/Notas
simple interest a percent of an amount that is borrowed or invested.	$I = Prt$ I = interest P = principal (amount borrowed or invested) r = interest rate t = time	
interés simple porcentaje de una cantidad que se toma prestada o se invierte.		
skewed left when most of the data points of a distribution are clustered near the greater values.	**Skewed Left**	
asimétrica a la izquierda cuando la mayoría de los datos de una distribución se agrupan cerca de los valores más altos.		
skewed right when most of the data points of a distribution are clustered near the lesser values.	**Skewed Right**	
asimétrica a la derecha cuando la mayoría de los datos de una distribución se agrupan cerca de los valores más bajos.		
slope for any two points on a line, the $\frac{\text{rise}}{\text{run}}$ or $\frac{\text{change in } y}{\text{change in } x}$. It is a measure of the steepness of a line. It is also called the *rate of change* of a linear function.	change in y (5, 2) (2.5, 1) change in x Slope: $\frac{1}{2.5} = 0.4$	
pendiente para dos puntos cualesquiera en una recta, la $\frac{\text{distancia vertical}}{\text{distancia horizontal}}$ o $\frac{\text{cambio en } y}{\text{cambio en } x}$. Es una medida de la inclinación de una recta. También se llama *tasa de cambio* de una función lineal.		
slope-intercept form a linear equation in the form $y = mx + b$, where m is the slope and b is the y-intercept.	equation: $y = 2x + 1$ slope: **2** y-intercept: (0, **1**)	
forma pendiente-intercepto ecuación lineal en la forma $y = mx + b$, en la que m es la pendiente y b es el intercepto en y.		

solution of an equation a value that can be substituted for a variable to make an equation true.

solución de una ecuación valor que puede sustituir a una variable para hacer que una ecuación sea verdadera.

The solution to
$19 = 4x - 1$ is $x = 5$.

solution of an inequality a value that can be substituted for a variable to make an inequality true.

solución de una desigualdad valor que puede sustituir a una variable para hacer que una desigualdad sea verdadera.

All values of x less than
5 ($x < 5$) are solutions to
the inequality $5x < 25$.

sphere a three-dimensional figure in which every point is the same distance from the center.

esfera figura tridimensional en la que todos los puntos están a la misma distancia del centro.

square a quadrilateral with 4 right angles and 4 sides of equal length.

cuadrado cuadrilátero que tiene 4 ángulos rectos y 4 lados de la misma longitud.

square root of x the number that when multiplied by itself is equal to x.

raíz cuadrada de x número que cuando se multiplica por sí mismo es igual a x.

$$\sqrt{16} = \sqrt{4 \cdot 4}$$
$$= 4$$
4 is the square root of 16.

statistical question a question that can be answered by collecting data that are expected to vary.

pregunta estadística pregunta que se puede responder reuniendo datos que se espera que varíen.

What is the typical amount of rain in April?

English/Español	Example/Ejemplo	Notes/Notas

straight angle an angle that measures 180°. The sides of a straight angle form a straight line.

ángulo llano ángulo que mide 180°. Los lados de un ángulo llano forman una línea recta.

A   B   C

$\angle ABC$ is a straight angle.

sum the result of addition.

total resultado de la suma.

$24 + 35 = 59$

supplementary angles two angles whose measures sum to 180°.

ángulos suplementarios dos ángulos cuyas medidas suman 180°.

$\angle WXZ$ and $\angle ZXY$ are supplementary angles.

surface area the sum of the areas of all the faces of a three-dimensional figure.

área total suma de las áreas de todas las caras de una figura tridimensional.

5 units
4 units
5 units

Surface Area: $2(4)(5) + 2(4)(5) + 2(5)(5) = 130$ unit^2

symmetric when a distribution has the same shape on both sides of a middle point.

simétrico cuando una distribución tiene la misma forma en ambos lados de un punto que está en el medio.

Symmetric

English/**Español**	**Example**/Ejemplo	**Notes**/Notas
system of linear equations a group of related linear equations in which a solution makes all the equations true at the same time. A system of equations can have zero, one, or infinitely many solutions.		
sistema de ecuaciones lineales grupo de ecuaciones lineales relacionadas en el que una solución hace que todas las ecuaciones sean verdaderas al mismo tiempo. Un sistema de ecuaciones puede tener cero, una o infinitas soluciones.	$y = 4x + 8$ $y = 3x + 8$	

Tt

tax a percent of income or of the cost of goods or services paid to the government.	A 7% sales tax on a purchase of $40 is $2.80	
impuesto porcentaje del ingreso o del costo de bienes o servicios que se paga al gobierno.		
term a number, a variable, or a product of numbers, variables, and/or expressions. A term may include an exponent.	$4x + 9 + y^2$ ↑ ↑ ↗ term	
término número, variable o el producto de números, variables y/o expresiones. Un término puede tener un exponente.		

English/Español	Example/Ejemplo	Notes/Notas
terminating decimals decimals that end, or end in repeated zeros.	0.25 5.6 -7.125	
decimal finito decimal en el que termina un número, o que termina en ceros repetidos.		
theoretical probability the probability of an event occurring based on what is expected to happen.	There are two equally likely outcomes to flipping a coin: heads up or tails up. The theoretical probability of the outcome heads up is $\frac{1}{2}$, or 50%.	
probabilidad teórica probabilidad de que ocurra un evento según lo que se espera que suceda.		
three-dimensional solid, or having length, width, and height. For example, a cube is three-dimensional.		
tridimensional sólido, o que tiene longitud, ancho y altura. Por ejemplo, un cubo es tridimensional.		
transformation a change in location, orientation, or size of a figure.	 $\triangle A'B'C'$ is a transformation of $\triangle ABC$.	
transformación cambio de ubicación, orientación o tamaño de una figura.		
translation a transformation that moves (slides) each point of a figure the same distance and in the same direction.	 $\triangle A'B'C'$ is a translation of $\triangle ABC$ 5 units down.	
traslación transformación que mueve (desplaza) cada punto de una figura la misma distancia y en la misma dirección.		

English/Español	Example/Ejemplo	Notes/Notas
transversal a line that cuts two or more lines. The lines cut by the transversal may or may not be parallel. **transversal** línea que corta dos o más rectas. Las rectas cortadas por la transversal pueden ser o no ser paralelas.	Line *a* is a transerval that cuts lines *b* and *c*.	
trapezoid (exclusive) a quadrilateral with exactly one pair of parallel sides. **trapecio (exclusivo)** cuadrilátero que tiene exactamente un par de lados paralelos.		
trapezoid (inclusive) a quadrilateral with at least one pair of parallel sides. **trapecio (inclusivo)** cuadrilátero que tiene al menos un par de lados paralelos.		
tree diagram a visual that shows all possible outcomes of an experiment. **diagrama de árbol** representación visual que muestra todos los resultados posibles de un experimento.	There are 8 possible outcomes from flipping a coin 3 times.	
trial a single performance of an experiment. **ensayo** ejecución única de un experimento.	Rolling a number cube once	
triangle a polygon with exactly 3 sides and 3 angles. **triángulo** polígono que tiene exactamente 3 lados y 3 ángulos.		
triangular prism a prism where the bases are triangles. **prisma triangular** prisma en el que las bases son triángulos.		

English/Español	Example/Ejemplo	Notes/Notas

two-dimensional flat, or having measurement in two directions, like length and width. For example, a rectangle is two-dimensional.

width

length

bidimensional plano, o que tiene medidas en dos direcciones, como longitud y ancho. Por ejemplo, un rectángulo es bidimensional.

two-way table a table that displays two-variable categorical data. One variable is shown along the top, the other down the side. Each entry in the table gives information about the frequency or relative frequency for the paired data.

	Red Car	Black Car
New Car	16	22
Used Car	23	14

tabla de doble entrada tabla que muestra datos categóricos de dos variables. Una variable se muestra arriba y la otra abajo al costado. Cada entrada en la tabla da información acerca de la frecuencia o frecuencia relativa para los pares de datos.

Uu

unit fraction a fraction with a numerator of 1. Other fractions are built from unit fractions.

fracción unitaria fracción que tiene un numerador de 1. Otras fracciones se construyen a partir de fracciones unitarias.

$$\frac{1}{5}$$

---

unit rate the numerical part of a rate. For the ratio $a : b$, the unit rate is the quotient $\frac{a}{b}$.

tasa por unidad parte numérica de una tasa. Para la razón $a : b$, la tasa por unidad es el cociente $\frac{a}{b}$.

Rate: 3 miles per hour

Unit rate: 3

---

unknown the value you need to find to solve a problem.

incógnita valor que hay que hallar para resolver un problema.

$$20.5 + x = 30$$

---

upper quartile the middle number between the median and the maximum in an ordered set of numbers. The upper quartile is also called the 3rd quartile or Q3.

cuartil superior número del medio entre la mediana y el máximo en un conjunto ordenado de números. El cuartil superior también se llama tercer cuartil, o Q3.

upper quartile

20 30 40 50 60 70 80 90

Vv

variability how spread out or close together values in a data set are.

variabilidad la dispersión o cercanía de los valores en un conjunto de datos.

Gavin's Handstand Times

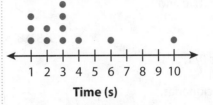

Time (s)

There is high variability in Gavin's handstand times.

---

variable a letter that represents an unknown number. In some cases, a variable may represent more than one number.

variable letra que representa un número desconocido. En algunos casos, una variable puede representar más de un número.

$$3x + 9 = 90$$

---

vertex the point where two rays, lines, or line segments meet to form an angle.

vértice punto en el que dos semirrectas, rectas o segmentos de recta se encuentran y forman un ángulo.

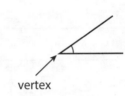

vertex

---

vertical angles opposite angles formed when two lines intersect. Vertical angles are congruent.

ángulos opuestos por el vértice ángulos opuestos que se forman cuando se intersecan dos rectas. Los ángulos opuestos por el vértice son congruentes.

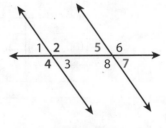

$\angle 5$ and $\angle 7$

$\angle 2$ and $\angle 4$

---

volume the amount of space inside a solid figure. Volume is measured in cubic units such as cubic inches.

volumen cantidad de espacio dentro de una figura sólida. El volumen se mide en unidades cúbicas como las pulgadas cúbicas.

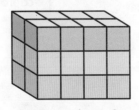

volume: 24 unit^3

English/Español	Example/Ejemplo	Notes/Notas

Ww

whole numbers the numbers 0, 1, 2, 3, 4, . . . Whole numbers are nonnegative and have no fractional part.

0, 8, 187

números enteros los números 0, 1, 2, 3, 4, . . . Los números enteros no son negativos y no tienen partes fraccionarias.

Xx

x-axis the horizontal number line in the coordinate plane.

eje x recta numérica horizontal en el plano de coordenadas.

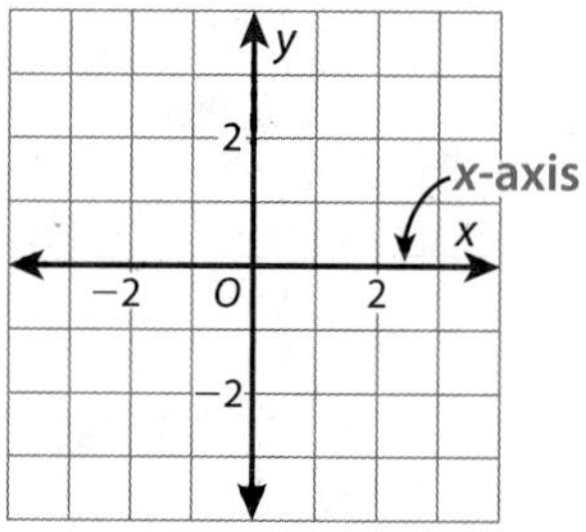

x-coordinate the first number in an ordered pair. It tells the point's horizontal distance from the *y*-axis.

(x, y)

x-coordinate

coordenada x primer número en un par ordenado. Indica la distancia horizontal del punto al eje *y*.

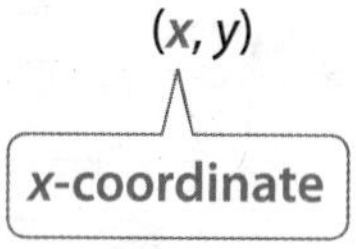

English/Español	Example/Ejemplo	Notes/Notas

x-intercept the x-coordinate of the point where a line, or graph of a function, intersects the x-axis.

intercepto en x coordenada x del punto en el que una recta, o gráfica de una función, interseca al eje x.

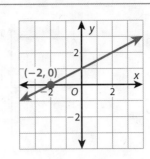

(−2, 0)

The x-intercept is −2.

Yy

y-axis the vertical number line in the coordinate plane.

eje y recta numérica vertical en el plano de coordenadas.

y-coordinate the second number in an ordered pair. It tells the point's vertical distance from the x-axis.

coordenada y el segundo número en un par ordenado. Indica la distancia vertical del punto al eje x.

(x, y)

y-coordinate

y-intercept the y-coordinate of the point where a line, or graph of a function, intersects the y-axis.

intercepto en y coordenada y del punto en el que una recta, o gráfica de una función, interseca al eje y.

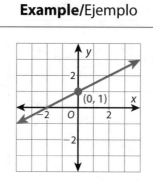

The y-intercept is 1.

Zz

zero pair two numbers whose sum is zero. Opposite numbers form a zero pair.

par cero dos números cuya suma es cero. Los números opuestos forman un par cero.

−3 and 3 form a zero pair.

1.2 and −1.2 form a zero pair.

Credits

Acknowledgment

Common Core State Standards © 2010. National Governors Association Center for Best Practices and Council of Chief State School Officers. All rights reserved.

Photography Credits

Cover: Taras Hipp/Shutterstock
Back Cover: 104 Aleksandar Grozdanovski/Shutterstock; 274 Bennyartist/Shutterstock, Tiger Images/Shutterstock, Nata-Lia/Shutterstock
Text: iii, 93 kuzmaphoto/Shutterstock, Artens/Shutterstock; iii, 79, 115 Makhh/Shutterstock; iv, 177 iStock.com/MR1805, solarseven/Shutterstock; iv, 214 Carlos Caetano/Shutterstock; iv, 294 Elena Noeva/Shutterstock, theendup/Shutterstock, IFH/Shutterstock; v, 349 JIANG DONGYAN/Shutterstock, Eddgars/Shutterstock; v, 435 CoolimagesCo/Shutterstock; vi, 459 StockImageFactory.com/Shutterstock; vi, 522 Sascha Burkard/Shutterstock, Vaclav Volrab/Shutterstock; vii, 642 Volodymyr Nikitenko/Shutterstock; viii, 747, 748 Photimageon/Alamy Stock Photo; viii, 774 Lopris/Shutterstock; 1, 3 kosolovskyy/Shutterstock; 4 Vadym Andrushchenko/Shutterstock, MarinaD/Shutterstock; 15 donsimon/Shutterstock.com; 16 Sarawut Aiemsinsuk/Shutterstock; 17 ne2pi/Shutterstock, Cube29/Shutterstock; 24 chanchai howharn/Shutterstock, eakasarn/Shutterstock; 31 NANTa SamRan/Shutterstock, MLWatts/Wikimedia Commons/CC0 1.0; 44 ma3d/Shutterstock, Alex Tuzhikov/Shutterstock; 45 Stock-Asso/Shutterstock, Amish Spirit; 48 Stanislav Samoylik/Shutterstock, MaxCab/Shutterstock; 65 GraphicsRF/Shutterstock; 73 FrameStockFootages/Shutterstock, Anna Komissarenko/Shutterstock; 81 Thomas Dutour/Shutterstock; 83 Michael Kraus/Shutterstock; 94 Daniel Doerfler/Shutterstock; 95 mTaira/Shutterstock, qonchajabrayilova/Shutterstock; 114 Piyawat Nandeenopparit/Shutterstock; 116 hrui/Shutterstock; 121, 122 Greg A Boiarsky/Shutterstock; 128 Photographee.eu/Shutterstock; 137 Anna Nahabed/Shutterstock; 138 Trompinex/Shutterstock; 139 ottoflick/Shutterstock; 142 Gearstd/Shutterstock; 143 Isaac Mok/Shutterstock.com; 159 iStock.com/Carol Hamilton; 164 Ambient Ideas/Shutterstock; 165 iStock.com/Talaj; 167 Yulia YasPe/Shutterstock; 173, 197 lovelyday12/Shutterstock; 175 denio109/Shutterstock; 180 Willyam Bradberry/Shutterstock; 181, 182 Julien Tromeur/Shutterstock; 185 LM Photos/Shutterstock; 186 CastecoDesign/Shutterstock; 187 Chandan Dubey/Moment/Getty Images; 188 Iakov Filimonov/Shutterstock.com; 190 sirtravelalot/Shutterstock; 191 Vaclav Sebek/Shutterstock; 195 foodonwhite/Shutterstock; 199 FocusDzign/Shutterstock.com; 202 Sergey Novikov/Shutterstock; 203 kurhan/Shutterstock; 204 MyImages - Micha/Shutterstock; 209 Denise Lett/Shutterstock, ppart/Shutterstock, Anne Kramer/Shutterstock; 210 Piotr Wytrazek/Shutterstock, Gina Stef/Shutterstock; 216 April Cat/Shutterstock; 218 Andrey_Kuzmin/Shutterstock, Vismar UK/Shutterstock; 220 Sergey Mironov/Shutterstock; 223 caimacanul/Shutterstock; 225 aradaphotography/Shutterstock; 227 Diane Garcia/Shutterstock; 230 Pratchaya.Lee/Shutterstock; 231 YAKOBCHUK VIACHESLAV/Shutterstock; 232 Naruedom Yaempongsa/Shutterstock, JIANG HONGYAN/Shutterstock; 234, 268, 348 Africa Studio/Shutterstock; 235 Ermolaev Alexander/Shutterstock; 237 Blake Alan/Shutterstock; 238 iStock.com/SarahPage; 240 pukkhoom_nokwila/Shutterstock.com; 242 David Porras/Shutterstock; 246, 448, 584 Eric Isselee/Shutterstock.com; 247 Manuel Ascanio/Shutterstock.com; 249 Anatoli Styf/Shutterstock; 253 ccarvalhophotography/Shutterstock; 254 Inspired by Maps/Shutterstock; 256 nullplus/Shutterstock, Anna Sastre Forrellad/Shutterstock; 259, 260 Thomas Soellner/Shutterstock; 260 Pop_Studio/Shutterstock; 268 Madlen/Shutterstock; 269 Parinya Feungchan/Shutterstock; 270 Cultura Creative (RF)/Alamy Stock Photo; 275 Dan Breckwoldt/Shutterstock; 278 WDG Photo/Shutterstock; 281 Nathapol Kongseang/Shutterstock; 282 home_sweet_home/Shutterstock; 286 Photo Melon/Shutterstock, Mego studio/Shutterstock; 288 Tim Jones/Alamy Stock Photo; 293 Marques/Shutterstock, Anton Kozyrev/Shutterstock, Felix Lipov/Shutterstock; 296 Dawid Galecki/Shutterstock; 302 Maria Kolpashchikova/Shutterstock; 309 Anton Gvozdikov/Shutterstock; 310 Lightspring/Shutterstock, Tyler Olson/Shutterstock; 314 Dmytro Zinkevych/Shutterstock; 315 Ev Thomas/Shutterstock; 316 Fascinadora/Shutterstock; 320 Mikayel Bartikyan/Shutterstock; 329 Kolpakova Daria/Shutterstock; 331 stephan kerkhofs/Shutterstock, Andre Seale/Alamy Stock Photo; 336 Konrawat/Shutterstock; 337 Seashell World/Shutterstock; 339 Volodymyr Goinyk/Shutterstock, Alex Stemmer/Shutterstock; 345, 387 ezphoto/Shutterstock.com; 347, 506, 668 New Africa/Shutterstock; 348 Archi_Viz/Shutterstock; 353 Dja65/Shutterstock, Picsfive/Shutterstock; 357 HEX LLC./Alamy Stock Photo; 359 Laura Crazy/Shutterstock; 360 theskaman306/Shutterstock; 361 adidas4747/Shutterstock; 364 dgbomb/Shutterstock; 365 Greg Epperson/Shutterstock; 366 worldinmyeyes.pl/Shutterstock; 368 bowoedane/Shutterstock, Infinity T29/Shutterstock; 370 spaxiax/Shutterstock, ben bryant/Shutterstock; 371, 372 Charlesy/Shutterstock, Kriengsuk Prasroetsung/Shutterstock; 372 fotorince/Shutterstock; 374 Mykola Mazuryk/Shutterstock, Iakov Filimonov/Shutterstock, elena09/Shutterstock; 377 Pixel-Shot/Shutterstock; 380 Chubarov Alexandr/Shutterstock;

381 leolintang/Shutterstock; 385, 498 Fotokostic/Shutterstock; 388, 393 adike/Shutterstock; 388 EVZ/Shutterstock; 389 iStock.com/ByronD; 392 Sugarless/Shutterstock; 393 RGB Ventures/SuperStock/Alamy Stock Photo, Linda Bucklin/Shutterstock, PHOTO JUNCTION/Shutterstock; 394 Willyam Bradberry/Shutterstock; 397 Brocreative/Shutterstock; 399 Marc Romanelli/Tetra Images/Getty Images; 400 Reid Dalland/Shutterstock; 403 Jim David/Shutterstock, iweta0077/Shutterstock; 407 Claudio Rampinini/Shutterstock, Olga Dubravina/Shutterstock; 409 jamesteohart/Shutterstock; 416 Gary Saxe/Shutterstock; 419 Ammit Jack/Shutterstock; 421 3DMAVR/Shutterstock; 422 Izf/Shutterstock; 436 Miceking/Shutterstock; 437 hobbit/Shutterstock; 439 TayebMEZAHDIA/Pixabay; 445, 447 Alina Lavrenova/Shutterstock; 453, 454 Rost9/Shutterstock; 460 Noah Seelam/AFP/Getty Images; 464 Marco Rubino/Shutterstock; 464 videoduck/Shutterstock; 468 aldarinho/Shutterstock; 469, 470 Fenton/Shutterstock; 474 Kateryna Kon/Shutterstock, Triff/Shutterstock; 475 Rvector/Shutterstock, KPG_Payless/Shutterstock; 476 Kia Nakriz/Shutterstock; 490 bluehand/Shutterstock; 491 View Apart/Shutterstock.com; 492 Maxx-Studio/Shutterstock; 493 r0ma4/Shutterstock; 496 imageBROKER/Alamy Stock Photo; 497 iStock.com/kyoshino; 500 Alex Mit/Shutterstock, BlueberryPie/Shutterstock, iStock.com/LueratSatichob; 502 Ermolaev Alexander/Shutterstock; 503 SoleilC/Shutterstock, kornn/Shutterstock; 504 Chatchai Somwat/Shutterstock; 506 Teacherx555/Shutterstock, iambasic_Studio/Shutterstock, Moolkum/Shutterstock; 511, 755 Tiger Images/Shutterstock; 511 soleilC/Shutterstock, Dancestrokes/Shutterstock, Ilya Andriyanov/Shutterstock, Khumthong/Shutterstock; 513 Neirfy/Shutterstock; 514 Oleksiy Mark/Shutterstock; 515 Aphelleon/Shutterstock; 518, 546 NASA; 519 Taiga/Shutterstock, mikeledray/Shutterstock, topseller/Shutterstock; 520 gg-foto/Shutterstock; 524 ixpert/Shutterstock; 525 Paul Crash/Shutterstock; 526 Chase Dekker/Shutterstock; 528 Lou Linwei/Alamy Stock Photo; 532 Poelzer Wolfgang/Alamy Stock Photo; 534 iStock.com/muendo; 534 iStock.com/Antagain; 539 Lidiya Oleandra/Shutterstock, iStock.com/Holcy, Goran Bogicevic/Shutterstock; 540 Checubus/Shutterstock; 541, 544 Christos Georghiou/Shutterstock; 541, 544, 548 Siberian Art/Shutterstock; 543 mijatmijatovic/Shutterstock; 546 nattha99/Shutterstock, John Rossie/AerospaceEd.org, 3D sculptor/Shutterstock; 547 Karl Yamashita/Shutterstock, Barry Diomede/Alamy Stock Photo; 548 Golden Sikorka/Shutterstock; 549 gyn9037/Shutterstock; 555, 595 oxygen/Moment/Getty Images; 557 Natalya Erofeeva/Shutterstock;

558 ma3d/Shutterstock; 559 akiyoko/Shutterstock; 562 Kwangmoozaa/Shutterstock, Take Photo/Shutterstock; 564 Sean Pavone/Shutterstock; 566 faak/Shutterstock; 569 prapann/Shutterstock, Peter Olsson/Shutterstock, Michal Ninger/Shutterstock, Elnur/Shutterstock; 570 vvoe/Shutterstock, Sementer/Shutterstock, serg_bimbirekov/Shutterstock, Andrej Antic/Shutterstock; 572 Rashevskyi Viacheslav/Shutterstock; 574 David P. Lewis/Shutterstock, Vitalii Hulai/Shutterstock; 577 xpixel/Shutterstock; 578 RinArte/Shutterstock, Kanunnikov Vasyl/Shutterstock; 579 Yayayoyo/Shutterstock; 581 Evgeny Karandaev/Shutterstock, Amitofo/Shutterstock; 586 Lydia Vero/Shutterstock; 588 Mike Flippo/Shutterstock, Sergiy Kuzmin/Shutterstock, Nataliia K/Shutterstock; 590 Sebastian Janicki/Shutterstock; 593 John Le/Shutterstock; 594 arka38/Shutterstock; 596 Gts/Shutterstock; 597 G. Ronald Lopez/Alamy Stock Photo; 601 GraphicsRF/Shutterstock; 602 Irina Fischer/Shutterstock; 606 Jango/Stockimo/Alamy Stock Photo; 607 Yoshed/Shutterstock; 608 B Christopher/Alamy Stock Photo; 612 Runrun2/Shutterstock, Ivailo Nikolov/Shutterstock; 617 Stanislav Samoylik/Shutterstock; 618 Photoexpert/Shutterstock; 626 HelloRF Zcool/Shutterstock; 630 mihalec/Shutterstock, You Touch Pix of EuToch/Shutterstock; 636 iStock.com/oonal; 657 alicanozgur/Shutterstock; 664 iStock.com/Katiekk2; 668 MACVON/Shutterstock, Macrovector/Shutterstock; 670 naramit/Shutterstock; 672 art of line/Shutterstock; 674 Nyura/Shutterstock; 679, 682 Gines Valera Marin/Shutterstock; 679 tgavrano/Shutterstock, Travelerpix/Shutterstock; 685 J Davidson/Shutterstock; 687 Seksun Guntanid/Shutterstock, Baronb/Shutterstock; 693, 695 Denis Belitsky/Shutterstock; 700 Erik Lam/Shutterstock; 707 Matushchak Anton/Shutterstock, JoemanjiArts/Shutterstock; 710 Racheal Gazias/Shutterstock; 716 freesoulproduction/Shutterstock; 718 JeniFoto/Shutterstock; 723 Rawpixel.com/Shutterstock; 724 3000ad/Shutterstock; 725 PixieMe/Shutterstock; 728 Monkey Business Images/Shutterstock; 730 Samuel Borges Photography/Shutterstock; 734 mipan/Shutterstock; 735, 736 Yaran/Shutterstock; 738 Sergey Korkin/Shutterstock; 741 PetlinDmitry/Shutterstock; 745 Jenna Hidinger/Shutterstock; 755 Tiger Images/Shutterstock; 756 MilkyM/Shutterstock; 757 Khaled ElAdawy/Shutterstock; 762 Grigorita Ko/Shutterstock; 766 Ienjoyeverytime/Shutterstock; 767 Venus Angel/Shutterstock; 772 Josep Curto/Shutterstock; 777 Ana Prego/Shutterstock; 779 9george/Shutterstock; 784 Michael D Brown/Shutterstock; 785 David P. Smith/Shutterstock; 786 Flat art/Shutterstock; 787 Jeff Zehnder/Shutterstock, Bushko Oleksandr/Shutterstock, Varavin88/Shutterstock; (smartphone and laptop) guteksk7/Shutterstock